GUIDE TO THE COLLECTIONS
IN THE HOOVER INSTITUTION ARCHIVES
RELATING TO IMPERIAL RUSSIA,
THE RUSSIAN REVOLUTIONS AND CIVIL WAR,
AND THE FIRST EMIGRATION

GUIDE TO THE COLLECTIONS
IN THE HOOVER INSTITUTION ARCHIVES
RELATING TO IMPERIAL RUSSIA,
THE RUSSIAN REVOLUTIONS AND CIVIL WAR,
AND THE FIRST EMIGRATION

Compiled by
CAROL A. LEADENHAM

HOOVER INSTITUTION PRESS
Stanford University, Stanford, California

The Hoover Institution on War, Revolution and Peace, founded at Stanford University in 1919 by the late President Herbert Hoover, is an interdisciplinary research center for advanced study on domestic and international affairs in the twentieth century. The views expressed in its publications are entirely those of the authors and do not necessarily reflect the views of the staff, officers, or Board of Overseers of the Hoover Institution.

Hoover Press Bibliographical Series 68
Copyright 1986 by the Board of Trustees of the
  Leland Stanford Junior University

All rights reserved. No part of this publication may be reproduced, stored in a retrieval system, photocopying, recording, or otherwise, without written permission of the publisher.

Manufactured in the United States of America
Photographs courtesy of Sondra Bierre

Library of Congress Cataloging in Publication Data
Hoover Institution on War, Revolution, and Peace.
  Guide to the collections in the Hoover Institution archives relating to Imperial Russia, the Russian revolutions and civil war, and the first emigration.

  (Hoover Press bibliographical series ; 68)
  Includes index.
  1. Soviet Union—Politics and government—1894–1917—Sources—Bibliography—Catalogs. 2. Soviet Union—History—Revolution, 1917–1921—Sources—Bibliography—Catalogs. 3. World War, 1914–1918—Soviet Union—Sources—Bibliography—Catalogs. 4. Soviet Union—History—Revolution, 1917–1921—Protest movements—Sources—Bibliography—Catalogs. 5. Soviet Union—History—Allied intervention, 1918–1920—Sources—Bibliography—Catalogs. 6. Hoover Institution on War, Revolution, and Peace—Archives—Catalogs.
I. Leadenham, Carol A., 1950–   . II. Title.
III. Series.
Z2510.H66 1986   [DK262]   016.94708   86-7513
ISBN 0-8179-2661-X

For Lascelle de Basily

CONTENTS

Foreword, *W. Glenn Campbell*	ix
Preface, *Marc Raeff*	xi
Acknowledgments	xiii
Introduction	xv
Photographs	following p. 14
List of Archival Collections Arranged Alphabetically	1
Descriptions of Archival Collections	15
Comprehensive Collections and Memorabilia	17
Imperial Russia	21
Revolutionary Movements	40
Imperial Russian Army Organization	46
Imperial Russian Army Before 1904	47
Russo-Japanese War, 1904–1905; 1905–1913	49
World War I	52
February Revolution, Provisional Government Period, October Revolution, and Civil War	65
Anti-Bolshevik Participants in the Civil War; Allied Intervention	81
Siberia	105
Mongolia	120
Relief Agencies	123
Emigré Activities	138
Index	147

FOREWORD

I am pleased to present this guide to the archival and manuscript collections in the Hoover Institution relating to the history of imperial Russia and the Russian emigrations since 1850 and to the early Soviet period. It is another in the series of bibliographic studies published to aid scholars using the world-renowned holdings of the Hoover Institution. The Hoover Institution Archives include more than 4,000 collections, 676 of which are described in this guide.

The collection of Russian materials dates from the earliest years of the Hoover Institution, beginning while the Civil War was still raging in Soviet Russia. In the intervening years, the processing and expansion of the Russian collections have consistently been assigned high priority. Today, experts throughout the world consider these collections to have few equals outside the Soviet Union. Publication of the guide to these materials reflects the Hoover Institution's commitment to publicizing its holdings and making them more accessible for scholarly research.

This guide is dedicated to Mrs. Lascelle de Basily. Her many gifts to the Hoover Institution over the years have included, among others, the papers, books, and art collection of her late husband, Nicholas de Basily, a diplomat and statesman who left Russia after the revolution of 1917. The Hoover Institution's Nicholas de Basily Room, which houses the collection's art objects, also is a result of Mrs. de Basily's generosity. My colleagues and I, as well as the scholarly community, are indebted to her for this continuing and farsighted support for the collection and preservation programs of the Hoover Institution Library and Archives.

W. Glenn Campbell, Director
Hoover Institution

PREFACE

Who controls the past . . . controls the future: who controls the
present controls the past.
George Orwell, 1984

Wars, revolutions, and especially civil wars destroy not only lives and goods, but records as well. Records are as valuable as material goods, for they are the basis of modern man's memory--and without memory there is no civilization, no culture. Anyone concerned with helping people to survive in times of crisis is also perforce confronted with the task--nay, duty--of salvaging the records of their time and lives. This is precisely what Herbert Hoover realized when he founded the library and archives of the institution that bears his name and encouraged the collecting of records in a Russia torn by civil strife and racked by famine and disease. Fortunately, too, in subsequent years the Hoover Institution kept enlarging its collection of documents pertaining to Russia by acquiring the records of the White armies and of the Russian émigrés. As a result, the Hoover Institution is now the depository of the largest archive pertaining to Russian affairs (mainly of the twentieth century) outside the Soviet Union. For some subjects it is indeed the only source; much has perished in the Soviet Union, and access to what is preserved is subject to the vagaries of the political climate and the needs of the Soviet government. The fact that the Russian Historical Archive, set up in Prague in the early 1920s, was donated to the Soviet Union by the Czechoslovak government in 1945 "in gratitude for the liberation by the Red Army" has made crucial the role of the Hoover Institution in preserving historical knowledge of and promoting research on twentieth-century Russia.

Two features of the Russian archival material at the Hoover Institution--a detailed catalog of which is published here for the first time--deserve special mention. First, the bulk of the materials pertain to political, diplomatic, and military matters. Of course, under the circumstances of émigré existence, political and cultural activities are not always kept separate, so that the historian of Russian literature and art in the twentieth century will find much of value as well. Second, the materials are of relevance not to Russian history alone; there is also much (especially in the fabulous Nicolaevsky Collection) on the general history of socialism and international revolutionary movements--not to speak of the interstate dimension of the events involving Russia and the Soviet Union. In conjunction with the Hoover Library's rich holdings of printed works (including serials, pamphlets, and monographs) and pictorial documentation (films, photographs, and posters), the Hoover Archives have transformed the institution into one of the world's major centers for research on Russia since the middle of the nineteenth century.

Archives are notoriously complex and difficult to use. Without a catalog the scholar is completely at sea, especially if he comes from far away and has only limited time at his disposal. The present guide goes a long way toward facilitating access to the Hoover Institution's riches in the field of Russian affairs. As historians know all too well, archival collections often arise accidentally, in a haphazard manner, and are rarely homogeneous in their contents. It is not enough, therefore, to have a description, however detailed, of individual collections; one needs a key to locate materials dispersed among various collections. The greatest service Carol A. Leadenham has performed in compiling the present guide has been to work up several detailed indexes that will facilitate efficient use of the materials on deposit at the Hoover Institution--not only by scholars on the premises, but also by those who lack access to computers or live in faraway places.

Amnesia is a disease that destroys the very humanity of the individual. Similarly, the loss of memories by a nation or society threatens the very survival of its culture. Orwell put it succinctly and trenchantly: "It was quite simple. All that was needed was an unending series of victories over your own memory. 'Reality control' they called it." That is why twentieth-century totalitarian tyrannies have made particularly strenuous efforts to obliterate historical memories by selecting what may be written or talked about and by destroying or refusing access to records of the past. Fortunately, in the case of the Soviet Union, the existence of the Hoover Institution's Russian collection--along with such other depositories as the Bakhmeteff Archive at Columbia University--will preclude a total victory over memory. In so doing, the Hoover Institution contributes to the survival and ongoing creativity of Russian culture; the present guide is a prime instrument to this end.

                                        Marc Raeff
                                        Columbia University

ACKNOWLEDGMENTS

I would like to thank the Hoover Institution and, especially, the staff of the Hoover Institution Archives, who contributed so much to the completion of this volume. The archivist, Charles G. Palm, initially suggested that this guide be compiled, and he has continued to provide valuable editorial advice and encouragement. Dale Reed, assistant archivist for technical services, revised the collection-level archival descriptions in preparation for entering all the archives' holdings into the Research Libraries Information Network (RLIN) in 1984-85. He provided me with his cataloging revision memos, which provided much information I was able to incorporate into this guide. His assistant, Linda Bernard, was also extremely helpful in providing information on the changes resulting from the RLIN project. Elena Danielson, assistant archivist for reference, made useful suggestions on the organization of the manuscript. Michael Jakobson aided in the selection of photographs. Ron Bulatoff generously shared his extensive knowledge of the Russian collections, gained during years of processing and providing reference services for them. My husband, Doug, deserves special gratitude for his editorial suggestions and for caring for our son during the hours I was working on this guide.

INTRODUCTION

In addition to taking an immense toll in human lives and uprooting millions of people, the Russian revolutions and Civil War also placed the documentary records of the times in peril. Many records of governmental agencies and papers of civilian and military leaders, collections that in normal times would never have left Russia, instead found a home in the Hoover Institution Archives.

The Hoover War Library, founded in 1919, was extremely well suited to serve as a repository for these displaced documentary records. The library's founder, Herbert Hoover, saw the need to collect documents relating to World War I, which were in danger of perishing in its aftermath. Similarly, he was one of the first foreigners to interest himself in preserving the documents created during the Russian revolutions and Civil War, and he encouraged timely collecting efforts in the early 1920s. Hoover's role as director of the American Relief Administration, which fed so many famine victims, especially children, in Soviet Russia in 1921-1923, has never been adequately appreciated. Scholars, also, owe him a debt of gratitude for ensuring the survival of many documents that otherwise would surely have perished during those chaotic times.

In the years that followed, exiles from tsarist Russia and émigrés belonging to groups that lost out to the Bolsheviks in the Civil War continued to donate materials to the Hoover Institution Archives. As a result, the archives' Russian collections, though rich in individual documentary treasures, such as drafts of the abdication proclamation of Nicholas II (in the Nicolas de Basily Collection), also have a depth that permits research on many topics in Russian history for the turbulent period from the 1880s to the end of the Civil War.

A glance at the subdivisions in the table of contents of this volume reveals areas of significant research potential in the Hoover Institution Archives' Russian collections. The most noteworthy inclusions in the Imperial Russian Collection (whose honorary curator is Prince Vasili Romanov) are the papers of imperial family members, such as Empress Mariia Feodorovna and Grand Duchess Kseniia, wife and daughter of Emperor Alexander III. The collection also contains many diplomatic records; specifically, those of Russian consulates and legations in various German states, which contain information on Russo-German economic relations during the period 1828-1914.

The Nicolas de Basily Room in the Hoover Tower Building is a focal point for the Imperial Russian Collection. Created by Mrs. Lascelle de Basily as a memorial to her husband, the room contains a remarkable collection of paintings. These are mainly by Russian artists, such as Dmitrii Levitskii, Fedor Rokotov, and Vladimir Borovikovskii, but the room also includes works by Western Europeans, such as Sir Joshua Reynolds and Marco Ricci, and other art objects from the Basily art collection. The collection especially emphasizes portraits of Russian emperors, courtiers, diplomats, and statesmen of the eighteenth century. This impressive room is used as a meeting place for scholarly sessions, a reception area for special guests of the Hoover Institution, and for other special occasions.

Among the archives' many collections dealing with revolutionary movements in late tsarist Russia, the most famous are the Boris I. Nicolaevsky and the Okhrana (Russia. Departament politsii. Zagranichnaia agentura, Paris) collections. Nicolaevsky, a Menshevik who was exiled from Soviet Russia, and his wife and co-worker, Anna Bourguina, spent years collecting materials relating to the history of the revolutionary parties, especially the Marxist ones. In their attempts to keep the documents--and themselves--out of the hands of the Nazis, they transferred the materials from Berlin to Amsterdam to Paris to New York. Finally, they accepted an offer to house the collection in the Hoover Institution Archives, where they subsequently served as its curators. They continued to collect materials and to prepare a guide to the collection until their respective deaths in 1966 and 1982.

The Okhrana Collection consists of the files of the tsarist secret police office in Paris, from which Russian revolutionaries living in Europe were kept under surveillance. Included are reports by agents on the day-to-day activities of the revolutionaries, intercepted letters, mug shots and descriptions acquired as part of arrest procedures, and information on the inner workings of the Okhrana itself. Besides these large collections, there are many smaller ones dealing with revolutionaries like Ekaterina Breshko-Breshkovskaia.

The subdivisions into which this guide is classified are not mutually exclusive. For example, many of the collections document the lives of men who served as officers in the Imperial Russian Army, later fought with the Whites in the Civil War, and finally were active in émigré groups in various countries. In these cases, the selection of the subdivisions into which to place the collections was based on what seemed to be the primary emphasis of the documents. Additional entries in the index indicate other topics covered.

The papers of tsarist military officers shed light on both the details of army organization and the history of specific military units. World War I campaigns are well covered (for example, General IUdenich's Turkish campaigns). General Alekseev, commander-in-chief of the Russian Imperial armies on the southwestern front and chief of staff to Nicholas II, is represented by a collection under his name and by one under the name of his daughter, Vera Alekseeva de Borel'. The World War I peace conferences are especially well documented in the archives' collections.

Collections relating to various anti-Bolshevik groups in the Civil War and to the Allied intervention make up a significant proportion of the Russian holdings. Anatolii Markov's <u>Entsiklopediia belago dvizheniia</u> (Encyclopedia of the White Movement) is a compilation of information on high- and low-ranking participants in the White armies and follows their activities in the emigration after the Civil War. Many White generals (such as IUdenich, Alekseev, and Vrangel'), along with lower-ranking White officers, military agents, and representatives of the various White generals in European capitals, are represented in the collections. There is substantial information on all the Civil War fronts, but especially on Siberia and the Allied intervention there (including the papers of William Sidney Graves, commanding general, American Expeditionary Force in Siberia, 1918-1920, and the papers of many high- and low-ranking American soldiers who served with him). Also included are the papers of the American diplomatic representative in Siberia and of members of groups like the U.S. Advisory Commission of Railway Experts to Russia, who were involved with the operations of the Trans-Siberian and Chinese Eastern railways during the period of disruption caused by the Civil War.

Another important group of Americans who intervened in the Civil War were the relief workers. The records of the American Relief Administration Russian Operations, which include graphic photographs of the suffering wrought by the famine and accounts of the successes of the famine relief efforts, are of great interest, as are the records of the other relief agencies that were active at the time, such as the YMCA, the American Friends Service Committee, and the American Red Cross. Besides the Herbert Hoover Collection, the archives also house the diaries and other papers of many individual relief workers. Among these, the Frank Alfred Golder Collection is especially interesting. Professor Golder was a historian who worked with professors E. D. Adams and Ralph H. Lutz in their pioneering efforts to collect materials on World War I for the Hoover War Library. The materials they collected during trips to Soviet Russia in 1921, 1925, and 1927 became the foundation of the library's Imperial Russian, Russian Revolution, and Soviet collections. The Golder Collection also includes information on Golder's activities as an ARA worker in the Ukraine.

Most of the holdings relating to émigrés concern those who fled to the Far East and the United States. There are also important diplomatic holdings, such as the records of the Provisional Government's ambassador and embassy in France and its embassy in the United States. (The embassy remained open as the officially recognized representative of the Russian government until the United States recognized the Soviet Union in 1933.)

Although the terms "Russia" and "Russian" have been used in this introduction for convenience, the collections contain extensive documentation on other ethnic groups inhabiting the Russian empire. For instance, by using the index one can locate numerous collections relating to Ukrainians and inhabitants of the Baltic region, especially during the Civil War period.

Two nondocumentary collections are especially noteworthy. The Axelbank Film Collection consists of 250,000 feet of motion picture film covering the period from 1900 to the 1970s. Much of the footage in the first 44 reels (up to 1930) is rare or unique. The first 28 reels (the part of the collection that is open for use at present) extend to 1921 and include footage of informal scenes of the tsar and his family, Leo Tolstoy and his family at his country estate and on a visit to his Moscow residence, the many demonstrations and parades of the Provisional Government period, Trotsky in his role as Red Army commander during the Civil War, and early meetings of the Comintern. The reel depicting Lenin's funeral is also open.

The Poster Collection includes about 4,000 Russian posters. Many date from World War I; besides the usual depictions of battle scenes, the collection includes posters done in the naive style of lubochnye knigi, which attempt to explain the war to peasant soldiers in their own terms. Other topics represented in the Russian posters include appeals to citizens to purchase bonds to help finance the war and to make charitable contributions to the widows and orphans of slain soldiers; campaign posters of the various parties for the Constituent Assembly; and Civil War posters, including some extremely rare ones produced by the Whites.

This guide includes collections acquired through June 30, 1984. The entries are, for the most part, the same as those that appear in the Hoover Institution Archives catalog. If the collection does not primarily relate to Russia, a few sentences have been added to the card catalog description to indicate what materials are present that would be of interest to users of this guide. As in the catalog, the Library of Congress transliteration system is used, except that ligatures have been omitted. For émigrés, the spelling of their names that they adopted has been employed (for example, Nicolaevsky, not Nikolaevskii).

The index is based on the archives' subject catalog, with certain additions and modifications. For instance, the indexing of the Okhrana Collection has been enhanced by index terms taken from the guidebook to the collection, such as the names of revolutionaries and revolutionary organizations that are listed separately in the guidebook. The Nicolaevsky Collection has been indexed at the series level, with index terms chosen for each of the 246 "numbers" into which the collection is divided. The Axelbank Film Collection also has additional index terms taken from the guide to the collection. Additional indexing for personal and place names has been taken from the collection descriptions, and the name of the donor has been added to the index if it does not already appear as the main entry of the collection. As a means of avoiding excessive repetition of the word "Russia" in the index, the following modification of the card catalog subject entries has been adopted: index terms that would normally be subdivided by country should be assumed to refer to Russia if there is no country mentioned. (For example, the heading "Labor and laboring classes" without country subdivision refers to Russia; when U.S.

workers are meant, the subdivision "U.S." is used.) The index employs the collection numbers assigned in this guide rather than page numbers.

In general, however, the index terms apply to collections as a whole. Therefore this guide and its index cannot take the place of the more detailed folder-by-folder guides available for some individual collections. These guides, called registers, are available for consultation in the Archives Reading Room. In many cases it is also possible to purchase copies of individual registers. Since the staff is constantly preparing additional registers, one should inquire about the availability of a register even if the present volume does not note the existence of one.

Materials may be examined in the Archives Reading Room in the Herbert Hoover Memorial Building (courtyard level) by anyone who presents personal identification, completes a registration form, and adheres to rules regarding use. Reading room hours are 8:15 a.m. to 4:45 p.m., Monday through Friday. Archives are not available through interlibrary loan. A limited number of photocopies may be purchased in accordance with a reproduction price list and policy statement (available on request). The Russian Pictorial Collection is one of many collections of photographs available in the archives; note that many of the documentary collections in this guide also contain photographs. The archives staff maintains a separate photograph catalog, which includes subject headings. Copies of photographs and slides from the archives' collections are also available for purchase. Reference services are provided to reading room users and to persons writing for information. For extensive searches involving detailed research, interpretation, or evaluation of materials, the names of qualified persons who work for a fee can be furnished. Inquiries should be addressed to the Archivist, Hoover Institution Archives, Stanford, CA 94305.

Some documentary materials on microfilm are housed in the Hoover Institution Library. For example, the library has the Records of the U.S. Advisory Commission of Railway Experts to Russia, the Russian Railway Service Corps, and the Interallied Railway Committee, 1917-1922 (40 reels). In cases in which the library holds a master negative, arrangements can be made to purchase microfilm copies. Inquiries on microfilm holdings in the Hoover Institution Library, and questions on the published holdings of the Hoover Institution should be addressed to the Reference Department, Hoover Institution Library, Stanford, CA 94305.

For those interested in obtaining more information on the Hoover Institution Archives, the following sources can be recommended. An overview of the history and collecting strengths of the archives can be found in the chapter by the archivist, Charles G. Palm, in Peter Duignan, ed., The Library of the Hoover Institution on War, Revolution and Peace (Stanford: Hoover Institution Press, 1985). The chapter by Joseph D. Dwyer, deputy curator, East European Collection, Hoover

Institution Library, also describes some of the archives' important Russian collections). Charles G. Palm and Dale Reed's <u>Guide to the Hoover Institution Archives</u> (Stanford: Hoover Institution Press, 1980) includes descriptions of the collections and an index, both based on entries in the archives' card catalog, and covers all collections acquired up to the end of 1978. Unpublished lists of the archives' collections relating to the Soviet Union and to the East European countries are available from the archivist. Collection-level descriptions of all the archives' holdings have been entered into the Research Libraries Information Network (RLIN). Those who would like to survey Russian and Soviet collections in repositories throughout the United States should turn to Steven A. Grant and John H. Brown, <u>The Russian Empire and Soviet Union: A Guide to Manuscripts and Archival Materials in the United States</u> (Boston: G. K. Hall, 1981).

LIST OF ARCHIVAL COLLECTION TITLES ARRANGED ALPHABETICALLY

Adams, Arthur E., 241
Aerenthal, Aloys Leopold Baptist Lexa von, Graf, 1854-1912, 20
Agence télégraphique de Petrograd, 169
Akaëmov, Nikolai, 328
Akintievskii, Konstantin Konstantinovich, 1884-1962, 329
Alekseev, Mikhail Vasil'evich, 1857-1918, 170
Alexander II, Emperor of Russia, 1818-1881, 21
American Committee for the Encouragement of Democratic Government in Russia, 242
American Slav Congress, 627
Anderson, Edgar, 1920- , 171
Anderson, Roy Scott, d. 1925, 330
Andreev, N. N., 243
Andrushkevich, Nikolai Aleksandrovich, 455
Anichkov, Vladimir Petrovich, 456
Annenkov, Boris Vladimirovich, 1890-1927, 457
Antonenko, V. P., 458
Arkhangel'skii, Aleksei Petrovich, 628
Asian pictorial collection, 1883-1948, 149
Austro-Hungarian Monarchy. Ministerium des K. und K. Hauses und des Aeussern, 172
Autograph collection, 1
Axelbank, Herman, 1900-1977, collector, 2
Axentieff, N., 552

Babb, Nancy, 1884-1948, 553
Balk, A., 22
Balykov, V. P., 629
Bane, Suda Lorena, 1886-1952, 554
Baratov, Nikolai Nikolaevich, 1864-1932, 173
Barber, Alvin B., 555
Barrett, William S., 459
Barringer, Thomas C., 556
Basily, Lascelle Meserve de, 23
Basily, Nicolas Alexandrovich de, 1883-1963, 24
Basily-Callimaki, Eva de, 1855-1913, 25
Bastunov, Vladimir J., collector, 146
Batiushin, N. S., 26
Baxter, Robert I., collector, 331
Bazarevich, Vladimir Iosifovich, 332
Bazarov, Pavel Aleksandrovich, 157
Bekeart, Laura Helene, 557
Benes, Eduard, 1884-1948, 244
Benjamin, Alfred, 245
Bennigsen, Emmanuil Pavlovich, Graf, 1875- , 333
Berk, Stephen M., 460
Bernatskii, Mikhail Vladimirovich, 1876- , collector, 174
Bielevskii, Lieutenant, collector, 27
Blagoev, Dimitur, 1856-1924, 122
Bland, Raymond L., 558

Bogdanov, A., 1872-   , 461
Bogoiavlensky, Nikolai Vasil'evich, 630
Boldyrev, Vasilii Georgievich, 1875-   , 462
Bookplates, 3
Borel', Vera Alekseeva de, 175
Botkine, Serge, <u>collector</u>, 631
Bourguina, Anna, 246
Bramhall, Burle, <u>collector</u>, 559
Branden, Albrecht Paul Maerker, 1888-   , 176
Breese, Alexander, 1889-1976, 632
Breese, Marie Annenkov, 633
Breitigam, Gerald B., 463
Breshko-Breshkovskaia, Ekaterina Konstantinovna, 1844-1934, 123
Browne, Louis Edgar, 1891-1951, 247
Brunelli, Paul, 150
Brunet, Court Councillor de, 28
Bublikov, Aleksandr Aleksandrovich, 248
Budberg, Aleksei Pavlovich, Baron, 1869-1945, 464
Bugbee, Fred William, 1876-1932, 465
Buliubash, Evgenii Grigor'evich, 334
Bungey, Grace Belle Reames, 560
Bunin, Viktor M., 1896-   , 335
Bunyan, James, 1898-1977, 249
Burlin, P. G., 336
Burtsev, Vladimir L'vovich, 1862-1942, 124
Byckoff, Michael M., <u>collector</u>, 4
Bykadorov, I., 337

Caldwell, John Kenneth, 1881-   , 29
Campbell, Hannah Brain, 1880-   , 561
Carbonnel, Francois de, 1873-1957, 30
Carroll, Philip H., 1885-1941, 562
Carter, Lieutenant, 338
Ceská druzina, 466
<u>Chasovoi</u> (Sentinel), 634
Cheriachoukin, A. V., 339
Cherkasskii family, 31
Chernov, Viktor Mikhailovich, 1873-1952, 340
Chicherin, Georgii Vasil'evich, 1872-1936, 250
Childs, James Rives, 1893-   , 563
Christoff, Peter K., <u>collector</u>, 32
Chuhnov, Nicholas, 635
Clark, Marmaduke R., d. 1964, 564
Clendenen, Clarence Clements, 1899-   , 251
Colton, Ethan Theodore, 1872-   , 565
Communist International, 252
Cooper, Merian C., 1894-1973, 341
Currency collection, n.d., 5

Daniloff, Karl B., 342
Darling, William Lafayette, 1856-1938, 343
Davies, E. Alfred, 467
Davis, Benjamin B., 566

Davis, Robert E., 567
Day, George Martin, 636
Demetropoulos, Constantine, <u>collector</u>, 6
Denikina, Kseniia, 344
Dmowski, Roman, 1864-1939, 177
Dobrynin, Vasilii A., 345
Dolgorouky, Barbara, Princess, 1885-   , 33
Domanenko, General, 147
Don Cossacks, Province of the, 178
Dorrian, Cecil, 253
Dotsenko, Paul, 468
Dratsenko, D. P., 346
Duncan, William Young, 568

"Economic Conditions of Kuban Black Sea Region," 254
Edison, J., 469
Egbert, Donald Drew, 1902-1973, 125
Egbert, Edward H., d. 1939, 569
"Egerskii Vestnik" (Egerskii [Regiment] Herald), 637
"Ekonomicheskoe polozhenie Sov. Rossii" (The economic situation of Soviet Russia), 255
Elachich, S. A., 470
Eliseev, Fedor Ivanovich, 1892-   , 347
Emerson, George H., 471
Epstein, Fritz Theodor, 1898-   , 348
Erasmus-Feit family, 638
Ergushov, P., 349
Erickson, Douglas, 350
Ermakov, Petr Zacharovich, 34
"Estoniia i pomoshch golodaiushchim" (Estonia and aid to the starving), 351
Etter, Maria von, 151
European subject collection, 1889-1962, 35

Far Eastern Republic collection, 1917-1921, 472
Faulstich, Edith M., d. 1972, <u>collector</u>, 473
Fedichkin, Dmitri I., 352
Fedorov, Georgii, 353
Ferguson, Alan, 474
"Finliandets" (Member of the Finland Regiment), 639
Finnish subject collection, 1900-1946, 36
Fisher, Harold Henry, 1890-1975, 570
Fleming, Harold M., 1900-   , 571
Flug, V. E., 179
Foss, F. F., 37
Free, Arthur M., <u>collector</u>, 180
French subject collection, 1665-1981, 256
Fried, Alfred Hermann, 1864-1921, 181
Friedlander, Ernst, 182
<u>The Frozen War: America Intervenes in Russia, 1918-1920</u>, 354
Frumkin, Jacob G., 183
Fuller, Adaline W., 1888-   , 572
Fuller, Benjamin Apthorp Gould, 1879-   , 257

Galvin, John A. T., collector, 158
Gankin, Olga Hess, 184
Garvi, Peter A., 1881-1944, 126
Gaskill, C. A., 573
Genkin, E., 540
Genoa. Economic and Financial Conference, 1922, 258
Georgievich, M., 185
Georgii Mikhailovich, Grand Duke of Russia, d. 1919, 186
Germany. Oberste Heeresleitung, 187
Gessen, B., 259
Gessen, Iosif Vladimirovich, 1866-1943, 355
Gibson, Hugh Simmons, 1883-1954, 574
Girs, Mikhail Nikolaevich, 1856-1932, 356
Gniessen, Vladimir F., 357
Golder, Frank Alfred, 1877-1929, 575
Golovan, Sergei Alexandrovich, 358
Golovin, Nikolai N., 1875-1944, 359
Golubev, 541
Gómez Gorkin, Julián, 1901-   , 38
Goodfellow, Millard Preston, 1892-1973, 640
Goodyear, A. Conger, 576
Gor´kii, (Maksim) collection (in Russian and English), 1921, 260
Graham, Malbone Watson, 1898-1965, 360
Gramotin, Aleksandr Aleksandrovich, 39
Grant, Donald, 1889-   , 577
Graves, William Sidney, 1865-1940, 475
Grayson, Walter A., 476
Green, Joseph Coy, 1887-   , 578
Grimm, David Davidovich, 1864-   , 641
Gronskii, Pavel Pavlovich, 1883-1937, 188
Group of English Speaking Communists, 261
Gubarev, P. D., 361
Gudelis, Petras, 362
Guins, George C., 1887-   , 477
Gulyga, Ivan Emel´ianovich, 1857-   , 189
Gurko, Vladimir Iosifovich, 1862-1927, 40

Hague International Peace Conference--Photographs, 1899-1907, 41
Halbrook, Stephen P., 262
Hall, Charles L., 579
Halonen, George, 263
Hamilton, Minard, 1891-1976, 580
Hammon, W. P., 1854-1938, 478
Harris, Ernest Lloyd, 1870-1946, 479
Harris, Gladys, collector, 480
Heiden, Dimitri F., Graf, 363
Helphand, Alexander, 1867-1924, 190
Henderson, Loy Wesley, 1892-   , 581
Heroys, Alexandre, 191
Heroys, Boris Vladimirovich, 364
Herron, George Davis, 1862-1925, 192
Hertmanowicz, Joseph John, 642
Hill, George Alexander, 1892-   , 365
Hilton, Ronald, 1911-   , 582

Hitoon, Serge E., 542
Holden, Frank Harvey, 583
Hoover, Herbert Clark, 1874-1964, 584
Hoover Institution on War, Revolution and Peace. Russian Provisional Government Project, 264; Soviet Treaty Series Project, 265; Supreme Economic Council and American Relief Administration Documents Project, 585
Hoover, John Elwood, 1924-   , 266
Horan, Brien Purcell, 42
Hoskin, Harry L., 1887-   , 481
Hoskins, Emmett A., 482
Hulse, James W., 267
Huston, Jay Calvin, 268

IAremenko, A. N., 483
Ilin, I. S., collector, 643
Istoricheskaia komissiia Markovskogo artilleriiskogo diviziona, 366
IUdenich, Nikolai Nikolaevich, 1862-1933, 367
IUnakov, N. L., 368
Ivanov, Vsevolod Nikanorovich, 484
"Iz vozzvaniia k karel´skomu naselneniiu kemskogo uezda" (From the appeal to the Karelian populace of the Kemsk region), 369
Izvestiia revoliutsionnoi nedeli (News of the revolutionary week), 269

Jacobs, John F. de, 586
Jacun, Konrad, 7
Jałowiecki, Mieczysław, 1886-   , 43
Janin, Pierre Thiébaut Charles Maurice, 1862-   , 485
Jennison, Harry A., 370
Jenny, Arnold E., 1895-1978, 587
Johnson, Benjamin O., 1878-   , 486
Johnson, William H., 487
Jones, Jefferson, collector, 159
Jordan, David Starr, 1851-1931, 270

Kader, Boris M., collector, 127
Kalnins, Eduards, 1876-1964, 371
Kapnist, Lieutenant, 488
Karcz, George F., 1917-1970, 44
Karmilof, Olga, 1897-   , 644
Kastchenko, Marie, 1902-   , 645
Kaul´bars, Aleksandr Vasil´evich, 1884-   , 193
Kautsky, Karl Johann, 1854-1938, 128
Kayden, Eugene M., 271
Kellock, Harold, 1879-   , 272
Kerenskii, Aleksandr Fedorovich, 1881-1970, 273
Keskűla, Aleksander, 1882-1963, 129
Kharbinskii komitet pomoshchi russkim bezhentsam, 646
Khorvat, Dmitrii Leonidovich, 1858-1937, 489
Khoshev, Boris Aleksandrovich, 1898-   , 372
Khrabroff, Nicholas, 1869-1940, 490
King, Gertrude, 194
Kititsyn, Captain, 491

Klemm, V., 1861-   , 373
Klimas, Petras, 1891-1969, 45
Kniazev, N. N., 543
Kocoj, Henryk, 46
Kokovtsov, Vladimir Nikolaevich, 1853-1942, 47
Kolchak, Aleksandr Vasil´evich, 1873-1920, 492
Kolobov, Mikhail Viktorovich, 493
Kologrivov, Constantine Nikolaevich, 195
Kolupaev, Eugenia Ritter, 588
Komor, Paul, 647
Konokovich, General, 196
Konstantin Nikolaevich, Grand Duke of Russia, 1827-1892, 48
Konstantinov, P. F., 49
Konstitutsionno-demokraticheskaia partiia, 648
Kornilov, Lavr Georgievich, 1870-1918, 274
Korol´kov, M., 160
Korvin-Kroukovsky, Eugenie A., 374
Kosinskii, Vladimir Andreevich, 1866-1938, 50
Koussonskii, Pavel Alekseevich, 375
Krajowa Agencja Wydawnicza, 275
Krasnov, Petr Nikolaevich, 1869-1947, 376
Krasnow, Wladislaw Georgievich, 1937-   , 51
Krassovskii, Vitol´d, 377
Kravchinskii, Sergei Mikhailovich, 1852-1895, 130
Kriukov, Boris Aleksandrovich, 1898-   , 494
"Krizis partii" (Party crisis), 131
Krupenskii, Aleksandr Nikolaevich, 197
Krymskoe kraevoe pravitel´stvo, 378
Krzeczunowicz, Kornel, 379
Kseniia Aleksandrovna, Grand Duchess of Russia, 52
Kuhn, Sylvester E., 495
Kurguz, Peter Nicholas, 276
Kutukov, Leonid Nikolaevich, 1897-   , 380
Kutzevalov, Boniface Semenovich, 381
Kwiatkowski, Antoni Wincenty, 1890-1970, 277

Lager Altengrabow, Germany, 198
Lampe, Aleksei Aleksandrovich von, 1885-1960, 382
Landesen, Arthur C., 649
Lansing, Robert, 1864-1928, 199
Lapteff, Alexis V., 589
Laserson, Maurice, 1880-   , 53
Lavrent´ev, K. I., 544
Lavrov, Sergei, 545
Lawrence, Eva, 590
LeGendre, William C., 200
Leikhtenberg, Nikolai Nikolaevich, Gertsog fon, 383
Leman, Rudolf, 1897-   , 278
Lenin, Vladimir Il´ich, 1870-1924, 279
L´Escaille, Mademoiselle de, 54
Levitsky, Eugene L., 384
Lewis, Roger L., d. 1936, 591
Lithuanian National Council in America, 650
Little, William Henry, 1937-   , 55

Liubimov, Dmitrii Nikolaevich, 1864-   , 56
Livermore, Edith, 57
Livingstead, Ivor M. V. Z., 58
Lodygensky, Georges, 385
Loehr, Mrs., <u>collector</u>, 280
Longuevan, Joseph B., <u>collector</u>, 496
Loucheur, Louis, 1872-1931, 201
Lovestone, Jay, 1898-   , 281
Lukomskii, Aleksandr Sergeevich, d. 1939, 386
Lykes, Gibbes, 592
Lyon, Bessie Eddy, 593
Lyons, Marvin, <u>collector</u>, 282

McCormick, Chauncey, 1884-1954, 594
McDonnell, Geoffrey, 497
McDuffee, Roy W., 283
McLean, Katherine S., 595
Makarov, N., 284
Makhno, Nestor Ivanovich, 1889-1935, 387
Maklakov, Vasilii Alekseevich, 1870-1957, 285
Makowiecki, Zygmunt, 202
Mariia Feodorovna, Empress Consort of Alexander III,
    Emperor of Russia, 1847-1928, 59
Maritime Province, Siberia. Komissiia po obsledovaniiu
    obstoiatel´stv sobytii 4-6 aprelia vo Vladivostoke, 498
Markov, Anatolii, 388
Martens, Ludwig Christian Alexander Karl, 1874-1948, 286
Martov, IUlii Osipovich, 1873-1923, 389
Martynov, A. P., d. 1951, 60
Martynov, General, 651
Martynov, Zakhar Nikiforovich, 390
Masaryk, Tomás Garrigue, Pres., Czechoslovakia, 1850-1937, 499
Maslovskii, Evgenii Vasil´evich, 203
Mason, Frank Earl, 1893-1979, 287
Mathews, Sarah E., 1880-   , 596
Matveev, General, 204
Maximova-Kulaev, Antonina Alexandrovna, 288
Medals collection, ca. 1914-1974, 8
Meiendorf, Maria F., Baronessa, 1869-1972, 61
Mel´gunov, Sergei Petrovich, 1897-1956, 289
Meyer, Henry Cord, 1913-   , 391
Michael, Louis Guy, 62
Miliukov, Pavel Nikolaevich, 1859-1943, 63
Miller, Evgenii Karlovich, 1867-1937, 392
Miroliubov, Nikander Ivanovich, 1870-1927, 64
Miroshnikov, Lev Ivanovich, 65
Mirovicz, General, 205
Mitchell, Anna V. S., 597
Mitkiewicz, Leon, 1896-1972, 393
Moran, Hugh Anderson, 1881-   , 598
Moravskii, Valerian Ivanovich, 1884-1940, 500
Mueller and Graeff photographic poster collection, ca. 1914-1945, 9
Mukhanov, Mikhail Georgievich, 66
Muraveiskii, S., 132

Murav´eva, Ekaterina Ivanovna, 652
Murphy, Merle Farmer, 599
Murray, A. C., 501

Naczelny Komitet Narodowy, 206
"Nakaz bol´shogo i malago voiskovogo kruga Voiska terskago"
    (Order of the Large and Small Military Union of the Tersk
    Unit), 394
National Polish Committee of America, 207
Naumov, Aleksandr Nikolaevich, 1868-1950, 67
Nekrasov, Nikolai Vissarionovich, 290
Newspaper Enterprise Association, 502
Nicholas I, Emperor of Russia, 1796-1855, 68
Nicholas II, Emperor of Russia, 1868-1918, 69
Nicolaevsky, Boris I., 1887-1966, 133
Nikolaieff, Alexander Mikhailovitch, 1876-   , 653
Nikol´skii, Evgenii Aleksandrovich, 161
Nilus, Evgenii Khristianovich, 1880-   , 503
Nirod, Feodor Maksimilianovich, Graf, 1871-   , 395
Nosovich, Anatolii, 396
Novaia zhizn´ (New life) (1917-1918) Leningrad, 291
Nowak, Jan, 397

Ob"edinenie russkikh v Marokko, 654
Oblastnoi komitet armii, flota i rabochikh Finliandii, 292
O´Brien, Charles A., 600
Obshchestva formirovaniia boevykh otriadov, 398
Obshchestva ob"edineniia i vzaimopomoshchi russkikh ofitserov
    i dobrovol´tsev, 399
Odintsov, Gleb Nikolaevich, 400
Oiderman, M., 401
"Olonetskaia Kareliia," 293
One Hundred Years of Revolutionary Internationals,
    Conference, Hoover Institution on War, Revolution
    and Peace, Stanford University, 1964, 134
Orbison, Thomas James, 1866-1938, 601
Ostroukhov, P., collector, 504
Otorchi, Ulan, 546
Ovchinnikov, Anton Zakharovich, 505
Ozels, Oskars, 1889-1975, 402

Paderewski, Ignacy Jan, 1860-1941, 208
Paleologue, Sergei Nikolaevich, 1887-   , 403
Paley, Olga Valerianovna, 1865-   , 404
Palitsyn, Fedor Fedorovich, 1851-1923, 405
Pantiukhov, Oleg Ivanovich, 1882-1974, 406
Pares, Sir Bernard, 1867-1949, 506
Paris. Congress, 1856, 70; Peace Conference, 1919. Commission on
    Baltic Affairs, 209; Peace Conference, 1919. U.S. Division of
    Territorial, Economic and Political Intelligence, 210
Partiia sotsialistov-revolutionerov, 135
Partridge, Stanley N., 507
Pash, Boris T., 407
Patouillet, Madame, 294

Pershin, Dimitrii Petrovich, 547
Pertsov, V. A., 508
Pertzoff, Constantin A., 1899-   , 509
Petrov, Arkadii Nikolaevich, 510
Petrushevich, Ivan, 1875-1950, 408
Philipp, Werner, 10
Pickett, Carrie, 602
Pierce, Richard A., 136
Pirnie, Malcolm, 603
Platonov, Valerian Platonovich, 1809?-   , 71
Pogrebetskii, Aleksandr I., 511
Poland. Ambasada (U.S.), 409
Poletika, W. P. von, 211
Polish Grey Samaritans, 604
Polish subject collection, 1908-1981, 212
Politicheskii ob"edinennyi komitet, 655
Das politische Leben in Russisch-Polen (Political life in Russian Poland), 72
"Poltavskiia eparkhial´nyia diela", 410
Popovskii, Mark Aleksandrovich, collector, 411
"The Port Arthur Diary," 162
Possony, Stefan Thomas, 1913-   , 295
Post, Wilbur E., 412
Poster collection, 11
Postnikova, E., 296
Pototskii, Sergei Nikolaevich, 1877-   , 213
Pravda (Truth), 297
Prianishnikov, Boris V., 656
Price, Hereward Thimbleby, 1880-1964, 214
Protocols of the Wise Men of Zion, 73
Puchkov, F. A., 512
Purington, Chester Wells, 513

Radek, Karl, 1885-1939, 298
Rakovskii, Khristian Georgievich, 1873-1941, 299
Ramplee-Smith, Winifred V., collector, 300
Rasputin, Grigorii Efimovich, 1871-1916, 74
Rayski, Ludomił, 1892-1976, 215
Red Cross. U.S. American National Red Cross, 605
Red Myth, 137
Reise, Lloyd, collector, 163
Rerberg, Fedor Petrovich, 1868-   , 413
"Revel´skaia gavan´ i bol´sheviki" (Revel harbor and the bolsheviks), 414
Reynolds, Elliott H., 514
Riabukhin, N. M., 548
Richardson, Gardner, 606
Riga, Treaty of, 1920, 415
Ringland, Arthur C., 607
Rodgers, Marvin, 608
Rodichev, Fedor Izmailovich, 1854-1933, 301
Rodzianko, Mikhail Vladimirovich, 1859-1924, 75
Rogers, Leighton W., 302
Rokitiansky, Nicholas John, 1912-   , collector, 76

Ronzhin, Sergei Aleksandrovich, 216
Rosenbluth, Robert, 609
Rossiiskaia sotsial-demokraticheskaia rabochaia partiia, 138
Rossiiskoe natsional´noe ob"edinenie, 657
Rostovtseff, Fedor, 658
Rozenshil´d-Paulin, Anatolii Nikolaevich, 217
Rudneff, Ilya Alexeevich, 1892-1969, 218
Russia. Armiia. 10. korpus, 219; Armiia. Kavkazskaia armiia, 220; Departament politsii. Zagranichnaia agentura, Paris, 139; Gosudarstvennaia duma--Collection (in Russian and English), 1906-1916, 77; Kabinet Ego Imperatorskago Velichestva. Ispolnitel´naia kommissiia po ustroistvu zemel´ Glukhoozerskoi fermy, 78; Konsul´stvo, Breslau, 79; Konsul´stvo, Leipzig, 80; Legatsiia (Hesse), 81; Legatsiia (Saxe-Weimar-Eisenach), 82; Legatsiia (Wuerttemberg), 83; Ministerstvo imperatorskogo dvora, 84; Posol´stvo (France), 303; Posol´stvo (U.S.), 304; Shtab verkhovnogo glavnokomanduiushchego, 221; Sovet ministrov, 222; Voenno-morskoi agent (Germany), 152; Voenoe ministerstvo, 223; Voennyi agent (France), 153; Voennyi agent (Japan), 164
Russia (1917. Provisional Government). Vserossiiskoe uchreditel´noe sobranie, 305;
Russia (1917- R.S.F.S.R.). Sovet narodnykh komissarov, 306; Tsentral´naia komissiia pomoshchi golodaiushchim, 307
Russia (1917-1922. Civil War Governments). Dobrovol´cheskaia armiia. Glavnyi kaznachei, 416; Donskaia armiia, 417; Vooruzhennye sily iuga Rossii. Nachal´nik snabzheniia, 418; Vooruzhennye sily iuga Rossii. Sudnoe otdielenie, 419; Vremennoe sibirskoe pravitel´stvo, 515
Russian National Committee, 659
Russian pictorial collection, 1887-1977, 12
"The Russian Public Debt," 308
Russian Review, 13
Russian subject collection, 1700-1975, 14
"Russie: Bulletin des anneés 1917-1922" (Russia: Report on the years 1917-1922), 15
Russiian, Viktor Nikolaevich, 85
Russing, John, 224
Russkaia narodnaia armiia (Russian people´s army), 420
Russkiia vedomosti (Russian news) (Moscow), 421
Russkoe aktsionernoe obshchestvo dlia primeneniia ozona, 86
Russkoe slovo (Russian word), 140
Ryskulov, T., 309

Sabine, Edward G., collector, 610
Sachs, Johannes, 225
Safonov, Ludmila, 1897-   , 660
Sakharov, Konstantin Viacheslavovich, 1881-   , 516
Salnais, Voldemars, 1886-1948, 517
Samsonow, Michael S., 1900-1973, 87
Sapon´ko, Angel Osipovich, 1876-1944, 88
Savich, N. V., 226
Savin, Petr Panteleimonovich, 661
Savinkov, Boris Viktorovich, 1879-1925, 422

Savintsev, Lieutenant, 518
Sazonov, Sergei Dmitrievich, 1861-1917, 89
Schakovskoy, Wladimir, Prince, 1904-1972, 423
Schauman, Georg Carl August, 1870-1930, 424
Schneider, Leo Victor, 1890-1963, 425
Schuyler, Eugene, 90
Scipio, Lynn A., 1876-   , collector, 611
Semenov, Evgenii Petrovich, 1861-   , 227
Semenov, Grigorii Mikhailovich, 1890-1945, 519
Serebrennikov, Ivan Innokentievich, 1882-   , 520
Sevastopoulo, Marc, 91
Shalikashvili, Dimitri, 426
Shapiro-Lavrova, Nadezhda L., 521
Shchepikhin, Sergei Afanasevich, 522
Shcherbachev, Dmitrii Grigor´evich, 1855-1932, 427
Shevelev, Klavdii Valentinovich, 1881-   , 428
Shil´nikov, Ivan Fedorovich, 228
Shinkarenko, Nikolai Vsevolodovich, 1890-1968, 429
Shkuro, Andrei Grigor´evich, 1887-1947, 662
Shneyeroff, M. M., 1880-   , 141
Shrewsbury, Kenneth O., 430
Shutko, IAkov, collector, 229
Shvarts, Aleksei Vladimirovich fon, 1874-1953, 431
Shvetzoff, Dimitrii Andreevich, 1902-   , 432
Skalskii, Vladimir Evgenievich, 433
"Slaviane v Amerikie" (Slavs in America), 92
Smith, Henry Bancroft, 1884-   , 612
Smith, Jack A., 523
Smith, Jessica, 613
Smolin, I. S., 93
Snigirevskii, Konstantin Vasil´evich, d. 1937, 154
Société agricole arménienne, 94
Sokolnicki, Michał, 1880-1967, 230
Sokolnikov, Grigorii IAkovlevich, 1888-1939, 310
Sokolnitskii, V., 549
Sokolov, Boris Fedorovich, 1893-   , 311
Sokolov, Nikolai Alekseevich, 1882-1924, 95
Solovei, Dmytro, 96
Solski, Wacław, 1896-   , 312
Soudakoff, Peter, 97
Sovet oppozitsii Man´chzhurii i Dal´niago vostoka, 663
"Soviet-Polish Dispute," 434
Spalding, Merrill Ten Broeck, 313
"Spravki o glavnokomanduiushchikh frontami, komandirakh armiiami, komandirakh korpusov i proch" (List of commanding officers of the Russian Imperial Army, arranged by units, at the time of the First World War), 231
Sprigg, Rodney Searle, 1894-   , 524
Stackelberg, Rudolf von, Baron, 98
Stafford, Clayton I., 435
Stamps, n.d., 16
Stanfield, Boris, 1888-   , 314
Steinberg, Isaac Nachman, 1888-1957, 436

Steinfeldt, Eric, <u>collector</u>, 525
Stenbock-Fermor, Ivan, Graf, 1897-   , <u>collector</u>, 99
Stepanov, Aleksandr Stepanovich, 526
Stepanova, Vanda Kazimirovna, 232
Stephens, Frederick Dorsey, 1891-   , 614
Stevens, John Frank, 1853-1943, 527
Stines, Norman Caswell, Jr., 1914-1980, 315
Story, Russell McCulloch, 1883-1942, 615
Strobridge, William S., 528
Struve, Petr Berngardovich, 1870-1944, 437
Sullivant, Robert Scott, 1925-   , 100
Sukacev, Lev Pavlovich, 1895-1974, 438
Sviatopolk-Mirsky, N., <u>collector</u>, 101
"Svodki o politicheskom i ekonomicheskom polozhenii v Sovetskoi
    Rossii za 1922 god" (Summaries of the political and economic
    situation in Soviet Russia for 1922), 316
Swinnerton, C. T., 317
Sworakowski, Witold S., 1903-1979, 102
Sychev, E., 529

Tal´, Georgii Aleksandrovich von, 103
Taneev, Sergei Aleksandrovich, 1887-1975, 104
Tarsaidze, Alexandre Georgievich, 1901-1978, 105
Tatistcheff, Alexis Borisovich, 1903-   , 106
Tchernigovetz, Nikolai, 664
Tikhon, Patriarch of Moscow and All Russia, 1865-1925, 439
Timofievich, Anatolii Pavlovich, d. 1976, 107
Tolstaia, Mariia Alekseevna, 108
Tolstaia, Sofiia Andreevna, 1844-1919, 109
Tolstoi, Lev Nikolaevich, 1828-1910, 110
Tolstoy, M.P., 111
Tomilov, P. A., 440
Treat, Payson J., 1879-1972, 165
Treloar, George D., 441
Tribunal Arbitral, The Hague, 1912, 155
"Trinadtsat´ let Oktiabria" (Thirteen years of October), 318
Trubetskoi, Vladimir S., Kniaz´, 166
Tschebotarioff, Gregory Porphyriewitch, 1899-   , 442
Tsurikov, N., 665
Tuban, Mark R., <u>collector</u>, 17
Turrou, Leon G., 616

"Ulany Ego Velichestva, 1876-1926" (His Majesty's Lancers,
    1876-1926), 443
Ungern-Shternberg (Roman Fedorovich, Baron) collection, 1921, 550
U.S. American Relief Administration. Russian Operations,
    1921-1923, 617; Army. A.E.F., 1917-1920, 530; Committee Upon
    the Arbitration of the Boundary Between Turkey and Armenia,
    444; Consulate, Leningrad, 319; Federal Security Agency, 666;
    Military Mission to Armenia, 445
Unruh, B. H., 112
Uperov, Vasilii Vasil´evich, 1877-1932, 233
Upovalov, Ivan, 446
Urquhart, Leslie, 320

Ustrialov, Nikolai Vasil'evich, 1890-   , 531

Vagner, Ekaterina Nikolaevna, 142
Vail, Edwin H., 618
Vaksmut, A. P., 447
Valkeapaeae, P. J., 619
Varneck, Elena, 532
Varnek, Tat'iana Aleksandrovna, 234
Varska, A. S., 533
Vasil'ev, Dimitrii Stepanovich, d. 1915, 167
Vasil'ev, E., 235
Vatatsi, Mariia Petrovna, 1860-   , 113
Vernadsky, George, 1887-1973, 321
Vernadsky, Nina, 322
Verstraete, Maurice, 1866-   , 114
Veselovzorov, Major General, 148
Vesselago, George M., 1892-   , 448
Viazemskii, Sergei Sergeevich, d. 1915, 236
Victor, George, 667
Vinaver, Rose Georgievna, 449
Vinogradoff, Igor, collector, 115
Vinogradov, A. K., 323
Violin, IA. A., 324
Vishniak, Mark Veniaminovich, 1883-1976, 143
Vitkovskii, Vladimir K., 450
Vladimir Kirillovich, Grand Duke of Russia, 1917-   , 668
Vladimirov, Ivan Alekseevich, 1870-1947, 325
Voitsekhovskii, Sergei L'vovich, 1900-   , 669
Volkhovskii, Feliks Vadimovich, 1846-1914, 144
Volkonskii, Vladimir Mikhailovich, 1868-1953, 116
Volkov, Boris, 551
Vologodskii, Petr Vasil'evich, 534
Vol'skii, Nikolai Vladislavovich, 1879-1964, 145
Von Arnold, Antonina R., 670
Von Mohrenschildt, Dimitri Sergius, 1902-   , 671
Vorotovov, Colonel, 535
Voyce, Arthur, d. 1977, 117
Vrangel', Mariia D., 451
Vrangel', Petr Nikolaevich, Baron, 1878-1928, 452
Vyrypaev, V. I., 453

Wachhold, Allen, 620
Wallen, E. Carl, 1889-1961, 621
Walsh, Warren B., translator, 118
Washington, Harold George, 1892-1961?, collector, 536
Wayne, Roy E., 237
Whitcomb, John M., collector, 326
Whitehead, James H., collector, 537
Wiasemsky, Serge, Prince, 672
Willis, Edward Frederick, 1904-   , 622
Wilson, Samuel Graham, 623
Wiren, Nicholas, 18
Wiskowski, Wlodzimierz, collector, 238
Wolfe, Henry Cutler, 1898-1976, 624

Wolkoff, A. de, 156
Woolf, Paul N., <u>collector</u>, 168
World War I pictorial collection, 1914-1919, 239
World War I subject collection, 1914-1920, 240
Woronzow-Daschkow, Hilarion, Graf, <u>collector</u>, 119

Yelsky, Isadore, 1896-1958, 538
Young Men's Christian Associations, 625
Yurchenko, Ivan, 673

Zakhartchenko, Constantine L., 1900-   , 674
Zavadskii, Sergei Vladislavovich, 120
Zavarin, Konstantin Nikolaevich, 539
Zawodny, Jay K., 327
Zebrak, Nicholas A., 675
Zershchikov, K., 121
Zinkin, Harold, <u>collector</u>, 19
Znamiecki, Alexander, 626
Zubets, Vladimir Aleksandrovich, 676
Zvegintsov, Nikolai, 454

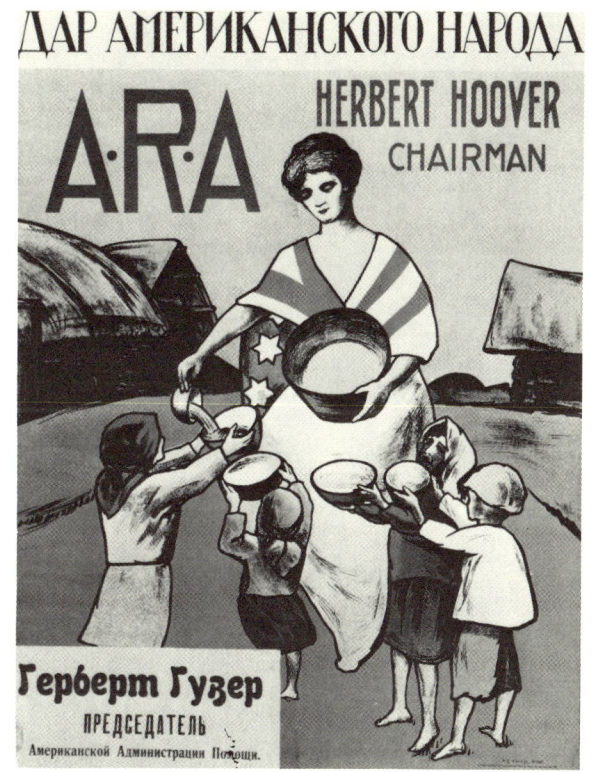

(Upper left) Comtesse Stroganov, painting by Dmitrii Levitskii (Nicolas de Basily Room)

(Left) Ivan Bunin, first Russian recipient of the Nobel Prize for literature (1933), and his wife, V. N. Muromtseva. Annotated by Bunin. (Boris I. Nicolaevsky Collection)

(Above) Poster commemorating the lifesaving work of the American Relief Administration and its chairman, Herbert Hoover, during the famine in Soviet Russia, 1921–1923

Nicolas de Basily Room in the Hoover Tower displays portraits, icons, paintings, and other artifacts from the Nicolas and Lascelle de Basily Collection

(Left) Photograph of Ekaterina Breshko-Breshkovskaia, Socialist Revolutionary leader, from the files of the Paris branch of the Okhrana

(Right) Dr. Frank A. Golder, first collector of Russian materials for the Hoover Institution

Odessa children wearing suits made from grain sacks and shoes supplied by the American Relief Administration

Imperial Russian World War I poster. Warns the Germans that while they are intent on capturing Paris, the Russians threaten Berlin

DESCRIPTIONS OF ARCHIVAL COLLECTIONS

COMPREHENSIVE COLLECTIONS AND MEMORABILIA

1. AUTOGRAPH COLLECTION. 1/2 ms. box.
    Collection of miscellaneous autographs of famous persons.
    Consult Archives staff for contents.

2. AXELBANK, HERMAN, 1900-1977, COLLECTOR.
    Motion picture film, ca. 1900-1977. 266 reels.
    Depicts major events in twentieth-century Russian history, including the Russian Revolution and World Wars I and II; the tsarist family and court; communist political and military leaders; and scenes of economic, social, and cultural activities in the Soviet Union.
    Register (reels 1-28).
    Preliminary inventory.
    Reels 1-28 and 40, ca. 1900-1924, are open; rest of collection is closed until processed.
    Purchase, Jay Axelbank, 1979.

3. BOOKPLATES. 1 ms. box.
    Many autographed by famous persons. Includes many autographed American Red Cross bookplates, collected by Noble E. Dawson, and prerevolutionary bookplates from the Baltic region.
    Gift, estate of N. E. Dawson, 1965. Incremental gifts, various sources, various dates.

4. BYCKOFF, MICHAEL M., COLLECTOR.
    Collection, 1769-1972. 18 albums (9 oversize boxes).
    Currency, banknotes, and stamps issued by the Imperial Russian and Soviet governments and by various regional and local governments and banks during the period of the Russian Civil War. In Russian and other languages.
    Gift, Natasha MacKenzie and Nadia Meigs, 1983.

5. CURRENCY COLLECTION, n.d. 8 ms. boxes.
    Coins, paper currency, and bonds from many countries and various periods of time; largely from Europe during World War I and the interwar period. Includes Russian currency, 1910-1922, and five tsarist bank notes.
    Gifts, various sources.

6. DEMETROPOULOS, CONSTANTINE, COLLECTOR.
    Postage stamps, ca. 1899-1923. 1 folder.
    Tsarist Russian stamps issued in China; stamps issued by German occupation forces in Russia during World War I; Russian Provisional Government, White Russian, and British occupation force stamps

issued in Russia during the Russian Revolution and Civil War; and early Soviet stamps.
Gift, C. Demetropoulos, 1979.

7. JACUN, KONRAD.
Study (in Polish), n.d. "Antagonizm Azyi i Europy" (Antagonism between Asia and Europe). 1 folder.
Typescript and printed.
Relates to the Eurasian nature of Russian civilization.

8. MEDALS COLLECTION, ca. 1914-1974. 20 ms. boxes.
Medals from many countries relating to the two world wars, to political events in the twentieth century, and to miscellaneous subjects. Includes tsarist Russian medals and a medal commemorating the fiftieth anniversary of the founding of the White Russian Army.
Preliminary inventory.
Gift, various sources.

9. MUELLER AND GRAEFF PHOTOGRAPHIC POSTER COLLECTION, ca. 1914-1945. 4 ms. boxes.
Photographs of posters relating primarily to Germany during World Wars I and II, German political events in the interwar period, and the Spanish Civil War. Includes Russian posters from the World War I and revolutionary periods and posters from France and a number of other countries.
Preliminary inventory.

10. PHILIPP, WERNER.
Translation of study, n.d. "The Historical Conditioning of Political Thought in Russia." 1 folder.
Typescript (mimeographed).
Relates to the Russian tradition of political theory. Original study, entitled "Historische Voraussetzungen des politischen Denkens in Russland," published in <u>Forschungen zur osteuropaeischen Geschichte</u> (Bd. 1, 1954).

11. POSTER COLLECTION. ca. 68,000 posters.
Posters from many countries relating to the two world wars, political conditions in the twentieth century, and various other subjects. Collection includes propaganda posters issued by the French, German, United States, and British governments during World Wars I and II and by the Russian Bolshevik and German Nazi parties and the Soviet government. Also includes materials printed in Paris, 1880-1900, relating to Russian revolutionary movements. The following collections have been incorporated into the Poster collection: Austria--Posters; Bolshevik posters; British poster collection; China--Posters; Disarmament--Posters; France--Posters; French election posters, 1951; Greece--Posters; Netherlands

--Posters; Odessa--History--Posters; Poland--Independence
movements--Posters; Russian revolutionary movements, 19th century
--Posters; U.S.S.R.--Posters; Ukraine--History--Revolution,
1917-1921--Posters; World War I--Posters; and World War II--Posters.
  Closed until the completion of the poster preservation project.
  Gifts and purchases, various sources, various dates.

12. RUSSIAN PICTORIAL COLLECTION, 1887-1977. 69 envelopes, 1 box of
    glass plates, 8 album boxes.
      Photographs and post cards depicting industrial, cultural,
    religious, and military scenes in Imperial Russia and the Soviet
    Union; scenes of daily life; scenes from notable historical events,
    especially the Russian Revolution; and prominent personalities from
    the tsarist and Soviet periods. The following collections have
    been incorporated into the Russian pictorial collection: Dniepro-
    stroi--Photographs; Ipatieff, Vladimir Nikolaevich, 1867-1952; Kra-
    matorsk Machine Tool Factory, Kramatorsk, Russia; Russia--
    Photographs; Russia (Provisional Government)--Photos; U.S.S.R.--
    Photographs; U.S.S.R. propaganda, 1945-1950--Photographs; Russian
    postcards; Alekseev, F.; Russian officer, 1839; Chichagoff, Lt.
    General; Goremykin, Ivan; Grigorovich, N. I.; Guchkov, Aleksandr I.;
    Kokovtsov, Vladimir N.; Krivoshein, Alexander; Miliukov, Pavel N.;
    Rodzianko, Mikhail V.; Rukhlov, Sergei V.; Sazonov, Sergei D.;
    Shingarev, Andrei I.; Stolypin, Petr A.; Sukhomlinov, Vladimir;
    Gairngrass, Alexander Alexeevich; Mendeleev Congress; Plehve,
    Viacheslav; Witte, Serge; Rasputin, Grigorii; Irina Aleksandrovna
    (Princess); Alexandra Fydorovna, Empress of Russia; Nicholas II,
    Czar of Russia; Nicholas II, Emperor of Russia, 1868-1918; American
    Russian Institute, San Francisco, CA; Voskevich, P.; Russia--History
    --Revolution of 1905; Russia--History--Duma; Russia--History--
    Revolution, 1917-1921; Maritime Regional People's Assembly; Russia
    --History--Allied Intervention, 1918-1920; Siberia--International
    Military Police; Chrezvychainaia komissiia po bor'be s kontr'-
    revoliutsiei i sabotazhem; Wrangel Army Camp--Gallipoli; Russia--
    Famines; Szamuely, Tibor; U.S.S.R.--History--Pictorial works,
    1930's; U.S.S.R.--Politbureau; and Molotov, Viacheslav M.
      Gift, various sources.

13. <u>RUSSIAN REVIEW</u>.
      Records, 1941-1973. 10 ms. boxes, 3 cu. ft. boxes.
      Monthly periodical published at the Hoover Institution on War,
    Revolution and Peace. Correspondence, subscription files,
    unpublished articles submitted for publication, clippings, and
    printed matter relating to Russian and Soviet literature, politics
    and government, history, and political and social movements before
    and after the Russian Revolution of 1917.
      Gift, <u>Russian Review</u>, 1973.

14. RUSSIAN SUBJECT COLLECTION, 1700-1975. 21 ms. boxes, 1 oversize
    box, 1 oversize folder, 1 phonorecord, 1 motion picture reel.
      Pamphlets, leaflets, serial issues, clippings, other printed

matter, correspondence, memoranda, reports, orders, and translations relating to political, social, and economic conditions in tsarist Russia and the Soviet Union, the Russian Revolution and Civil War, and American engineers in Russia. Mainly in Russian. The following collections have been incorporated into the Russian subject collection: American engineers in Russia, 1927-1933; Bint, Henri Jean, 1851-   ; Fedorov, Grigorii Fedorovich, 1891-   ; Gold mines and mining--Russia; Kappel´, Vladimir Oskarovich, 1881-1920; Partiia narodnoi voli; Posolskaya incident; Press--Archangel, Russia; Propaganda, Communist--Russia; Propaganda, Russian; Rossiisko-amerikanskaia kompaniia; Russia. Armiia. Leib-gvardii kirasirskii Ego Velichestva polk; Russia--History--Revolution, 1917-1921; Russia--Miscellanea; Russian Civil War in Georgia; Russo-Japanese War; Russo-Romanian relations; Samizdat; Soviet Union--Emigration; Stepno-Badzheiskyi volost´, Russia; Trotskii, Lev, 1879-1940 (including motion picture); and U.S. Advisory Commission of Railway Experts to Russia, etc.
   Register.
   Gift, various sources.

15. "RUSSIE: BULLETIN DES ANNEES 1917-1922" (RUSSIA: REPORT ON THE YEARS 1917-1922).
   Bibliographical essay (in French), ca. 1922. 1 folder.
   Typescript.
   Relates to publications during the period 1917-1922 on the subject of Russian history.

16. STAMPS, n.d. 15 albums, 3 boxes, 4 folders.
   Postage stamps from many countries issued at various times.
   Consult Archives staff for contents of collection.

17. TUBAN, MARK R., <u>COLLECTOR</u>.
   Napkin, n.d.
   Russian linen napkin with Romanov imperial crest and design.
   Gift, M. R. Tuban, 1981.

18. WIREN, NICHOLAS.
   Sword, n.d.
   Belonged to N. Wiren, Russian émigré who was probably an Imperial Russian military officer.
   Gift, David Tennant Bryan, 1976.

19. ZINKIN, HAROLD, <u>COLLECTOR</u>.
   Tabernacle, ca. 1835-1845.
   Russian tabernacle inscribed "Ral´k, Supplier for the Imperial Court."
   Gift, H. Zinkin, 1977.

IMPERIAL RUSSIA

20. AEHRENTHAL, ALOYS LEOPOLD BAPTIST LEXA von, GRAF, 1854-1912.
Memoirs (in German), 1895. "Memorie des Freiherrn von Aehrenthal über die Beziehungen zwischen Oesterreich-Ungarn und Russland, 1872-1894" (Memoirs of Baron von Aehrenthal on relations between Austria-Hungary and Russia, 1872-1894). 1 vol.
Typescript.

21. ALEXANDER II, EMPEROR OF RUSSIA, 1818-1881.
Decree (in Russian), 1859. 1 folder.
Printed.
Emperor of Russia. Relates to the status of Russian 5 percent bank notes and of investments in Russian banks.

22. BALK, A.
Memoirs (in Russian), 1929. "Posliednie piat´ dnei tsarskago Petrograda, 23-28 fevralia 1917 g.: dnevnik posliedniago petrogradskago gradonachal´nika" (The last five days of tsarist Petrograd, February 23-28, 1917: The diary of the last Petrograd mayor). 1 vol.
Typescript (carbon copy).
For translation, see collection number 118.

23. BASILY, LASCELLE MESERVE de.
Papers. 3 ms. boxes.
Wife of Nicolas A. de Basily, tsarist Russian diplomat. Includes drafts and galley proofs of the autobiography of L. M. de Basily, Memoirs of a Lost World (Stanford: Hoover Institution Press, 1975) relating to life in Russia before the Russian Revolution, Russian émigré life and world travel, and miscellaneous printed matter.

24. BASILY, NICOLAS ALEXANDROVICH de, 1883-1963.
Papers (in Russian and French), 1881-1957. 25 ms. boxes, 4 envelopes.
Imperial Russian diplomat; deputy director, Chancellery of Foreign Affairs, 1911-1914; member, Council of Ministry of Foreign Affairs, 1917. Correspondence, memoranda, reports, notes, and photographs relating to Russian political and foreign affairs, 1900-1917, Russian involvement in World War I, the abdication of Tsar Nicholas II, and the Russian Revolution and Civil War. Includes drafts of N. A. de Basily's book Russia Under Soviet Rule and the paintings and other art works in the Nicolas de Basily Room.
Register.
Gift, Mrs. N. A. de Basily, 1965. Subsequent increments.

25. BASILY-CALLIMAKI, EVA de, 1855-1913.
    Papers (in French), 1867-1913. 2 1/2 ms. boxes.
    Russian art critic and author. Correspondence, writings, notes, clippings, printed matter, photographs, and memorabilia relating to French and Western European art history and to Jean Baptiste Isabey, the French miniaturist. Includes the biography Isabey by E. de Basily-Callimaki and a draft of the book.
    Gift, Mrs. Nicolas A. de Basily, 1965. Increment, 1978.

26. BATIUSHIN, N. S.
    History (in Russian), n.d. "V chem byla sila Rasputina" (What comprised the strength of Rasputin). 1 vol.
    Typescript (carbon copy).
    Relates to Grigorii Rasputin, 1871-1916.

27. BIELEVSKII, LIEUTENANT, COLLECTOR.
    Miscellany (in Russian), 1917. 1 folder.
    Military reports and memoranda relating to the abdication of Tsar Nicholas II and to disintegration of discipline in the Russian army during the Russian Revolution.
    Preliminary inventory.

28. BRUNET, COURT COUNCILLOR de.
    Papers (in French, Russian, Swedish, and German), 1809-1814. 1 ms. box.
    Russian consul general in Norway. Correspondence, proclamations, and reports relating to Russian foreign policy and commerce in the Baltic.

29. CALDWELL, JOHN KENNETH, 1881-
    Memoirs, n.d. 1 folder.
    Typescript.
    American diplomat; consul at Vladivostok, 1914-1920. Relates to U.S. foreign relations and commerce with Japan, Russia, Australia, China, and Ethiopia, 1906-1945, and to U.S. participation in international narcotics control agencies.
    Gift, J. K. Caldwell, 1976.

30. CARBONNEL, FRANCOIS de, 1873-1957.
    Diary (in French), 1904-1905. 104 p.
    Typewritten transcript (photocopy).
    French diplomat in Russia, 1904-1906. Relates mainly to the Russian revolution of 1905.
    Gift, Anne Gasztowtt, 1982.

31. CHERKASSKII FAMILY.
    Papers (in Russian), 1837-1974. 1 1/2 ms. boxes, 1 oversize roll.
    Imperial Russian noble family. Diaries, correspondence, books,

memorabilia, writings, genealogy, clippings, printed matter, and
photographs relating to the careers, experiences, and genealogy of
the Cherkasskii family, the Russian Revolution and Civil War, the
Russian Orthodox Church abroad, and the Imperial Russian Army.
 Gift, Russian Historical Archive and Repository, 1975.

32. CHRISTOFF, PETER K., COLLECTOR.
 Collection (in Russian), 1840-1956. 1 ms. box, 2 envelopes.
 Photocopies of originals located in the Lenin Library, Moscow.
 Correspondence, diaries, and writings of prominent Moscow
Slavophils, 1840-1864, and photographs depicting social conditions
in the Soviet Union, 1931-1956.
 Gift, P. K. Christoff, 1980.

33. DOLGOROUKY, BARBARA, PRINCESS, 1885-
 Memoirs (in Russian), n.d. 1/2 ms. box.
 Typescript (photocopy).
 Russian aristocrat. Relates to the Romanov family, the Russian
imperial court, and the Russian Revolution and Civil War,
1885-1919.
 Purchase, B. Dolgorouky, 1973.

34. ERMAKOV, PETR ZACHAROVICH.
 Memoirs, n.d. "The Massacre of the Romanoffs." 1 folder.
 Typescript (photocopy).
 Participant in the execution of the Russian royal family, 1918.
Written by Richard Haliburton, as told by P. Z. Ermakov.
 Gift, M. Lyons, 1971.

35. EUROPEAN SUBJECT COLLECTION, 1889-1962. 7 ms. boxes.
 Pamphlets, leaflets, serial issues, posters, proclamations,
certificates, reports, and correspondence relating to miscellaneous
aspects of twentieth-century European history, especially to the
socialist movement in Europe between the two world wars. In various
languages. The following collections have been incorporated into
the European subject collection: Baltic states--Politics, Finnish
independence movement.
 Register.
 Gift, various sources.

36. FINNISH SUBJECT COLLECTION, 1900-1946. 5 ms. boxes, memorabilia.
 Trial transcripts, maps, pamphlets, and bulletins relating to
the Finnish independence movement before World War I and to the
trial of former Finnish government leaders accused of responsibility for Finnish participation in World War II. Includes a
flag of the Grand Duchy of Finland. Mainly in Finnish.
 Register.
 Gift, various sources.

37. FOSS, F. F.
    Papers, 1890-1917. 20 envelopes, 4 albums, 38 oversize prints, 1 oversize package (1/2 l. ft.).
    Engineer in Russia. Photographs and memorabilia relating to the development of industry in prerevolutionary Russia. Includes two albums with 59 prints depicting places of interest in Kiev.
    Gift, F. F. Foss, 1936.

38. GOMEZ GORKIN, JULIAN, 1901-
    Translation of play (in French), n.d. "Douze fantomes revivent leur histoire" (Twelve phantoms relive their history). 1 folder.
    Typescript.
    Relates to conditions in tsarist Russia during the early twentieth century.

39. GRAMOTIN, ALEKSANDR ALEKSANDROVICH.
    Report (in Russian), 1919. 1 folder.
    Holograph (photocopy).
    Captain, Imperial Russian Army. Relates to the activities of the Russian imperial family during the Russian Revolution.
    Gift, Marvin M. Lyons, 1965.

40. GURKO, VLADIMIR IOSIFOVICH, 1862-1927.
    History (in Russian), n.d. "Cherty i siluety proshlago: pravitel´stvo i obshchestvennost´ v tsarstvovanie Nikolaia II" (Features and figures of the past: Government and opinion in the reign of Nicholas II). 1 ms. box.
    Typescript.
    Imperial Russian government official. Translation published (Stanford, 1939). Russian manuscript includes two chapters omitted from published translation.

41. HAGUE INTERNATIONAL PEACE CONFERENCE--PHOTOGRAPHS, 1899-1907.
    2 framed photographs.
    Depicts delegates to the first and second Hague Peace Conferences, 1899 and 1907. Includes an identification chart for the second photograph.
    Gift, Mrs. Otto Lorenz, 1960.

42. HORAN, BRIEN PURCELL.
    Study, 1981. "Anastasia? The Anna Anderson-Anastasia Case." 201 p.
    Typescript (photocopy).
    American lawyer. Relates to the claim of one Anna Anderson to be the Grand Duchess Anastasia of Russia.
    Gift, B. P. Horan, 1982.

43. JAŁOWIECKI, MIECZYSŁAW, 1886-
    Memoirs (in Polish), 1964. 7 1/2 ms. boxes, 8 oversize boxes.
    Typescript.
    Polish-Lithuanian agricultural expert, architect, and engineer; chairman, Vilnius Agrarian Association. Relates to historical events in Russia and Lithuania before, during, and after the Russian Revolution and Civil War; Poles in Lithuania; and agricultural developments in Lithuania, 1881-1939. Includes watercolor drawings and sketches of scenes and manor houses in Lithuania and Poland.

44. KARCZ, GEORGE F., 1917-1970.
    Papers, 1917-1970. 37 ms. boxes, 4 card file boxes (2/3 l. ft.), 1 phonotape.
    American agricultural economist; professor, University of California, Santa Barbara. Correspondence, writings, research notes, statistical surveys and reports, and miscellanea relating to Soviet and Eastern European agriculture and economics. Includes "Agricultural Administration in Russia from the Stolypin Land Reform to Forced Collectivization: An Interpretive Survey" by George L. Yaney.
    Register.
    Purchase, Irene Karcz, 1971.

45. KLIMAS, PETRAS, 1891-1969.
    Diary excerpts (in Lithuanian), 1910-1939. 1 folder.
    Typescript.
    Lithuanian diplomat; minister to France, 1925-1940. Relates to Lithuanian student organization in tsarist Moscow, Lithuanian diplomacy after the outbreak of World War II, and political activities of the Lithuanian diplomat and writer Oskaras Milasius. Excerpts selected and edited by Zibuntas Miksys.
    Gift, Z. Miksys, 1982.

46. KOCOJ, HENRYK.
    Study (in Polish), n.d. "Prusy wobec powstania listopadowego" (Prussia and the November Uprising). 224 p.
    Typescript.
    Relates to Prussian diplomacy during the Polish revolution of 1831.

47. KOKOVTSOV, VLADIMIR NIKOLAEVICH, 1853-1942.
    Translations of memoirs, 1935. <u>Out of My Past: The Memoirs of Count Kokovtsov.</u> 1 ms. box, 1 envelope.
    Typescript.
    Russian statesman; minister of finance, 1904-1914; chairman of the Council of Ministers, 1911-1914. Relates to Russian political conditions, 1904-1917, and to the Russian Revolution. Translation published (Stanford: Stanford University Press, 1935). Edited by H. H. Fisher and translated by Laura Matveev. Includes photographs used to illustrate the book.

48. KONSTANTIN NIKOLAEVICH, GRAND DUKE OF RUSSIA, 1827-1892.
   Extracts from letters (in Russian), 1881-1882, to State Secretary Aleksandr Golovnin. 1 folder.
   Typescript.
   Relates to his travels in Western Europe and the political situation in Russia.

49. KONSTANTINOV, P. F.
   Newspaper article (in Russian), 1947. "Zhizn´ i vstrechi" (Life and encounters). 1 folder.
   Relates to Professor V. P. Ipat´ev´s memoir Zhizn´ odnogo khimika (Life of a chemist) and conditions in Russia before and after the revolution of 1917.

50. KOSINSKII, VLADIMIR ANDREEVICH, 1866-1938.
   Study (in Russian), n.d. "Russkaia agrarnaia revoliutsiia" (Russian agrarian revolution). 2 ms. boxes, 1 envelope.
   Typescript.
   Professor of political science and economics, Moscow University. Relates to agrarian reforms in Russia from 1905 until 1917.
   Gift, Sister Seraphim, 1972.

51. KRASNOW, WLADISLAW GEORGIEVICH, 1937-
   Dissertation, 1974. "Polyphony of The First Circle: A Study in Solzenicyn´s Affinity with Dostoevskij." 1/2 ms. box.
   Typescript (photocopy).
   Relates to the Russian novelist Aleksandr Solzhenitsyn. Ph.D. dissertation, University of Washington, Seattle.
   Gift, W. G. Krasnow, 1976.

52. KSENIIA ALEKSANDROVNA, GRAND DUCHESS OF RUSSIA.
   Papers (in Russian and French), 1912-1929. 11 ms. boxes.
   Daughter of Tsar Alexander III and sister of Tsar Nicholas II of Russia. Correspondence, diaries, and printed matter relating to events in Russia before, during, and after the Russian Revolution and Russian imperial family matters. Includes letters of Nicholas II and his mother, Mariia Fedorovna.
   May not be used without permission of depositors.
   Deposit, Prince Andrew and others, 1978.

53. LASERSON, MAURICE, 1880-
   Papers (in English, French, German, and Russian), 1920-1949. 1 1/2 ms. boxes, 1 envelope.
   Russian finance, commerce, and law expert. Correspondence, writings, reports, government documents, printed matter, and photographs relating to life in Russia prior to the 1917 revolution; the persecution of Jews in Russia and their emigration to Germany, 1904-1906; Soviet financial and commercial policy, 1918-1925; the

purchase of 600 locomotives by the Soviet government from Sweden, 1920; and the German socialist Karl Liebknecht.
   Gift, M. Laserson, 1948.

54. L'ESCAILLE, MADEMOISELLE de.
   Letters (in French), 1863-1921. 1 folder.
   Holograph.
   French governess. Letters from individuals connected closely with the Russian imperial family relating to personal matters in the lives of the Russian imperial family. Includes translations of some letters.
   Gift, Russian Historical Archive and Repository, 1974.

55. LITTLE, WILLIAM HENRY, 1937-
   Thesis, n.d. "The Tsarist Secret Police." 1 vol.
   Typescript (carbon copy).
   M.A. thesis, University of Texas.

56. LIUBIMOV, DMITRII NIKOLAEVICH, 1864-
   Memoirs (in Russian), n.d. 1/2 ms. box.
   Holograph.
   Chief of staff, Imperial Russian Ministry of the Interior. Relates to political conditions in Russia, 1902-1906.

57. LIVERMORE, EDITH.
   Photographs, 1913-1920. 1 envelope.
   Depicts activities of the German army during World War I, military parades and training exercises in Berlin, war damage in France, a 1913 parade in honor of Tsar Nicholas II at Potsdam, and British troops on parade in London.
   Gift, E. Livermore, 1940.

58. LIVINGSTEAD, IVOR M. V. Z.
   History, n.d. "The Downfall of a Dynasty." 1 vol.
   Typescript (carbon copy).
   Relates to the fall of the House of Romanov in Russia.

59. MARIIA FEODOROVNA, EMPRESS CONSORT OF ALEXANDER III, EMPEROR OF RUSSIA, 1847-1928.
   Letters (in Danish), 1881-1925, to Alexandra, queen consort of Edward VII, king of Great Britain. 15 ms. boxes.
   Holograph.
   Relates to matters of state and family.
   Preliminary inventory.
   Closed until January 2, 2001 or until publication of the letters by Princess Eugenie of Greece. Thereafter, may be used with written permission of Princess Eugenie, or, after her death, of

Prince Vasili Romanov or the director of the Hoover Institution.
Gift, Princess Eugenie, 1975.

60. MARTYNOV, A. P., d. 1951.
Memoir (in Russian), n.d. 1 ms. box.
Holograph.
Director, Moscow Office, Okhrana (Imperial Russian Police), 1912-1917. Relates to activities of the Okhrana, 1906-1917.
Purchase, Museum of Russian Culture, San Francisco, 1963.

61. MEIENDORF, MARIA F., BARONESSA, 1869-1972.
Memoirs (in Russian), n.d. "Moi vospominaniia" (My reminiscences). 1/2 ms. box, 1 scrapbook.
Typescript.
Russian aristocrat. Relates to social conditions in tsarist Russia, the Russian Revolution and Civil War, and Russian émigré life afterwards. Includes a printed copy of the memoirs (clippings from Russkaia zhizn' (San Francisco).
Purchase, Sophie Koulomzin, 1975.

62. MICHAEL, LOUIS GUY.
Memoir, n.d. "Russian Experience, 1910-1917." 3 vols.
Mimeograph.
American agricultural expert in Russia, 1910-1917.
Relates to agriculture and social conditions in Bessarabia, 1910-1916, and to the Russian revolution of November 1917.
May not be reproduced. Chapters 8 and 19 of Part I may not be quoted from.
Gift, Mrs. L. G. Michael, 1979.

63. MILIUKOV, PAVEL NIKOLAEVICH, 1859-1943.
History, n.d. "From Nicholas II to Stalin: Half a Century of Foreign Politics." 1 vol.
Typescript (carbon copy).
Russian historian. Relates to Russian diplomatic history.

64. MIROLIUBOV, NIKANDER IVANOVICH, 1870-1927.
Papers (in Russian), 1918-1927. 1 1/2 ms. boxes, 1 envelope.
White Russian political leader; chairman, Special Committee for the Investigation of the Murder of the Romanov Family.
Correspondence, memoranda, reports, and clippings relating to the investigation of the deaths of the Romanovs, 1918-1920, the creation of the first Far Eastern Republic, and Russian émigré organizations in the Far East, 1921-1927.
Register.
Gift, anonymous, 1936.

65. MIROSHNIKOV, LEV IVANOVICH.
Study, 1962. "The Development of Soviet Orientalism." 1 folder.
Typescript (photocopy).
Member of the Institute of the Peoples of Asia of the Academy of Sciences of the USSR. Relates to the history of Asian studies in prerevolutionary Russia and in the Soviet Union.

66. MUKHANOV, MIKHAIL GEORGIEVICH.
Papers (in Russian), 1862-1963. 1/2 ms. box.
Russian aristocrat. Correspondence, printed matter, reports, and photographs relating to conditions in Russia before, during, and after the revolution of 1917 and to experiences of various members of the Mukhanov family. Includes letters from the great-uncle of M. G. Mukhanov, Georgii Bakhmeteff, imperial Russian diplomat; from the great-great grandfather of M. G. Mukhanov, Marshal Mikhail Kutuzov, to his wife; and from Grand Duke Nikolai Nikolaevich to the father of M. G. Mukhanov, 1924.
Gift, Russian Historical Archive and Repository, 1975.

67. NAUMOV, ALEKSANDR NIKOLAEVICH, 1868-1950.
Memoirs (in Russian), 1929-1937. "Iz utsielievshikh vospominanii" (From surviving memories). 12 vols.
Typescript.
Imperial Russian minister of agriculture, 1915-1916. Relates to political conditions in Russia during the reign of Tsar Nicholas II and during the Russian Revolution and Civil War.

68. NICHOLAS I, EMPEROR OF RUSSIA, 1796-1855.
Order (in Russian), 1828. 1 folder.
Illustrates and describes various medals and awards.
Gift, Russian Historical Archive and Repository, 1974.

69. NICHOLAS II, EMPEROR OF RUSSIA, 1868-1918.
Miscellaneous papers (in Russian), 1890-1917. 1 1/2 ms. boxes, 1 oversize roll.
Two imperial orders (printed) signed by Tsar Nicholas II, 1905 and 1908; letters (handwritten and typewritten copies) from Nicholas II to Prime Minister P. A. Stolypin, 1906-1911; facsimile of the abdications of Nicholas II and Grand Duke Michael, 1917; Nicholas II's diary (handwritten copy); two religious books belonging to the Romanov family, which were found in Ekaterinburg after their murder; and other materials relating to the reign of Nicholas II. Includes a color reproduction of a painting of Nicholas II.

70. PARIS. CONGRESS, 1856.
Miscellaneous records (in French), 1857-1858. 1/2 ms. box.
Holograph.
Commission established by the Congress of Paris of 1856. Protocols of meetings and report relating to the reorganization

of the Romanian principalities of Wallachia and Moldavia.
Gift, Mrs. Lascelle de Basily, 1964.

71. PLATONOV, VALERIAN PLATONOVICH, 1809?-
Papers (in Russian, French, and Polish), 1815-1884. 3 ms. boxes.
Russian state secretary for Polish affairs, 1864-1884.
Correspondence, reports, and printed matter relating to Russian governmental administration in Poland; political, economic, and religious conditions in Poland; and the Polish revolution of 1863-1864.
Gift, Ksenia Denikin, 1936.

72. <u>DAS POLITISCHE LEBEN IN RUSSISCH-POLEN</u> (POLITICAL LIFE IN RUSSIAN POLAND).
Pamphlet (in German), ca. 1912. 1 folder.
Printed.
Gift, Stanford University Library, 1977.

73. <u>PROTOCOLS OF THE WISE MEN OF ZION.</u>
Writings (in Russian), n.d. "Sioniskie protokoly" (Protocols of Zion). 1 folder.
Handwritten.
Anti-Semitic propaganda tract.

74. RASPUTIN, GRIGORII EFIMOVICH, 1871-1916.
Note (in Russian), 1916. 1 folder.
Holograph (photocopy).
Adviser to Tsar Nicholas II and Tsarina Alexandra of Russia. Includes explanatory letter by Peter S. Soudakoff, March 4, 1956, and an affidavit copy certifying the authenticity of Rasputin's handwriting.

75. RODZIANKO, MIKHAIL VLADIMIROVICH, 1859-1924.
Papers (in Russian), 1914-1921. 1/2 ms. box.
President, Gosudarstvennaia duma of Russia. Correspondence, writings, and reports relating to Russian efforts in World War I, the Russian Revolution and Civil War, and the anti-Bolshevik movements. Includes letters and reports to Generals Vrangel´ and Denikin.
Preliminary inventory.
Gift, Nikolai Golovin, 1927.

76. ROKITIANSKY, NICHOLAS JOHN, 1912-   , <u>COLLECTOR.</u>
Collection (in Russian), 1817. 1 folder.
Photographic copy of originals in the Central Main Navy Archives of the U.S.S.R.
Map and sketches of Fort Ross, California.
Gift, N. J. Rokitiansky, 1979.

RUSSIA. DEPARTAMENT POLITSII. ZAGRANICHNAIA AGENTURA, PARIS, see collection number 139.

77. RUSSIA. GOSUDARSTVENNAIA DUMA--COLLECTION (IN RUSSIAN AND ENGLISH), 1906-1916. 1 ms. box, 1 envelope.
Proclamations, speeches, photograph, and translation of proceedings of the Russian Duma relating to activities of the Duma and to political conditions in Russia.

78. RUSSIA. KABINET EGO IMPERATORSKAGO VELICHESTVA ISPOLNITEL´NAIA KOMMISSIIA PO USTROISTVU ZEMEL´ GLUKHOOZERSKOI FERMY.
Account book (in Russian), 1900. 1 vol.
Holograph.
Imperial Russian Cabinet Executive Commission for the Organization of Lands of the Glukhoozerskaia Farm. Relates to expenses of digging canals on the Glukhoozerskaia Farm, an estate of Nicholas II, Tsar of Russia.

79. RUSSIA. KONSUL´STVO, BRESLAU.
Records (in Russian and German), 1860-1914. 10 ms. boxes.
Russian consulate in Breslau. Correspondence, intelligence reports, orders, and printed matter relating to Russian-German relations, especially commercial relations.
Preliminary inventory.
Gift, Serge Botkine, 1929.

80. RUSSIA. KONSUL´STVO, LEIPZIG.
Records (in Russian and German), 1830-1914. 7 ms. boxes.
Russian consulate in Leipzig. Correspondence, reports, and printed matter relating to Russian-German relations, especially commercial relations.
Preliminary inventory.
Gift, Serge Botkine, 1934.

81. RUSSIA. LEGATSIIA (HESSE).
Records (in Russian and German), 1857-1913. 17 ms. boxes.
Russian legation in Hesse (Hesse-Darmstadt until 1866). Correspondence, reports, circulars, instructions, telegrams, and printed matter relating to Russian-German relations.
Preliminary inventory.
Gift, Serge Botkine, 1929.

82. RUSSIA. LEGATSIIA (SAXE-WEIMAR-EISENACH).
Records (in Russian, French, and German), 1902-1908. 2 ms. boxes.
Russian legation in Saxe-Weimar-Eisenach. Correspondence, orders, reports, and printed matter relating to Russian-German relations.

Preliminary inventory.
Gift, Serge Botkine, 1934.

83. RUSSIA. LEGATSIIA (WUERTTEMBERG).
Records (in French, Russian, and German), 1828-1904. 16 ms. boxes.
Russian legation in Wuerttemberg. Correspondence, reports, orders, memoranda, and notes relating to Russian-Wuertemberg relations.
Preliminary inventory.
Gift, Serge Botkine, 1928.

84. RUSSIA. MINISTERSTVO IMPERATORSKOGO DVORA.
Bulletins (in Russian), 1894. 1 folder.
Printed.
Ministry of the Imperial Court of Russia. Relates to the illness and death of Alexander III, Tsar of Russia.

85. RUSSIIAN, VIKTOR NIKOLAEVICH.
Study, n.d. "The Work of Okhrana Departments in Russia." 1 folder.
Typescript.
Major general, Imperial Russian Army. Relates to the structure and operations of the Russian secret service in Russia before the revolution of 1917. Includes a draft with corrections and annotations.

86. RUSSKOE AKTSIONERNOE OBSHCHESTVO DLIA PRIMENENIIA OZONA.
Issuances (in Russian), 1911-1912. 1 folder.
Russian Joint Stock Company for the Adaptation of Ozone. Relates to the establishment of a filter-ozonizing station in St. Petersburg.

87. SAMSONOW, MICHAEL S., 1900-1973.
Papers (in English and French), 1919-1967. 1/2 ms. box, 1 envelope.
Hungarian-American historian. Memoirs, writings, and a photograph relating to Tsar Alexander III of Russia, Russian émigrés in Hungary after the Russian Revolution, and the provisions for a veto in the United Nations Charter.
Gift, M. S. Samsonow, 1970. Subsequent increments.

88. SAPON´KO, ANGEL OSIPOVICH, 1876-1944.
Papers (in Russian), 1900-1944. 11 ms. boxes.
Russian sociologist, political scientist, pacifist, and chief of the Stenographic and Records Division of the Duma until its dissolution. Correspondence, reports, essays, studies, articles, notes, clippings, printed matter, and photographs relating to

Christianity, disarmament, pacifism, religion and science, the
Russian Revolution and Civil War, fascism, world politics, Russians
in foreign countries, and the Russian Orthodox Church. Includes
papers of Zoia G. Brandt, his assistant, and materials pertaining
to A. V. Kossiakovskaia, exiled fiancée of Grand Duke Mikhail
Aleksandrovich.

89. SAZONOV, SERGEI DMITRIEVICH, 1861-1927.
   Papers (in English, French, German, and Russian), 1915-1927.
4 ms. boxes, 1 envelope.
   Russian diplomat; minister of foreign affairs, 1910-1916.
Memoirs, clippings, photograph, and correspondence relating to
imperial Russian foreign policy and the Russian Revolution and
Civil War.
   Gift, Lascelle de Basily, 1965.

90. SCHUYLER, EUGENE.
   Biography, 1883. "Peter the Great, Emperor of Russia: A Study
of Historical Biography." 1 ms. box.
   Holograph.

91. SEVASTOPOULO, MARC.
   Letters (in French), 1957-1959, received from Nicolas A. de
Basily. 1 folder.
   Holograph.
   Relates to the Sevastopoulo family genealogy.
   Gift, Elizabeth Stenbock-Fermor, 1977.

92. "SLAVIANE V AMERIKIE" (SLAVS IN AMERICA).
   Report (in Russian), 1917. 1 folder.
   Typescript.
   Relates to Czechs, Slovaks, Russians, Ukrainians, Yugoslavs,
and Poles in North and South America, their national organizations
and political activities during World War I. Written by a Russian
diplomatic agent in the United States.

93. SMOLIN, I. S.
   Translation of memoir, n.d. "The Alapaevsk Tragedy: The Murder
of the Russian Grand Dukes by the Bolsheviks." 1 folder.
   Typescript.
   White Russian army general. Relates to the discovery of the
bodies of members of the Russian royal family at Alapaevsk,
Russia, in 1918. Translated by W. Yourieff.

94. SOCIETE AGRICOLE ARMENIENNE.
   Report (in French), ca. 1919. "La situation agricole en
Arménie occidentale, années 1913 et 1917-1918: rapport" (The
agricultural situation in western Armenia, for the years 1913 and

1917-1918: Report). 1 vol.
Typescript (mimeographed).

95. SOKOLOV, NIKOLAI ALEKSEEVICH, 1882-1924.
Report (in Russian), 1919. 2 folders.
Holograph.
White Russian official; judicial investigator for especially important cases. Relates to the investigation of the murder of Tsar Nicholas II and his family. Intended as a supplement to the report by Lieutenant General M. K. Dieterichs. Includes translation (typewritten).
Gift, E. L. Harris.

96. SOLOVEI, DMYTRO.
Memorandum (in Ukrainian), 1944. "Istoriia ukrains´koi kooperatsii: korotkyi populiarnyi vyklad," Krynytsia, Ukraine. 1 folder (24 p.).
Typescript.
Relates to the history of agrarian cooperatives in the Ukraine.

97. SOUDAKOFF, PETER.
Writings (in Russian and English), n.d. 1 vol.
Typescript.
Relates to the Romanov dynasty, Lev Trotskii, and the Russo-Japanese War.

98. STACKELBERG, RUDOLF von, BARON.
Memoir (in German), 1919. 1 folder.
Typescript (photocopy).
Chief of the Field Chancellery of the Russian Ministry of the Court, 1914-1917. Relates to activities of Tsar Nicholas II and his court during World War I and the Russian Revolution.

99. STENBOCK-FERMOR, IVAN, GRAF, 1897-   , COLLECTOR.
Miscellany, ca. 1800-1913. 6 coins, 1 map.
Six imperial Russian coins and one nineteenth-century map of St. Petersburg.
Gift, I. Stenbock-Fermor, 1974.

100. SULLIVANT, ROBERT SCOTT, 1925-
Master's thesis, "The Problem of Eastern Galicia," submitted to the University of California at Los Angeles, 1948. 1 folder.
Typescript.
American political scientist. Relates to the national question in eastern Galicia, 1772-1939.

101. SVIATOPOLK-MIRSKY, N., <u>COLLECTOR</u>.
Postcards, n.d. 1 envelope.
Patriotic imperial Russian postcards, three from the collection of Tsarina Alexandra. Includes a photograph of Tsar Nicholas II and Tsarina Alexandra.
Preliminary inventory.
Gift, N. Sviatopolk-Mirsky, 1971.

102. SWORAKOWSKI, WITOLD S., 1903-1979.
Papers (mainly in Polish and English), 1921-1971. 2 1/2 ms. boxes.
Polish-American historian; assistant and associate director, Hoover Institution on War, Revolution and Peace, 1956-1970. Statistics, writings, translations, notes, maps, and printed matter relating to the ethnography of Upper Silesia in 1910, Polish boundary questions, 1918-1945, the Paris Peace Conference of 1919, communism in Eastern Europe after World War II, and the authorship of the 1917 abdication proclamation of Tsar Nicholas II.
Gift, estate of W. S. Sworakowski, 1979.

103. TAL´, GEORGII ALEKSANDROVICH von.
Memoir (in Russian), n.d. "Memuary ob otrechenii ot prestola rossiiskago Gosudaria Imperatora Nikolaia II" (Memoirs on the abdication of Emperor Nicholas II). 1 folder.
Typescript.
Commandant, imperial train of Nicholas II, Tsar of Russia, 1917.

104. TANEEV, SERGEI ALEKSANDROVICH, 1887-1975.
Papers (in Russian), 1883-1923. 1/2 ms. box, 1 album box.
Captain, Imperial Russian Army. Correspondence, notes, government documents, certificates, printed matter, photographs, and books relating to the Imperial Russian Army and Russian émigré life. Includes papers of the father and grandfather of S. A. Taneev, both tsarist government officials.
May not be published without permission of Tinatine Taneyew or her executor.
Gift, Tinatine Taneyew, 1979.

105. TARSAIDZE, ALEXANDRE GEORGIEVICH, 1901-1978.
Papers (in English, Russian, French, German, and Georgian), 1648-1978. 33 ms. boxes, 9 oversize boxes, 16 reels of film, 1 box of film fragments.
Georgian-American author and public relations executive. Correspondence, speeches and writings, research notes, printed matter, photographs, engravings, lithographs, and maps relating to the history of Georgia (Transcaucasia), the Romanov family, Russian-American relations, and the Association of Russian Imperial Naval Officers in America. Includes photocopies of Romanov family letters, photographs of Russia during World War I by Donald C. Thompson, and a documentary film of Nicholas II.

Preliminary inventory.
Bequest, A. G. Tarsaidze, 1978.

106. TATISTCHEFF, ALEXIS BORISOVICH, 1903-
Papers (in English and Russian), 1900-1978. 14 ms. boxes, 1 oversize album.
Russian-American economist and engineer. Correspondence, memoranda, writings, printed matter, and photographs relating to the Russian nobility, the Romanov dynasty, the Russian Revolution and Civil War, and Soviet-American relations during the 1960s and 1970s. Includes a history, "The Family of the Princes Obolensky," 1971.

107. TIMOFIEVICH, ANATOLII PAVLOVICH, d. 1976.
Papers (in Russian), 1890-1976. 2 1/2 ms. boxes, 1 memorabilia box (1/2 l. ft.).
Russian physician. Correspondence, clippings, and printed matter relating to various members of the Romanov family and other Russian dignitaries and nobility; events in Russia before, during, and after the Russian Revolution; and the Russian emigration. Includes a towel and cloth napkin with the crest of Tsar Nicholas II from Ekaterinburg and a hand-made rug presented to the Dowager Empress Mariia Fedorovna by the students of the Kievo-Fundukleevskaia zhenskaia gimnaziia in Kiev, 1915.
Gift, A. P. Timofievich, 1975.

108. TOLSTAIA, MARIIA ALEKSEEVNA.
Genealogy (in Russian), 1970. "Semeinaia khronika ot Krotkovykh do Meshcheriakovykh" (Family chronicle from the Krotkovs to the Meshcheriakovs). 170 p., 1 envelope.
Typescript.
Russian aristocrat. Relates to Krotkov and Meshcheriakov family history from 1760 to 1917. Includes excerpts from family correspondence, 1913-1917, and family photographs. By M. A. Tolstaia and Mariia Vladimirovna L'vova.
Gift, Prince Vasili Romanov, 1980.

109. TOLSTAIA, SOFIIA ANDREEVNA, 1844-1919.
Diary (in Russian), 1893-1910. 1 ms. box.
Typescript.
Wife of the Russian author Lev Tolstoi. Relates to Lev Tolstoi. May not be published without permission of the Tolstoy Foundation.
Gift, Tolstoy Foundation, 1981.

110. TOLSTOI, LEV NIKOLAEVICH, 1828-1910.
Miscellaneous papers (in Russian), 1853-1904. 3 1/2 ms. boxes.
Handwritten and typewritten transcripts of originals located in the Biblioteka SSSR imeni V. I. Lenina, Moscow.
Russian novelist. Diaries and writings relating to the life and

works of L. N. Tolstoi. Includes drafts of the novels <u>Anna Karenina</u> and <u>War and Peace</u> by L. N. Tolstoi.
  Preliminary inventory.
  Gift, S. Melgunov, 1932.

111. TOLSTOY, M. P.
  Miscellaneous papers (in Russian), 1858-1903. 1/2 ms. box.
  Russian countess. Memorandum notebook listing major military and state officials, 1858, and photographs of the 1903 Russian imperial costume ball in St. Petersburg.
  Gift, Russian Historical Archive and Repository, 1974.

112. UNRUH, B. H.
  Studies (in German), 1948. 1 1/2 ms. boxes.
  Typescript.
  German historian. Relates to the emigration of German Mennonites from the Soviet Union, 1921-1933. Includes typewritten copies (in German) of documents relating to the Mennonites in Russia from 1820 until 1870.
  Deposit, Margarete Woltner, 1948.

113. VATATSI, MARIIA PETROVNA, 1860-
  Papers (in Russian), 1917-1934. 1 1/2 ms. boxes.
  Wife of a tsarist government official in the Caucasus. Memoirs and correspondence relating to family affairs, political conditions in Russia, 1904-1917, White Russian activities during the Russian Civil War, and the Kuban Republic.

114. VERSTRAETE, MAURICE, 1866-
  Memoirs (in French), 1949. "Sur les routes de mon passé" (On the paths of my past). 1 ms. box.
  Typescript.
  French diplomat; consul in Moscow, 1894-1896; secretary of embassy to Russia, 1897-1900; consul general in St. Petersburg, 1901-1918.
  Relates to French relations with Russia and historical and political events in Russia from 1894 to 1918.
  Gift, M. Verstraete, 1949.

115. VINOGRADOFF, IGOR, <u>COLLECTOR</u>.
  Collection, 1824-1919. 1 ms. box.
  In part, typed copies of originals in possession of Count Alexei Bobrinski and Count Alfred Solmes-Sonnenwalde.
  Diary of Countess Mariia Benkendorf´ and letters of her sons Aleksandr and Vasilii Dolgorukii, 1915-1919, relating to the Russian army in World War I and to the Russian Revolution; photographs of the family of the tsar in captivity at Tobolsk, 1917; and diary of the journey of a noble Dutch family to Russia, 1824-1825. In French and Russian.
  Purchase, I. Vinogradoff, 1983.

116. VOLKONSKII, VLADIMIR MIKHAILOVICH, 1868-1953.
   Memoir, n.d. 1 folder.
   Typescript (photocopy).
   Relates to the canonization of Saint Serafim of Sarov by the Russian Orthodox Church, 1903.
   Gift, Vasili Romanov, 1977.

117. VOYCE, ARTHUR, d. 1977.
   Papers, ca. 1948-1960. 27 1/2 ms. boxes, 2 card file boxes (1/4 l. ft.).
   American art historian. Correspondence, writings, notes, photographs, slides, clippings, and other printed matter relating to Russian art and architecture from the fifteenth to the twentieth century.
   Gift, estate of A. Voyce, 1977.

118. WALSH, WARREN B., TRANSLATOR.
   Translations, n.d. 1/2 ms. box.
   Transcript (photocopy).
   Diary of A. Balk, prefect of police of Petrograd, 1917, relating to the Russian revolution of March 1917, and correspondence between Nicholas II, tsar of Russia, and P. A. Stolypin, president of the Council of Ministers of Russia, 1906-1911, relating to political conditions in Russia. Includes explanatory notes by W. B. Walsh.
   May not be quoted without permission of W. B. Walsh.
   Gift, W. B. Walsh, 1975.
   For Balk's diary in Russian, see collection number 22.

119. WORONZOW-DASCHKOW, HILARION, GRAF, COLLECTOR.
   Count H. Woronzow-Daschkow collection on imperial Russia (in Russian), 1903-1911. 3 oversize boxes (2 l. ft.).
   Printed photographs from the "Album of the Masquerade Ball at the Winter Palace in February 1903," depicting members of the Russian nobility, and a book entitled Kazanskii sobor, 1811-1911, v Sanktpeterburge (The Kazan Cathedral, 1811-1911, in Saint Petersburg).
   Gift, Count Woronzow-Daschkow, 1976.

120. ZAVADSKII, SERGEI VLADISLAVOVICH.
   Biography (in Russian), 1933-1935. "Zhizn' V. R. Zavadskago, razskazannaia synom" (The life of V. R. Zavadskii, as told by his son). 6 vols.
   Typescript.
   Relates to Vladislav Romual'dovich Zavadskii, imperial Russian courtier.

121. ZERSHCHIKOV, K.
    Memoir (in Russian), n.d. "Sobstvennyi Ego Velichestva konvoi v dni revoliutsii" (His Majesty's personal convoy in the days of the Revolution). 1 folder.
    Typescript (photocopy).
    Colonel, Imperial Russian Army. Relates to the bodyguard of Tsar Nicholas II in 1917.
    Gift, M. Lyons, 1971.

REVOLUTIONARY MOVEMENTS

122. BLAGOEV, DIMITUR, 1856-1924.
   Translations of writings, n.d. 1/2 ms. box.
   Bulgarian communist leader; student in Russia and social democratic leader, 1883-1886. Unpublished translations by Olga Hess Gankin of two published books by D. Blagoev, Prinos kum istoriiata na sotsializma v Bulgariia (Contributions to the history of socialism in Bulgaria), 1906, and Moi vospominaniia (Memoirs), 1928.

123. BRESHKO-BRESHKOVSKAIA, EKATERINA KONSTANTINOVNA, 1844-1934.
   Miscellaneous papers (in Russian and English), 1919-1931. 2 ms. boxes, 5 envelopes.
   Russian Socialist Revolutionary Party leader. Writings, correspondence, biographical data, and photographs relating to the life of E. Breshko-Breshkovskaia. Includes drafts of the book by E. Breshko-Breshkovskaia, The Hidden Springs of the Russian Revolution (Stanford University Press, 1931); a biographical sketch of E. Breshko-Breshkovskaia by Aleksandr Kerenskii; and three letters by E. Breshko-Breshkovskaia.
   Preliminary inventory.

124. BURTSEV, VLADIMIR L'VOVICH, 1862-1942.
   Papers (in Russian), 1906-1935. 1 ms. box.
   Russian revolutionist; later anti-Bolshevik. Memoirs, essays, correspondence, and printed matter relating to the Menshevik and Socialist Revolutionary movements before 1917, Evno Azef and other Okhrana agents, and counterrevolutionary movements during the Russian Revolution.

125. EGBERT, DONALD DREW, 1902-1973.
   Study, n.d. "Communism, Radicalism and the Arts: American Developments in Relation to the Background in Western Europe and in Russia from the Sevententh Century to 1959." 2 ms. boxes.
   Typescript (photocopy).
   American historian. Relates to the effects of Marxism and communism on American art and the relationships between works of art and the social, economic, and political beliefs of the artists who produced them, 1680-1959. A revised version of this study was published under the title Socialism and American Art in the Light of European Utopianism, Marxism and Anarchism (Princeton, 1967).
   Gift, Theodore Draper, 1964.

126. GARVI, PETER A., 1881-1944.
   Writings (in Russian), n.d. 1/2 ms. box.
   Typescript.
   Russian socialist. "Vospominaniia sotsialdemokrata" (Memoirs of a

social democrat), relating to the Russian Social Democratic Workers' Party, 1906-1917; "Professional'nye soiuzy Rossii v pervye gody revoliutsii" (Trade unions of Russia in the first years of the Revolution); and "Rabochaia kooperatsiia v pervye gody russkoi revoliutsii, 1917-1921" (Workers' cooperatives in the first years of the Russian Revolution, 1917-1921).
   Gift, Columbia University Research Program on the History of the C.P.S.U., 1956.

127. KADER, BORIS M., <u>COLLECTOR</u>.
   B. M. Kader collection on Peresylnaia tiurma (in Russian), 1906. 1 folder.
   Articles, notes, and poems written by the prisoners of Peresylnaia tiurma in Petrograd for their secret magazine "Tiurma" (Prison). Includes description of the material by B. M. Kader, editor of "Tiurma."
   Preliminary inventory.
   Gift, B. M. Kader, 1957.

128. KAUTSKY, KARL JOHANN, 1854-1938.
   Essay (in German), 1938. "Der demokratische Marxismus: zum vierzigsten Geburtstag der russischen Sozialdemokratie" (Democratic Marxism: On the fortieth anniversary of Russian social democracy). 1 folder.
   Typescript (photocopy).
   German socialist leader. Relates to the history and future prospects of socialism in Russia. Includes postcard photograph of K. J. Kautsky.
   Gift, Karl Kautsky, Jr., 1977.

129. KESKULA, ALEKSANDER, 1882-1963.
   Papers (in German), 1915-1963. 2 ms. boxes.
   Estonian socialist; reputed intermediary between V. I. Lenin and the German government during World War I. Correspondence, writings, and memoranda relating to personal experiences and to international socialist and communist movements.
   Preliminary inventory.
   Purchase, Ingeborg K. Weidmann, 1966.

130. KRAVCHINSKII, SERGEI MIKHAILOVICH, 1852-1895.
   Papers (in Russian), 1892-1908. 1 ms. box.
   Russian socialist and novelist. Correspondence, writings, and extracts from printed matter relating to nineteenth-century Russian revolutionary movements. Includes material relating to S. M. Kravchinskii.

131. "KRIZIS PARTII" (PARTY CRISIS).
   History (in Russian), n.d. 1 folder.
   Typescript.

Relates to the history and structure of the Communist Party of the Soviet Union, 1905-1923.

132. MURAVEISKII, S.
Translation of pamphlet, n.d. "Data on the History of the Revolutionary Movement in Central Asia: Result of a Brief Study of the Soviet Party Schools and Political Primary Schools." 1 folder.
Typescript.
Translation by Xenia J. Eudin of <u>Ocherki po istorii revoliutsionnogo dvizheniia v srednei Azii: opyt kratkogo posobiia dlia sovpartshkol i shkol politgramoty</u>, published in Tashkent in 1926.

133. NICOLAEVSKY, BORIS I., 1887-1966.
B. I. Nicolaevsky collection (in Russian, also partly in German, French, and English), 1850-1966. ca. 400 ms. boxes.
Russian social democrat, historian, author, publicist, collector of historical material on social and revolutionary movements in Russia and abroad. Letters, memoranda, writings, speeches, memoirs, minutes of meetings, underground leaflets, photographs, clippings, and other miscellaneous historical documents relating primarily to the Russian revolutionary movements (radicals, populists, anarchists, and, more specifically and extensively, the Russian Social Democratic Party and the Socialist Revolutionary Party); the tsarist government; the 1905 revolution; the Imperial Duma; the February and October Revolutions; the Civil War; Russian émigré politics; the Vlasov movement during World War II; history and activities of the First, Second, and Third Internationals; and the labor and socialist movements in Europe and the United States. Consists of approximately 300 units of collected materials, including records of such organizations as the Social Democratic and Socialist Revolutionary parties, and personal papers of such political figures as A. Herzen, M. Bakunin, P. Lavrov, G. Plekhanov, P. Akselrod, IU. Martov, I. Tsereteli, V. Chernov, and L. Trotsky. Includes material on the Shevchenko Library in L'vov, the Ukraine in the post-October period, the Ukrainian movement, and Ukrainian postwar émigré organizations.
Register prepared by Curator Anna Bourguina.
Purchase, B. I. Nicolaevsky, 1963; several incremental gifts.

134. ONE HUNDRED YEARS OF REVOLUTIONARY INTERNATIONALS, CONFERENCE, HOOVER INSTITUTION ON WAR, REVOLUTION AND PEACE, STANFORD UNIVERSITY, 1964.
Proceedings, 1964. 1 ms. box, 10 phonotapes.
Sound recordings and conference papers relating to the history of Marxist doctrine and of the communist movement.

135. PARTIIA SOTSIALISTOV-REVOLUTIONEROV.
Miscellaneous records (in Russian), 1914-1923. 1 ms. box.

Russian Socialist Revolutionary Party. Reports and minutes relating to the activities and views of the party and to the Russian Revolution.

136. PIERCE, RICHARD A.
   Study, 1957. "The Origins of Bolshevism in Russian Central Asia." 1 vol.
   Typescript (carbon copy).
   Prepared for the Columbia University Research Program on the History of the Communist Party of the Soviet Union.

137. RED MYTH.
   Motion picture, 1961. 13 reels.
   Relates to the history of communism. Produced for television by KQED-TV, San Francisco, in cooperation with the Hoover Institution on War, Revolution and Peace.
   Gift, National Educational Television, 1961.

138. ROSSIISKAIA SOTSIAL-DEMOKRATICHESKAIA RABOCHAIA PARTIIA.
   Miscellaneous issuances (in Russian), ca. 1904-1910. 1 folder.
   Printed.
   Russian Social Democratic Labor Party. Notice of change of address of party headquarters in Geneva, 1904; broadside relating to tsarist agents provocateurs and the trial of socialist deputies of the Duma, 1907; and proclamation by the Vpered Group relating to internal party politics, ca. 1910.
   Gift, Antony Sutton, 1970.

139. RUSSIA. DEPARTAMENT POLITSII. ZAGRANICHNAIA AGENTURA, PARIS.
   Records (mainly in Russian), 1883-1917. 203 ms. boxes, 10 vols. of clippings, 163,802 biographical and reference cards, 8 linear feet of photographs.
   Imperial Russian secret police (Okhrana), Paris office. Intelligence reports from agents in the field and the Paris office, dispatches, circulars, headquarters studies, correspondence of revolutionaries, and photographs relating to activities of Russian revolutionists abroad. Contains files relating to the Ukrainian revolutionary movement, including the Galician revolutionaries of 1914; the Berlin-based Ukrainian nationalists; a survey of the Ukrainian nationalist movement in 1916; the "Mazeppa group" in Canada; the Ukrainian Congress in Canada, 1916-1917; and M. Sichynsky, the leader of a "Mazeppa group" in the United States.
   Preliminary inventory.
   Deposit, Vasilii Maklakov, 1926. One item purchased from Jacob Rubin, 1976.

140. RUSSKOE SLOVO (RUSSIAN WORD).
   Translation of excerpts from articles, n.d. 1 folder.
   Typescript.

Russian newspaper. Relates to the activities of Roman Malinovskii, a tsarist agent who infiltrated the Bolshevik Party in Russia.

141. SHNEYEROFF, M. M., 1880-
Papers (in Russian and English), 1918-1957. 1 ms. box.
Member of the Russian Socialist Revolutionary Party. Memoirs, writings, and photographs relating to the Russian revolutionary movement in the early twentieth century.
Preliminary inventory.
Quotations limited to 500 consecutive words and to 5,000 words from any one manuscript.
Gift, M. M. Shneyeroff, 1959.

142. VAGNER, EKATERINA NIKOLAEVNA.
Papers (in Russian), 1876-1936. 2 ms. boxes.
Russian Socialist Revolutionary. Correspondence, writings, diaries, and printed matter relating to revolutionary movements and events in Russia. Includes the "Reminiscences" of N. N. Dzvonkevich (father of E. N. Vagner), a study of the Strelnikovskii trial in Odessa, and letters from Ekaterina Breshko-Breshkovskaia.
Preliminary inventory.
Purchase, E. N. Vagner, 1937.

143. VISHNIAK, MARK VENIAMINOVICH, 1883-1976.
Papers (in Russian and English), ca. 1910-1968. 14 ms. boxes.
Russian historian; Socialist Revolutionary Party leader. Correspondence, writings, and clippings relating to Russian and Soviet history, Russian revolutionists, Russian émigrés, and political conditions in the Soviet Union.
Preliminary inventory.
Gift, M. V. Vishniak, 1970.

144. VOLKHOVSKII, FELIKS VADIMOVICH, 1846-1914.
Papers (in Russian), 1875-1914. 24 ms. boxes.
Russian revolutionary and journalist; Socialist Revolutionary Party leader; editor, Free Russia (London). Correspondence, writings, photographs, periodicals, and clippings relating to revolutionary movements in imperial Russia.
Preliminary inventory.

145. VOL´SKII, NIKOLAI VLADISLAVOVICH, 1879-1964.
   Papers (in Russian and English), 1908-1964. 10 ms. boxes, 1 envelope.
   Russian revolutionary and author. Correspondence, writings, clippings, reports, and photographs relating to Russian revolutionary movements and émigré life, imperial Russian and Soviet agricultural and economic policies, labor movements, Menshevism, and political events in Russia.
   Preliminary inventory.
   Purchase, Vera Vol´skii, 1965. Purchase, International Institute of Social History, 1976.

IMPERIAL RUSSIAN ARMY ORGANIZATION

146. BASTUNOV, VLADIMIR J., COLLECTOR.
 V. J. Bastunov collection on the Imperial Russian Army (in Russian), 1897-1917. 4 ms. boxes.
 Imperial orders, military orders, personnel rosters, and casualty reports relating to the operations of the Imperial Russian Army and its personnel.
 Gift, V. J. Bastunov, 1975.

147. DOMANENKO, GENERAL.
 Study (in Russian), n.d. "Sluzhba General'nago shtaba v divizii i korpusie" (General staff service in the division and corps).
 1 vol.
 Holograph.
 Relates to the organization of the Imperial Russian Army.

148. VESELOVZOROV, MAJOR GENERAL.
 Commentary (in Russian), n.d. "Ustav unutrennei sluzhby" (Regulations of routine garrison service). 1 folder.
 Holograph.
 Imperial Russian Army officer. Relates to regulations of the Imperial Russian Army.

IMPERIAL RUSSIAN ARMY BEFORE 1904

149. ASIAN PICTORIAL COLLECTION, 1883-1948. 7 envelopes, 1 album box.
Photographs depicting miscellaneous scenes and personalities in Asia, including scenes of revolutionary disturbances in Iran, ca. 1908. Includes photograph, ca. 1877-1878, of General Etterg, commandant of Adrianopol´ during the Russo-Turkish War.
Gift, various sources.

150. BRUNELLI, PAUL.
Memoirs (in Russian), n.d. "Moia letopis´--Leib gvardii v Ismailovskom polku" (My chronicle--A life guard in the Ismailovskii Regiment). 1 folder.
Typescript (photocopy).
Colonel, Imperial Russian Army. Relates to the activities of the regiment during the year 1897.
Gift, M. Lyons, 1971.

151. ETTER, MARIA von.
Papers (in Russian), 1895-1916.
Russian aristocrat. Letters of appointment, commendation, and appreciation, certificates, and awards relating to the charitable volunteer work of M. von Etter. Includes a record book of patients at the Russian Red Cross von Etter Infirmary, 1915-1916, and a memorial album with an engraved sterling silver plaque dedicated to Ivan Sevastianovich von Etter from the imperial Russian Kiev officers under his command, containing photographs and autographs of the officers.
Gift, Russian Historical Archive and Repository, 1974.

152. RUSSIA. VOENNO-MORSKOI AGENT (GERMANY).
Records (in Russian and German), 1873-1912. 3 ms. boxes.
Russian naval agent in Germany. Correspondence, reports, orders, and printed matter relating to Russian-German naval relations and to Russian purchases of ships, ordnance, and naval equipment from German firms.
Preliminary inventory.
Gift, Serge Botkine, 1930.

153. RUSSIA. VOENNYI AGENT (FRANCE).
Records (in French and Russian), 1835-1876. 6 ms. boxes.
Office of the Russian military attaché in France. Correspondence, memoranda, reports, studies, lists, charts, and printed matter relating to military relations between Russia and France.

154. SNIGIREVSKII, KONSTANTIN VASIL´EVICH, d. 1937.
    History (in Russian), 1937. "Aleksandrovskii komitet o ranenykh" (Aleksadrovskii Committee for the Wounded). 1 folder.
    Holograph.
    Major general, Imperial Russian Army. Relates to a Russian organization founded in the nineteenth century for the care of wounded soldiers.

155. TRIBUNAL ARBITRAL, THE HAGUE, 1912.
    Issuances (in French), 1912. 1 folder.
    Printed.
    Arguments of the Russian and Turkish governments and decision of the tribunal relating to a dispute over reparations owed Russia by Turkey as a result of the Russo-Turkish War of 1877-1878.

156. WOLKOFF, A. de.
    Biography, n.d. "Lazarev of _Mirny_: Russia's Greatest Admiral." 504 p.
    Typescript (photocopy).
    Great-granddaughter of Mikhail Lazarev. Relates to the nineteenth-century Russian admiral Mikhail Petrovich Lazarev, explorer of the Pacific and Antarctic oceans and commander of the Black Sea Fleet, 1834-1851.
    Gift, Prince Vasili Romanov, 1980.

RUSSO-JAPANESE WAR, 1904-1905; 1905-1913

157. BAZAROV, PAVEL ALEKSANDROVICH.
   Papers (in Russian), 1904-1905. 1 ms. box.
   Lieutenant-colonel attached to the staff of commander in chief of the Russian armies, General A. N. Kuropatkin, during the Russo-Japanese War. Correspondence, memoranda, reports, orders, instructions, studies, maps, clippings, and printed matter relating to the Russo-Japanese War.
   Register.

158. GALVIN, JOHN A. T., COLLECTOR.
   Reproductions of paintings, n.d. 1 envelope.
   Depicts scenes from the Franco-Prussian War, the Boxer Rebellion, and the Russo-Japanese War, including the Battle of Tsushima Straits. Also includes misellaneous scenes, mainly of Japan.
   Gift, J. A. T. Galvin, 1955.

159. JONES, JEFFERSON, COLLECTOR.
   Miscellany, 1914-1918. 1/2 ms. box, 4 envelopes.
   Photographs, drawings, posters, printed matter, and miscellanea relating to activities of the Japanese army in China during World War I, especially the siege of Tsingtao, 1914; to the Russo-Japanese War of 1904-1905; and the palace of Kaiser Wilhelm II on the island of Corfu.
   Gift, J. Jones, 1959.

160. KOROL´KOV, M.
   Memoir (in Russian), 1928. "Iz vospominanii voennago iurista" (From the reminiscences of a military lawyer). 1 vol.
   Typescript.
   Relates to administration of military justice in the Imperial Russian Army and to military discipline at the time of the Russo-Japanese War.

161. NIKOL´SKII, EVGENII ALEKSANDROVICH.
   Memoirs (in Russian), 1934. 1 folder.
   Typescript.
   Imperial Russian Army officer. Memoirs entitled "Sluzhba v Glavnom shtabie i Glavnom upravlenii General´nago shtaba" (Service in the Main Headquarters and Main Directorate of the General Staff) and "Biezhentsy v velikuiu voinu (Refugees in the Great War), relating to the Russian general staff, 1903-1908, and Russian refugees during World War I.

162. "THE PORT ARTHUR DIARY."
   Translation of table of contents, n.d. 1 folder.

Typescript.

Diary of an unknown Russian relating to the siege of Port Arthur during the Russo-Japanese War, January 1904-April 1905. Translated by Elena Varneck.

163. REISE, LLOYD, COLLECTOR.
Photographs, ca. 1904-1918. 2 envelopes.
Depicts World War I scenes in France, especially aerial operations, and scenes in China, especially of the Russian fleet, during the Russo-Japanese War.
Gift, L. Reise, 1980.

164. RUSSIA. VOENNYI AGENT (JAPAN).
Records (in Russian), 1906-1921. 16 ms. boxes.
Russian military attaché in Japan. Letters, telegrams, contracts, minutes, receipts, memoranda, reports, accounts, declarations, requests, orders, instructions, packing and shipping specifications, invoices, insurance policies, bills of lading, blueprints, tables, diagrams, certificates, and lists relating to the Japanese army, political movements in Japan, and the purchase by the Russian army of military supplies from Japanese firms.
Register.
Gift, Nikolai Golovin, 1928.

165. TREAT, PAYSON J., 1879-1972.
Papers, 1855-1973. 63 ms. boxes, 1 album, 7 envelopes, 12 maps, 4 scrolls.
American historian. Correspondence, reports, interviews, copies of diplomatic records, speeches, writings, notes, photographs, maps, memorabilia, and printed matter relating to the diplomatic history of Japan, China, and other countries in the Far East. Includes a pamphlet collection on World War I. Also includes 3 oversize photographs of the negotiators of the Russo-Japanese treaty and, in box 59, "U.S. State Department records. Russia. Dispatches, instructions, etc., 1879-1905."
Register.
Gift, P. J. Treat, 1960. Subsequent increments.

166. TRUBETSKOI, VLADIMIR S., KNIAZ´.
Memoirs (in Russian), n.d. "Zapiski kirasira" (Notes of a kirasir). 139 p.
Typescript (photocopy).
Russian prince and army officer. Relates to the imperial Russian Kirasir Household Troops Regiment of Her Majesty Mariia Fedorovna during the period 1911-1913.
Gift, Prince Vasili Romanov, 1980.

167. VASIL´EV, DIMITRII STEPANOVICH, d. 1915.
Miscellanea (in Russian), 1907-1975. 1 folder.

Imperial Russian naval attaché in the United States. Marriage and death certificates, 1907 and 1915. Includes <u>Bulletins</u> of the Russian Imperial Naval Academy, 1973-1975, and a <u>document</u> concerning the Russian Military-Naval Agency in the United States, 1915-18, with which D. S. Vasil´ev was associated.
   Gift, Constantine Zakhartchenko, 1975.

168. WOOLF, PAUL N., <u>COLLECTOR</u>.
   Photographs, 1906. 1 envelope.
   Depicts people, scenic views, military parades, and captured weapons in Japan after the end of the Russo-Japanese War.
   Preliminary inventory.
   Gift, P. N. Woolf, 1963.

WORLD WAR I

169. AGENCE TELEGRAPHIQUE DE PETROGRAD.
   Daily news bulletins (in French), 1915-1916. 5 vols.
   Typescript.
   Press service. Relates to world military and political events.
   Purchase, Phyllis J. Walsh, 1971.

170. ALEKSEEV, MIKHAIL VASIL´EVICH, 1857-1918.
   Miscellaneous papers (in Russian), 1905-1918. 1/2 ms. box.
   Photocopy.
   General, Imperial Russian Army; commander in chief, Russian imperial armies on the southwestern front during World War I; chief of staff to Tsar Nicholas II, 1915-1917. Correspondence, notes, diaries, and military orders relating to Russian military activities during World War I and to the Russian Revolution and Civil War.
   Preliminary inventory.
   Gift, Vera Alexeyeva de Borel, 1977.

171. ANDERSON, EDGAR, 1920-
   Miscellaneous papers (in English and Latvian), 1944-1976. 1 ms. box.
   Latvian-American historian. Includes a typescript study "The Baltic Area in World Affairs, 1914-1920: A Military-Political History" and writings, correspondence, notes, and photographs relating to Latvian nationalist underground organizations during World War II.

172. AUSTRO-HUNGARIAN MONARCHY. MINISTERIUM DES K. UND K. HAUSES UND DES AEUSSERN.
   Dispatches (in German), 1914. 1 folder.
   Typewritten transcripts.
   Austro-Hungarian Foreign Ministry. Dispatches from the Austro-Hungarian embassy in Turkey and from the Austro-Hungarian legation in Switzerland relating to activities of Ukrainian nationalist organizations.

173. BARATOV, NIKOLAI NIKOLAEVICH, 1864-1932.
   Papers (in Russian), 1890-1934. 3 ms. boxes.
   General, Imperial Russian Army; commander, expeditionary corps in Persia, 1914-1917. Correspondence, memoranda, diaries, reports, military documents, maps, clippings, and printed matter relating to Russian military activities in Persia and the Caucasus during World War I.
   Gift, Eugenie Baratoff, 1981.

174. BERNATSKII, MIKHAIL VLADIMIROVICH, 1876-   , COLLECTOR.
    Miscellany (in Russian, French, and English), 1916-1918. 1 folder.
    Reports, correspondence, and statistics relating to the financing of the Russian war effort during World War I.
    Preliminary inventory.

175. BOREL', VERA ALEKSEEVA de.
    Biography (in Russian), n.d. "Sorok let v riadakh Russkoi imperatorskoi armii" (Forty years in the ranks of the Russian Imperial Army). 2 vols.
    Typescript.
    Daughter of Mikhail Vasil'evich Alekseev. Relates to General Alekseev, Imperial Russian Army, chief of staff to the Tsar, 1915-1917, and organizer of the White Russian Volunteer Army, 1918.
    Gift, V. A. de Borel', 1980.

176. BRANDEN, ALBRECHT PAUL MAERKER, 1888-
    History, n.d. "Submarines in World War I." 7 vols.
    Typescript (carbon copy).
    Relates to British, German, Austrian, French, Italian, and Russian submarines.

177. DMOWSKI, ROMAN, 1864-1939.
    Study, 1917. "Central and Eastern Europe." 1 vol.
    Typescript (carbon copy).
    Accompanied by explanatory letters by E. D. Adams and Ray Lyman Wilbur. Relates to Polish and other territorial questions of the World War I peace settlement. Privately printed under title Problems of Central and Eastern Europe. London, 1917.

178. DON COSSACKS, PROVINCE OF THE.
    Memorandum (in Russian), 1919. 1 folder.
    Printed.
    Relates to the Don national question and the World War I peace settlement. Presented by the delegation of the Don Republic to the Paris Peace Conference.

179. FLUG, V. E.
    Writings (in Russian), 1926-1933. 2 ms. boxes.
    Holograph.
    General, Imperial Russian Army. Includes a study entitled "Pekhota" (Infantry), 1926, relating to infantry organization and tactics, and a memorandum, 1933, relating to activities of the Russian 10th Army in September 1914.
    Register.
    Gift, N. N. Golovin, 1947.

180. FREE, ARTHUR M., COLLECTOR.
Photographs, 1914-1918. 8 envelopes.
Depicts German troops and war scenes on the eastern and western fronts during World War I and scenes of the negotiation of the Treaty of Brest-Litovsk, 1918. Captions in German.
Gift, A. M. Free, 1933.

181. FRIED, ALFRED HERMANN, 1864-1921.
Papers (in German), 1914-1919. 5 ms. boxes.
Austrian pacifist. Diaries, correspondence, clippings, and notes relating to the international peace movement (particularly during World War I), pacifism, international cooperation, and the World War I guilt question.

182. FRIEDLANDER, ERNST.
Memoir (in German), ca. 1920. "Imprisonment in Siberia." 1 vol.
Typescript.
Austrian soldier taken prisoner during World War I. Includes incomplete translation.

183. FRUMKIN, JACOB G.
Statement, 1957. 1 folder.
Typescript.
Notarized statement relating to a German offer to negotiate a separate peace with Russia in 1917. Includes second statement on same subject by Ilja Trotzky.
Gift, J. G. Frumkin, 1969.

184. GANKIN, OLGA HESS.
History, 1940. 2 ms. boxes.
Typescript and holograph.
Research associate, Hoover Institution on War, Revolution and Peace. Drafts and notes for her book, The Bolsheviks and the World War: The Origin of the Third International. Relates to Russian political events and the Russian army during World War I, Bulgarian political events during World War I, and the Communist International.

185. GEORGIEVICH, M.
Study (in Russian), n.d. "Vstriechnyi boi divizii i korpusa" (Encounters of battle divisions and corps). 1 folder.
Typescript.
Relates to Russian military organization during World War I.

186. GEORGII MIKHAILOVICH, GRAND DUKE OF RUSSIA, d. 1919.
Letters (in Russian), 1914-1918, to his daughter, Princess Kseniia. 2 ms. boxes.

Holograph.

Russian aristocrat; special military representative of Tsar Nicholas II during World War I. Relates to political and military conditions in Russia during World War I, the Russian Revolution, and family matters.

Register.

Gift, Nancy Wynkoop, 1976.

187. GERMANY. OBERSTE HEERESLEITUNG.
Records (in German), 1914-1918. 2 ms. boxes.
Intelligence and other reports, leaflets, radio news scripts, clippings, and press releases relating to political conditions in Russia and the Netherlands, Allied and Bolshevik propaganda, German propaganda, and military positions at the front during World War I.

188. GRONSKII, PAVEL PAVLOVICH, 1883-1937.
Study, n.d. "The Effects of the War upon the Central Government Institutions of Russia." 1 vol.
Typescript (carbon copy).
Relates to the political structure of Russia during World War I and the period of the 1917 Provisional Government.

189. GULYGA, IVAN EMEL´IANOVICH, 1857-
Memoirs (in Russian), 1923. "Vospominaniia starago plastuna o velikoi voinie, 1914-1917" (Reminiscences of an old scout about the Great War, 1914-1917). 1 vol.
Holograph.
Imperial Russian Army officer; commanding officer, Kubansko-Terskii plastunskii korpus, during World War I. Includes a biography (typewritten in Russian) of I. E. Gulyga by Karaushin.

190. HELPHAND, ALEXANDER, 1867-1924.
Receipt (in German), 1915. 1 folder.
Holograph (photocopy).
Russian-German socialist. Receipt for funds from the German government for furtherance of revolutionary activities in Russia.
Gift, Witold S. Sworakowski, 1978.

191. HEROYS, ALEXANDRE.
Memorandum (in French), 1918. "Situation politique et stratégique sur le front roumain et en Russie en 1917 et 1918" (Political and strategic situation on the Romanian front and in Russia in 1917 and 1918). 1 folder.
Typescript.
Relates to Russo-Romanian military activities during World War I and to the Russian Revolution.
Gift, A. Heroys.

192. HERRON, GEORGE DAVIS, 1862-1925.
   Papers, 1916-1927. 26 1/2 ms. boxes, 16 vols., 4 scrapbooks.
   American clergyman and lecturer; unofficial adviser to Woodrow
Wilson, president of the United States. Correspondence, interviews,
lectures, essays, notes, and clippings relating to the League of
Nations, territorial questions, prisoners of war, and other
political and economic issues at the Paris Peace Conference. Vol.
10 includes documents on Russia.
   Preliminary inventory.
   Gift, G. D. Herron, 1922. Subsequent increments.

193. KAUL´BARS, ALEKSANDR VASIL´EVICH, 1884-
   Study (in Russian), n.d. "Vozdushnyia voiska" (The Air Force).
 1 folder.
   Typescript.
   Relates to Russian aerial operations during World War I.

194. KING, GERTRUDE.
   Writings, 1915. 1 folder.
   Photocopy.
   American visitor to Europe, 1915. Letters and newspaper
   dispatches relating to conditions in Russia, Romania, and
 Bulgaria during World War I.
   May not be quoted without permission of Lyman B. Burbank.
   Gift, L. B. Burbank, 1980.

195. KOLOGRIVOV, CONSTANTINE NIKOLAEVICH.
   Memorandum, 1917. 1 folder.
   Typescript (photocopy).
   Captain, Imperial Russian Army. Relates to Tsar Nicholas II´s
Personal Combined Infantry Regiment and 4th Imperial Family Guards
Regiment. Memorandum addressed to Cornet Sergei Vladimirovich
Markov of the Crimean Horse Regiment.
   Gift, M. Lyons, 1971.

196. KONOKOVICH, GENERAL.
   Report (in Russian), n.d. "Opisanie boia 15 iulia 1916 goda
pri der. Trysten, kol. Kurgan i der. Voronchin" (An account of the
battle of July 15, 1916, near Trysten Village, Kurgan Settlement
and Voronchin Village). 1 folder.
   Typescript.
   Major general, Imperial Russian Army.

197. KRUPENSKII, ALEKSANDR NIKOLAEVICH.
   Papers (in Russian, French, and Romanian), 1918-1935. 9 ms.
 boxes.
   Marshal of the Bessarabian nobility; president, Bessarabian
 Provincial Zemstvo; Bessarabian delegate to the Paris Peace

Conference, 1919-1920. Correspondence, memoranda, lists, extracts, summaries, reports, appeals, protests, protocols, press analyses, maps, forms, notes, drafts, clippings, newspaper issues, journals, bulletins, and pamphlets relating to the Bessarabian question; to the relations among Russia, Romania, and Bessarabia; to the occupation and annexation of Bessarabia by Romania, 1918; and to the Paris Peace Conference.
   Register.
   Consult archivist for restrictions.
   Gift, A. N. Krupenskii, 1936.

198. LAGER ALTENGRABOW, GERMANY.
   Prison camp newspaper issues (in Russian and German), 1920. 1 folder.
   Typescript (mimeographed).
   Relates to conditions at Lager Altengrabow, Germany, and to political events in Russia and Germany. Issued by Russian prisoners of war in the camp.
   Preliminary inventory.

199. LANSING, ROBERT, 1864-1928.
   Miscellaneous papers, 1916-1927. 1 folder.
   Photocopy of originals at the Library of Congress. Secretary of state of the United States, 1915-1920. Diaries, correspondence, and memoranda relating to U.S. foreign policy during World War I and to the Paris Peace Conference in 1919.
   Gift, U.S. Library of Congress.

200. LEGENDRE, WILLIAM C.
   Letter, 1925. 1 folder.
   Holograph.
   American businessman. Relates to proposals in the United States for a negotiated end to World War I and Polish independence, 1916-1917. Also includes translations (typewritten) of excerpts from <u>Prawda dziejowa, 1914-1917</u> (The truth of history, 1914-1917) by Jerzy Jan Sosnowski, Russian diplomatic representative in the United States during World War I.

201. LOUCHEUR, LOUIS, 1872-1931.
   Papers (in French), 1916-1931. 12 ms. boxes, 1 envelope.
   French industrialist, statesman, and diplomat. Correspondence, speeches, notes, reports, and photographs relating to industry in Russia during World War I, inter-Allied diplomacy during World War I, war reparations, and postwar French and international politics.
   Preliminary inventory.
   Gift, Loucheur family, 1960. Subsequent increments.

202. MAKOWIECKI, ZYGMUNT.
   Memorandum (in German), 1916. "Nach der Feier" (After the

celebration). 1 folder.
  Typescript.
  Relates to the Polish national independence movement.

203. MASLOVSKII, EVGENII VASIL'EVICH.
  Letters (in Russian), 1945, to Baron Sergei Evgen'evich Ludinkhausen-Wolff. 1 folder.
  Holograph.
  Imperial Russian Army officer. Relates to Russian military activities in northern Persia before World War I and to the Turkish campaigns of General IUdenich during World War I.
  Gift, Valery Kuharets, 1977.

204. MATVEEV, GENERAL.
  Study (in Russian), 1939. "Gibel Rigo-Shavel'skago otriada" (Downfall of the Rigo-Shavel'skii Detachment). 1 vol.
  Holograph.
  General, Imperial Russian Army. Relates to Russian military operations during World War I.

205. MIROVICZ, GENERAL.
  Papers (in Russian), 1914-1916. 1 folder, 1 envelope.
  General, Imperial Russian Army. Reports, orders, maps, and photographs relating to military operations of the Second and Third Finland Rifle Brigades in four battles on the Riga front and in the Carpathian Mountains.
  Preliminary inventory.
  Gift, General Mirovicz.

206. NACZELNY KOMITET NARODOWY.
  Miscellaneous records (in Polish), 1915-1916. 1 folder.
  Polish National People's Committee. Drafts (handwritten) of minutes of meetings in Warsaw, 1915, relating to the Polish question and World War I and leaflets (printed), 1915-1916, relating to recruitment for the Legiony Polskie in the Austrian army.

207. NATIONAL POLISH COMMITTEE OF AMERICA.
  Postcards, ca. 1914-1918. 1 envelope.
  Depicts scenes of destruction in Poland during World War I, coins of Lithuania and Poland, and Polish-American soldiers in France during World War I.

208. PADEREWSKI, IGNACY JAN, 1860-1941.
  Papers (in Polish, English, and French), 1894-1941. 6 1/2 ms. boxes, 1 envelope, 1 album
  Polish statesman and musician; premier, 1919. Correspondence, speeches and writings, clippings, printed matter, and photographs relating primarily to the establishment of an independent Polish

state, the Paris Peace Conference, Polish politics in the interwar period, the occupation of Poland during World War II, and the musical career of I. J. Paderewski.
   Preliminary inventory.
   Personal financial materials in four folders closed until January 1, 1992. No handwritten material may be reproduced.
   Gift, Helena Liibke, 1975. Gift, Anne Appleton, 1976.

209. PARIS. PEACE CONFERENCE, 1919. COMMISSION ON BALTIC AFFAIRS.
   Minutes (mainly in French), 1919. 1 folder.
   Typed copy.
   Relates to aspects of the World War I peace settlement regarding the Baltic states. Includes some notes on proceedings of the commission.

210. PARIS. PEACE CONFERENCE, 1919. U.S. DIVISION OF TERRITORIAL, ECONOMIC AND POLITICAL INTELLIGENCE.
   Miscellaneous records, 1917-1918. 7 ms. boxes, 3 card file boxes (1/2 l. ft.).
   Organization created to prepare background information for the U.S. delegation to the Paris Peace Conference; known as "The Inquiry." Memoranda, notes, and reports relating to political and economic conditions in the Ottoman empire and Latin America, proposals for new boundaries in Asia Minor, creation of an independent Armenia, and boundary disputes in South America.

211. POLETIKA, W. P. VON.
   Miscellaneous papers (in German), 1941-1947. 1 folder.
   German economist. Reports, studies, bibliographies, and proclamations relating to Soviet agricultural policy and to German agricultural policy in occupied parts of Russia during the two world wars.

212. POLISH SUBJECT COLLECTION, 1908-1981. 5 ms. boxes, 1 microfilm reel, 7 phonotapes, 3 videotapes, memorabilia.
   Leaflets, serial issues, proclamations, pamphlets, other printed matter, and report relating to the movement for Polish independence, especially during World War I; miscellaneous aspects of subsequent Polish history; and the Solidarność trade union movement beginning in 1980. Mainly in Polish.
   Register.
   Gift, various sources.

213. POTOTSKII, SERGEI NIKOLAEVICH, 1877-
   Papers (mainly in Russian), 1930-1946. 40 ms. boxes, 2 card file boxes (1/3 l. ft.), 1 envelope.
   Major general, Imperial Russian Army; military attaché to Denmark, 1915. Correspondence, telegrams, reports, protocols, lists, orders, circulars, accounts and receipts, card file, and photographs

relating to imperial Russian military agencies in Copenhagen and Berlin, the Imperial Russian Passport Control Office in Copenhagen, the Russian prisoner-of-war and refugee camp at Horserød, the Russian Red Cross, military benevolent émigré organizations and activities, and Russian participation in World War I and the Russian Civil War.
   Register.
   Consult archivist for restriction.
   Gift, S. N. Potoskii, 1947.

214. PRICE, HEREWARD THIMBLEBY, 1880-1964.
   Papers (in English and German), 1914-1922. 3 ms. boxes.
   Anglo-German soldier during World War I; Russian prisoner, 1915-1918. Correspondence, post cards, and clippings relating to German prisoners of war in Siberia during World War I, the Russian Revolution, and social conditions in China.
   Gift, Arnold H. Price, 1982.

215. RAYSKI, LUDOMIL, 1892-1976.
   Papers (in Polish and English), 1966-1975. 1 ms. box.
   General, Polish air force; commander of the air force, 1926-1939. Photographs, correspondence, and two histories--entitled "Fakty" (Facts) and "Poland's Treason"--relating to the Polish air force from World War I to World War II.
   Gift, L. Rayski, 1969. Incremental gift, 1977.

216. RONZHIN, SERGEI ALEKSANDROVICH.
   Study (in Russian), 1925. "Zheliezn´yia dorogoi v voennoe vremia" (Railroads in wartime). 1 folder.
   Typescript.
   General, Imperial Russian Army. Relates to the use of railroads in Russia during World War I.

217. ROZENSHIL´D-PAULIN, ANATOLII NIKOLAEVICH.
   Diary extracts (in Russian), 1915-1916. 1 vol.
   Typescript (carbon copy).
   General, Imperial Russian Army; commanding general, 29th Infantry Division. Relates to operations of the division during World War I and to the imprisonment of A. N. Rozenshil´d in a German prison camp.

218. RUDNEFF, ILYA ALEXEEVICH, 1892-1969.
   Papers (in Russian), 1913-1923. 1 ms. box, 3 envelopes.
   Colonel, Imperial Russian air forces. Correspondence, photographs, and miscellany relating to Russian aviation in World War I and White Russian military activities during the Russian Civil War.
   Gift, Bertha Rudneff, 1970.

219. RUSSIA. ARMIIA. 10. KORPUS.
   War journal (in Russian), 1914. 1 vol.
   Typescript.
   Imperial Russian 10th Army Corps. Relates to activities of the corps at the outbreak of World War I, August 10-31, 1914.

220. RUSSIA. ARMIIA. KAVKAZSKAIA ARMIIA.
   Miscellaneous records (in Russian), 1915-1916. 1 folder.
   Imperial Russian Caucasian army. Orders, reports, and a map relating to Russian military operations in Transcaucasia during World War I.

221. RUSSIA. SHTAB VERKHOVNOGO GLAVNOKOMANDUIUSHCHEGO.
   Miscellaneous records (in Russian), 1914-1917. 1 ms. box.
   Supreme command, Imperial Russian Army. Military orders and directives issued by the supreme command, 1914-1915, and clippings collected by the supreme command, 1914-1917, relating to World War I military campaigns, principally on the eastern front.

222. RUSSIA. SOVET MINISTROV.
   Miscellany, 1914. 1 folder.
   Translation (typewritten) of a summary report of the meeting of the Council of Ministers of Russia, July 11, 1914, relating to the reaction of the Russian Government to Austro-Hungarian demands made against Serbia and a memorandum (typewritten) by Robert C. Binkley relating to the significance of this document in assessing war guilt for the outbreak of World War I.

223. RUSSIA. VOENNOE MINISTERSTVO.
   Report (in Russian), ca. 1916. "Kratkii otchet o dieiatel´nosti Voennago ministerstva za 1916 god" (Brief report on the activities of the War Ministry for the year 1916). 1 vol.
   Typescript (carbon copy).
   Imperial Russian War Ministry. Relates to Russian military activities in World War I.

224. RUSSING, JOHN.
   History, n.d. "Petrograd Lancers in Service to their Country."
   1 folder.
   Typescript.
   Relates to activities of a Russian army regiment during World War I.
   Deposit, J. Russing, 1974.

225. SACHS, JOHANNES.
   Speech (in German), 1916. "Die polnische Frage" (The Polish question). 1 folder.

Typescript (mimeographed).
Relates to World War I and the question of an independent Polish state. Speech delivered in Frankfurt am Main, April 6, 1916.

226. SAVICH, N. V.
Memoir (in Russian), n.d. 1 folder.
Typescript.
Member of the Russian Duma. Relates to the Russian war program of 1917.

227. SEMENOV, EVGENII PETROVICH, 1861-
Translation of articles, 1921. "German Money to Lenin."
1 folder.
Typescript.
Relates to allegations of German government subsidies to the Bolsheviks. Written by E. P. Semenov and Pavel Miliukov. Published in Poslednie novosti, April 1921.

228. SHIL'NIKOV, IVAN FEDOROVICH.
History (in Russian), 1933. "Voevyia dieistviia 1. Zabaikal'skogoi kazachei divizii v velikoi voine 1914-1918 goda" (Military operations of the 1st Zabaikal Cossack Division in the Great War of 1914-1918). 1 folder.
Typescript.
Published as 1-aia Zabaikal'skaia kazach'ia diviziia v velikoi evropeiskoi voine 1914-1918 g. (1st Zabaikal Cossack Division in the Great European War, 1914-1918) (Harbin, 1933).

229. SHUTKO, IAKOV, COLLECTOR.
Miscellany (in Russian), 1916-1917. 1 folder.
Reports, orders, and correspondence relating to Russian troops stationed at La Courtine, France during World War I, and to revolutionary movements among the troops.

230. SOKOLNICKI, MICHAL, 1880-1967.
Papers (in Polish, French, and English), 1908-1968. 15 ms. boxes, 10 microfilm reels.
Polish diplomat; minister to Denmark, 1931-1935; ambassador to Turkey, 1935-1945. Diaries, correspondence, writings, dispatches, memoranda, and printed matter relating to the Polish nationalist movement before and during World War I, Polish relations with Denmark and Turkey, and the Polish government-in-exile during World War II.
Quotations limited to 250 consecutive words and 2,000 words total.
Purchase, Mrs. M. Sokolnicki, 1968. Subsequent increments.

231. "SPRAVKI O GLAVOKOMANDUIUSHCHIKH FRONTAMI, KOMANDIRAKH ARMIIAMI, KOMANDIRAKH KORPUSOV I PROCH" (LIST OF COMMANDING OFFICERS OF THE RUSSIAN IMPERIAL ARMY, ARRANGED BY UNITS, AT THE TIME OF THE FIRST WORLD WAR).
    List (in Russian), ca. 1916. 1 vol.
    Holograph.

232. STEPANOVA, VANDA KAZIMIROVNA.
    Memoirs (in Russian), ca. 1918. "Zapiski velikoi voiny 1914-1918 g." (Notes on the Great War, 1914-1918). 1 vol.
    Holograph.
    Nurse, Imperial Russian 12th Army. Relates to activities of this army during World War I.

233. UPEROV, VASILII VASIL´EVICH, 1877-1932.
    Papers (in Russian), 1916-1917. 1 ms. box.
    Major, Imperial Russian Army; chief of staff, 5th Infantry Division, 1915-1917. Reports, orders, maps, and diaries relating to activities of the 5th Infantry Division on the western front during World War I.
    Gift, Nikolai N. Golovin, 1938.

234. VARNEK, TAT´IANA ALEKSANDROVNA.
    Memoir (in Russian), 1921. "Vospominaniia, 1912-1921" (Reminiscences, 1912-1921). 1 folder.
    Typescript.
    Russian nurse. Relates to the training of nurses in Petrograd and nursing on the eastern front during World War I.

235. VASIL´EV, E.
    Memoirs (in Russian), n.d. "Zapiski o plienie" (Notes on prison). 1/2 ms. box.
    Holograph.
    Russian soldier. Relates to the imprisonment of E. Vasil´ev in a German prison camp during World War I.
    Gift, E. Vasil´ev, 1925.

236. VIAZEMSKII, SERGEI SERGEEVICH, d. 1915.
    Correspondence (in Russian), 1915. 1 folder.
    Captain, Imperial Russian Navy. Relates to Russian naval operations during World War I, especially the battles in Riga Bay in defense of the Irbenskii Strait.
    Gift, Olga Karpova, 1975.

237. WAYNE, ROY E.
    Photographs, ca. 1918-1919. 1 envelope.
    U.S. Navy photographer. Depicts social conditions and refugees in Yugoslavia, Russia, and Turkey at the end of World War I.

238. WISKOWSKI, WŁODZIMIERZ, COLLECTOR.
   W. Wiskowski collection on Poland (in Polish), 1914-1919. 5 ms. boxes.
   Writings, reports, memoranda, booklets, leaflets, magazines, newspapers, memorials, and speeches relating to political conditions in Poland during World War I and the development of Polish nationalism.
   Register.
   Purchase, W. Wiskowski, 1921.

239. WORLD WAR I PICTORIAL COLLECTION, 1914-1919. 102 envelopes, 22 album boxes, 13 ms. boxes, 12 card file boxes, 1 wooden box of glass plates.
   Photographs, cartoons, and postcards depicting a variety of scenes and personalities from World War I. The collections Russian military cemetery (France)--Photographs, U.S. Army. A.E.F., 1917-1920, and German army--World War I--Photographs, ca. 1914-1918 (which includes scenes on the Russian-Polish border) have been incorporated into the World War I pictorial collection.
   Gift, various sources.

240. WORLD WAR I SUBJECT COLLECTION, 1914-1920. 24 ms. boxes, 1 scrapbook.
   Leaflets, pamphlets, proclamations, clippings, propaganda, other printed matter, miscellaneous orders and other military documents, soldiers' letters, maps, memorabilia, and miscellany relating to military operations and home front conditions in many countries, especially Germany, during World War I. The following collections have been incorporated into the World War I subject collection: European War, 1914-1918--Propaganda; European War, 1914-1918--Russia; German occupation proclamations--Lithuania; Russia--World War I: and Russian imperial military documents--World War I.
   In various languages.
   Register.
   Gift, various sources.

FEBRUARY REVOLUTION, PROVISIONAL GOVERNMENT PERIOD, OCTOBER REVOLUTION, AND CIVIL WAR

241. ADAMS, ARTHUR E.
History, 1960. "Bolsheviks in the Ukraine: The Second Campaign, 1918-1919." 2 vols.
Typescript (Carbon copy).
Includes bibliography.

242. AMERICAN COMMITTEE FOR THE ENCOURAGEMENT OF DEMOCRATIC GOVERNMENT IN RUSSIA.
Records, 1917. 1 folder.
Organization of American civic leaders sympathizing with the Russian revolution of February 1917. Correspondence and printed matter relating to American public opinion regarding the February Revolution.

243. ANDREEV, N. N.
Letters received (in Russian), 1921-1923, from his son.
1 folder.
Photocopy.
Relates to impressions of the Civil War in Russia formed during a trip from the Crimea to Vladivostok.
Gift, Mrs. Constantine Zakhartchenko, 1975.

244. BENES, EDUARD, 1884-1948.
Speech (in Russian), 1921. 1 folder.
Typescript.
Foreign minister of Czechoslovakia, 1918-1935; president of Czechoslovakia, 1935-1938 and 1939-1948. Relates to Soviet-Czechoslovakian foreign relations.

245. BENJAMIN, ALFRED.
Thesis, 1950. "The Great Dilemma." 1 ms. box.
Typescript.
Relates to the foreign policy of the Russian Provisional Government, March-May 1917. Political science thesis, Columbia University.

246. BOURGUINA, ANNA.
Study (in Russian), 1938. "Rabochii vopros pri Arkhangel'skom Pravitel'stve" (The labor question in the Archangel government).
1 vol.
Typescript.
Relates to the period of the Civil War in Russia, 1918-1920.
Gift, Anna Bourguina.

247. BROWNE, LOUIS EDGAR, 1891-1951.
   Papers, 1917-1956. 2 ms. boxes.
   Correspondent of the Chicago Daily News in Russia and Turkey, 1917-1919. Dispatches, correspondence, printed matter, and photographs relating to political conditions in Russia during the Russian Revolution, Allied intervention in Russia, and political conditions in Turkey at the end of World War I.
   Preliminary inventory.

248. BUBLIKOV, ALEKSANDR ALEKSANDROVICH.
   Essay (in Russian), 1923. "Likvidatsiia likholiet´ia" (Liquidation of troubled times). 1 vol.
   Typescript.
   Relates to Russian reconstruction and public finance after the Russian Civil War.

249. BUNYAN, JAMES, 1898-1977.
   Papers (in Russian and English), 1917-1963. 2 1/2 ms. boxes.
   Russian-American historian. Excerpts from published sources, documents, and notes (primarily in Russian) relating to the Ukrainian government, Russia, Siberia, and the Far Eastern Republic during the Russian Civil War in 1919, used by J. Bunyan as research material for his book The Bolshevik Revolution, 1917-1918 (1934); drafts, notes, charts, and printed matter (primarily in English) relating to Soviet economic, administrative, agricultural, and industrial organization and planning, 1917-1963, used by J. Bunyan as research material for his book, The Origin of Forced Labor in the Soviet State, 1917-1921 (1967); and drafts of the latter book.
   Gift, J. Bunyan, 1975. Subsequent increments.

250. CHICHERIN, GEORGII VASIL´EVICH, 1872-1936.
   Letter, 1918, to Allen Wardwell. 1 folder.
   Typescript (photocopy).
   Soviet commissar of foreign affairs, 1918-1930. Calls for the condemnation of atrocities by anti-Bolshevik forces in Russia.

251. CLENDENEN, CLARENCE CLEMENTS, 1899-
   Papers, 1881-1968. 13 1/2 ms. boxes, 4 card file boxes (2/3 l. ft.), 7 envelopes, 14 phonotapes.
   Colonel, U.S. Army; Curator of Special Collections, Hoover Institution on War, Revolution and Peace. Printed matter, biographical notes, interviews, diaries, correspondence, army manuals, research notes, photographs, and maps relating to American military history, especially during World War II and the Vietnamese war, and to the punitive expedition in Mexico in 1916. Includes 33 miscellaneous photos concerning World War I and the Red Army.

Preliminary inventory.
Gift, C. C. Clendenen, 1968. Subsequent increments.

252. COMMUNIST INTERNATIONAL.
Instructions, 1922. "Concerning the Next Tasks of the CP of A."
1 vol.
Typescript (photocopy).
From the Executive Committee of the Communist International to the Communist Party of the United States. Seized by U.S. Department of Justice during a raid on a secret convention of the Communist Party, U.S.A., at Bridgman, Michigan, 1922. Includes a cover letter signed by Nikolai Bukharin, Karl Radek, and Otto Kuusinen. Collection also includes transcripts, typewritten in German, of instructions from the Communist International and the Red International of Labor Unions to their Central European offices, 1921, relating to organization and activities.

253. DORRIAN, CECIL.
Papers, 1912-1926. 1 ms. box, 6 envelopes.
American journalist; war correspondent, Newark Evening News, 1914-1926. Clippings, writings, postcards, and photographs relating to World War I; postwar reconstruction in Western Europe, the Balkans, and the Near East; and the Russian Revolution and Civil War.

254. "ECONOMIC CONDITIONS OF KUBAN BLACK SEA REGION."
Translation of study, n.d. 1 folder.
Typescript.
Relates to the topography and economic conditions of the Kuban District, Russia, during the Russian Civil War.

255. "EKONOMICHESKOE POLOZHENIE SOV. ROSSII" (THE ECONOMIC SITUATION OF SOVIET RUSSIA).
Memorandum (in Russian), ca. 1923. 1 folder.
Typescript.

256. FRENCH SUBJECT COLLECTION, 1665-1981. 88 ms. boxes, 8 phonotapes, 17 microfilm reels, 8 videotapes.
Pamphlets, leaflets, clippings, serial issues, campaign literature, and other printed matter relating to political conditions in France, especially during the Fifth Republic; socialist and communist movements in France; French radicalism, especially student radicalism, during the events of 1968; Freemasonry in France; and miscellaneous aspects of French history, 1665-1871. In French.
Register.
Gift, various sources.

257. FULLER, BENJAMIN APTHORP GOULD, 1879-
   Papers, 1918-1919. 4 ms. boxes, 2 envelopes.
   Captain, U.S. Army; member, American Section, Supreme War Council of the Allied and Associated Powers during World War I. Memoranda, daily bulletins, and photographs relating to military developments, especially on the Italian front, and to political conditions in Europe and Russia.
   Preliminary inventory.
   Gift, B. A. G. Fuller.

258. GENOA. ECONOMIC AND FINANCIAL CONFERENCE, 1922.
   Records (in English, French, and Italian), 1922. 2 ms. boxes.
   Minutes of meetings, agenda, committee reports, draft proposals, a roster of delegates, and telegrams sent and received by the Italian delegation relating to European economic reconstruction and to European economic relations with Russia.

259. GESSEN, B.
   Memorandum (in Russian), n.d. "Transportnyia sredstva i transportirovanie" (Means of transport and transportation).
   1 folder.
   Typescript.
   Relates to transportation systems in Russia during the Russian Civil War.

260. GOR´KII (MAKSIM) COLLECTION (IN RUSSIAN AND ENGLISH), 1921. 1 folder.
   Appeal (handwritten in Russian) by M. Gor´kii (1868-1936), Russian novelist, 1921, relating to the need for foreign relief to aid Russian intellectuals, and four essays (typewritten) by Soviet scholars relating to the literary, political, and humanitarian ideas of M. Gor´kii.
   Gift, Edgar Ammende, 1963. Gift, Soviet Embassy to the United States, 1943.

261. GROUP OF ENGLISH SPEAKING COMMUNISTS.
   Leaflet, 1919. 1 folder.
   Printed.
   Bolshevik propaganda leaflet distributed to American and British soldiers in Russia.

262. HALBROOK, STEPHEN P.
   Study, 1973. "Anarchism and Marxism in the Twentieth Century Revolution." 1/2 ms. box.
   Typescript.
   Relates to the influence of anarchist and Marxist theories on the Russian and Chinese revolutions and on revolutionary movements throughout the world.
   Gift, S. P. Halbrook, 1974.

263. HALONEN, GEORGE.
   Miscellaneous papers, 1918-1922. 1 ms. box.
   Karelian Worker's Commune representative in the United States, 1918-1919. Correspondence, writings, reports, and printed matter relating to activities of the Finnish Information Bureau in the United States in publicizing and seeking United States recognition of the Soviet government of Finland. Includes writings and correspondence of Santeri Nuorteva, head of the Finnish Information Bureau.
   Preliminary inventory.
   Gift, G. Halonen, 1950.

264. HOOVER INSTITUTION ON WAR, REVOLUTION AND PEACE. RUSSIAN PROVISIONAL GOVERNMENT PROJECT.
   Translations of documents, 1955-1960. 10 ms. boxes.
   Project for publication of a documentary history of the Russian Provisional Government of 1917. Results published as Robert Browder and Alexander Kerensky, eds. The Russian Provisional Government, 1917 (Stanford: Stanford University Press, 1961).
   Preliminary inventory.

265. HOOVER INSTITUTION ON WAR, REVOLUTION AND PEACE. SOVIET TREATY SERIES PROJECT.
   Records, 1957-1959. 12 cu. ft. boxes, 2 file drawers (1 l. ft.).
   Correspondence, memoranda, notes, bibliographies, and translations of published material used in preparation of A Calendar of Soviet Treaties, 1917-1957 by Robert M. Slusser and Jan F. Triska (Stanford: Stanford University Press, 1959; Hoover Institution Document Series #4).

266. HOOVER, JOHN ELWOOD, 1924-
   Thesis, 1955. "The American Congress and the Russian Revolution, March 1917 to February 1918." 1/2 ms. box.
   Typescript (photocopy).
   Major general, U.S. Army. Relates to U.S. congressional opinions and actions regarding the Russian Revolution. M.A. thesis, Georgetown University.
   Gift, Stefan T. Possony, 1978.

267. HULSE, JAMES W.
   History. "The Communist International in Its Formative Stage, 1919-1920." 1/2 ms. box.
   Typescript.
   Later published as The Forming of the Communist International (Stanford: Stanford University Press, 1964).

268. HUSTON, JAY CALVIN.
Papers (in English and Russian), 1917-1931. 14 ms. boxes, 2 envelopes.
American consular official in China, 1917-1932. Writings, pamphlets, leaflets, and clippings relating to cultural, political, and economic conditions in China and to communism and Soviet influence in China.
Preliminary inventory.
Gift, Payson J. Treat, 1935.

269. IZVESTIIA REVOLIUTSIONNOI NEDELI (NEWS OF THE REVOLUTIONARY WEEK).
Extracts from newspaper articles (in Russian), 1917. 1 folder.
Typescript.
Petrograd newspaper. Relates to the February 1917 revolution in Petrograd. Includes texts of Russian government decrees and appeals and resolutions of Russian political groups.

270. JORDAN, DAVID STARR, 1851-1931.
Papers, 1814-1947. 77 ms. boxes, 4 envelopes, 5 scrapbooks, 8 posters.
American educator and pacifist; president, Stanford University, 1891-1913; chancellor, Stanford University, 1913-1916. Correspondence, writings, pamphlets, leaflets, clippings, and photographs relating to pacifism and the movement for world peace, disarmament, international relations, U.S. neutrality in World War I, United States foreign and domestic policy, civil liberties in the United States, problems of minorities in the United States, and personal and family matters. Subject file contains references to material on Russian foreign policy with regard to Asia and on the Russian Revolution, 1917-1921.
Register.
Boxes 70-77 are closed until processed.
Gift, Jessie Knight Jordan.

271. KAYDEN, EUGENE M.
Memorandum, 1918. "A Memorandum on the Political Changes in Russia Since the Revolution." 1 folder.
Typescript.
Staff member, Bureau of Research, U.S. War Trade Board.

272. KELLOCK, HAROLD, 1879-
Letter, 1918, to Lincoln Steffens. 1 vol.
Holograph.
Publicity secretary, Finnish Information Bureau in the United States. Relates to American relations with the revolutionary governments of Finland and Russia.

273. KERENSKII, ALEKSANDR FEDOROVICH, 1881-1970.
   Miscellaneous papers (in Russian and English), 1945-1965. 1 ms. box.
   Premier, Russian Provisional Government, 1917. Correspondence and writings relating to the Russian Revolution and personal matters. Inludes a history by Kerenskii entitled "The Genesis of the 'October Revolution' of 1917" and correspondence with Vasilii Maklakov, Michael Karpovich, and Anatole G. Mazour.
   Preliminary inventory.
   Gift, A. F. Kerenskii. Gift, A. G. Mazour, 1976.

274. KORNILOV, LAVR GEORGIEVICH, 1870-1918.
   Writings (in Russian and English), 1917. 1 folder.
   General and commander in chief, Russian army, 1917. Translation (typewritten) of a speech and copy (typewritten in Russian) of an order, both relating to conditions of morale and discipline in the Russian army in 1917.

275. KRAJOWA AGENCJA WYDAWNICZA.
   Posters (in Polish), 1971-1975. 24 posters.
   Printed.
   National Publishing Agency of Poland. Relates to social and political conditions in Poland, including posters on the subject of the career of Feliks Dzerzhinskii.
   Purchase, 1976.

276. KURGUZ, PETER NICHOLAS.
   Dissertation, 1963. "Historical Investigation of the Church-State Conflict Caused by the Philosophy of Communism in Russia, 1917-1919." 1 vol.
   Typescript (carbon copy).
   Ph.D. dissertation, Lincoln University.

277. KWIATKOWSKI, ANTONI WINCENTY, 1890-1970.
   Papers (mainly in Polish and Russian), 1917-1969. 45 ms. boxes, 1 album, 4 envelopes.
   Polish scholar. Writings, correspondence, reports, memoranda, research and reference notes, clippings, and photographs relating to Marxism-Leninism, dialectical and historical materialism, communism and religion, and the Communist International. Includes an autobiography and biography.
   Register.
   Gift, Annemarie Buschman-Brandes, 1971.

278. LEMAN, RUDOLF, 1897-
   Memoirs (in German), n.d. "Geschichte der goldenen zwanziger Jahre in Russland" (History of twenty golden years in Russia).
   1/2 ms. box.
   Typescript.

German chemist in Russia, 1920-1930. Relates to economic
conditions in Russia, especially Siberia, in the interwar period
and to the economic policy of the Vysshii sovet nagodnogo
khoziaistva.
   Gift, R. Leman, 1974.

279. LENIN, VLADIMIR IL'ICH, 1870-1924.
   Miscellaneous speeches and writings (in Russian), 1903-1940.
1 folder, 1 phonotape.
   Russian revolutionary leader; premier of Russia, 1917-1924.
Pamphlet by V. I. Lenin entitled "K studenchestvu: zadachi
revoliutsionnoi molodezhi" (To the students: The tasks of
revolutionary youth), 1903 (mimeographed); leaflet by V. I. Lenin
and V. Bonch-Bruevich entitled "Usluzhlivyi liberal" (The obliging
liberal) (printed); photocopy of the table of contents (printed) of
Stat'i i rechi o srednei Azii i Uzbekistane (Articles and speeches
about Central Asia and Uzbekistan) by V. I. Lenin and Iosif Stalin,
1940: and recordings of speeches by V. I. Lenin, 1919-1920.

280. LOEHR, MRS., COLLECTOR.
   Collection of photographs, notes, and printed matter, 1917.
1 folder, 1 envelope.
   Relates to conditions in Petrograd during the Russian Revolution.

281. LOVESTONE, JAY, 1898-
   Papers, 1906-1976. 634 ms. boxes.
   General secretary of the Communist Party, U.S.A., 1927-1929, and
of the Communist Party (Opposition), 1929-1940, executive secretary
of the Free Trade Union Committee of the American Federation of
Labor-Congress of Industrial Organizations, 1955-1974.
Correspondence, reports, memoranda, bulletins, clippings, serial
issues, pamphlets, other printed matter, and photographs relating
to the Communist International, the communist movement in the United
States and elsewhere, communist influence in United States and
foreign trade unions, and organized labor movements in the United
States and abroad.
   Register.
   Collection closed except for printed material (Boxes 1-191).

282. LYONS, MARVIN, COLLECTOR.
   Collection, 1966. 1 folder.
   Biographical sketch of Major General Aleksandr Aleksandrovich
   Drentel'n, adjutant to Tsar Nicholas II, and summary of an interview
of Joseph Germek, a member of the Cheka
   during the Russian Revolution. In Russian and English.
   Gift, M. Lyons, 1971.

283. MCDUFFEE, ROY W.
   Dissertation, 1953. "The Department of State and the Russian Revolution, March-November, 1917." 1/2 ms. box.
   Mimeograph.
   Relates to evaluation of the Russian Revolution and formation of American policy toward it by the U.S. Department of State. Ph.D. dissertation, Georgetown University.
   Gift, Stefan T. Possony, 1978.

284. MAKAROV, N.
   Study (in Russian), n.d. "Na puti k krizismu sotsial'nago rationalizma: sotsial'no-ekonomicheskie ocherki o Rossii i eia revoliutsii, 1917-1920" (On the path to a crisis of social rationalism: Socioeconomic essays on Russia and its revolution, 1917-1920). 1 folder.
   Holograph.

285. MAKLAKOV, VASILII ALEKSEEVICH, 1870-1957.
   Papers (in Russian and French), 1917-1956. 22 ms. boxes.
   Ambassador of the Provisional Government of Russia to France, 1917-1924. Correspondence, reports, diaries, and clippings relating to Russian foreign relations with France, the Russian Revolution, and Russian émigrés in France after the Revolution.
   Preliminary inventory.
   Gift, V. A. Maklakov, 1957.

286. MARTENS, LUDWIG CHRISTIAN ALEXANDER KARL, 1874-1948.
   Letter, 1919, to Boris Bakhmetev. 1 folder.
   Typescript (photocopy).
   Demands that B. Bakhmetev, ambassador of the Russian Provisional Government to the United States, hand over all property of the Russian government in the United States. Written by L. C. A. K. Martens and Santeri Nuorteva, Soviet diplomatic representatives in the United States.

287. MASON, FRANK EARL, 1893-1979.
   Papers (in English and German), 1915-1975. 4 ms. boxes, 7 envelopes.
   American journalist; Berlin correspondent and president, International News Service. Correspondence, reports, journalistic dispatches, and other material relating to German and Soviet politics and diplomacy in the interwar period and to the Allied military administration of Germany at the end of World War II. Includes a copy of the logbook of the submarine that sank the Lusitania, 1915, correspondence with Georgii Chicherin and Karl von Wiegand, and Louise Bryant's and Anna Louise Strong's Moscow dispatches, 1920-1921.
   Preliminary inventory.
   Gift, F. E. Mason, 1955. Subsequent increments.

288. MAXIMOVA-KULAEV, ANTONINA ALEXANDROVNA.
   Memoir, 1932. 1 folder.
   Typescript.
   Russian physician. Relates to her service as a surgeon in a Red Army hospital in Koslov, Russia, and to the occupation of Koslov by White Russian forces in 1919.

289. MEL'GUNOV, SERGEI PETROVICH, 1897-1956.
   Papers (in Russian), 1918-1933. 17 ms. boxes.
   Russian historian and editor; author of <u>The Red Terror in Russia</u>. Clippings, writings, correspondence, and reports relating to the Russian Revolution and Civil War and the operations of the Soviet secret police.
   Preliminary inventory.
   Gift, S. P. Mel'gunov, 1938.

290. NEKRASOV, NIKOLAI VISSARIONOVICH.
   Translation of speech, 1917. 1 folder.
   Typescript.
   Minister of finance, Russian Provisional Government. Relates to the financial situation of the Provisional Government. Speech delivered in Moscow, August 1917.

291. <u>NOVAIA ZHIZN'</u> (NEW LIFE) (1917-1918) LENINGRAD.
   Newspaper articles (in Russian), 1917-1918. 1 vol.
   Typewritten transcripts.
   Petrograd newspaper. Relates to the role of the All-Russian Executive Committee of the Railroad Workers' Union, Vserossiiskii ispolnitel'nyi komitet Zheleznodorozhnogo soiuza (Vikzhel'), in the Russian Revolution.

292. OBLASTNOI KOMITET ARMII, FLOTA I RABOCHIKH FINLIANDII.
   Proclamation (in Russian), 1917. "Pravitel'stvo spaseniia revoliutsii" (Government for the rescue of the Revolution).
   Printed.
   Regional Committee of the Army, Navy, and Workers of Finland. Supports the Russian revolutionaries.
   Gift, Ivan Blums, 1970.

293. "OLONETSKAIA KARELIIA."
   Memorandum (in Russian), 1919. 1 folder.
   Typescript.
   Relates to Russian influence in Karelia during the Russian Civil War.

294. PATOUILLET, MADAME.
   Diary (in French), 1916-1918. 1 vol.

Typescript (carbon copy).
Frenchwoman in Russia. Relates to conditions in Petrograd and Moscow during World War I and the Russian Revolution, October 1916-August 1918.

295. POSSONY, STEFAN THOMAS, 1913-
Papers (in English and French), 1940-1977. 27 ms. boxes.
American political scientist; Senior Fellow, Hoover Institution on War, Revolution and Peace. Correspondence, writings, reports, research notes, bibliographic card files, term papers, examination papers, periodical articles, and newspaper clippings relating to military science, technology, national defense, international relations, Soviet foreign policy, revolution in the twentieth century, and communism.
Gift, S. T. Possony, 1978.

296. POSTNIKOVA, E.
History (in Russian), 1924. "R.S.F.S.R." 1 vol.
Typescript.
Relates to the Russian Socialist Federated Soviet Republic during the Russian Civil War, 1919-1921.

297. PRAVDA (TRUTH).
Translation of newspaper article excerpts (in German), 1917. 1 folder.
Typescript.
Bolshevik newspaper. Relates to the social democratic peace conference in Stockholm and to the suppression of the Bolsheviks in Russia during the "July Days." Excerpts are dated July-August 1917.

298. RADEK, KARL, 1885-1939.
Letter (in German), 1919, to Paul Levi. 1 folder.
Holograph (photocopy).
Revolutionary; Soviet and international communist leader. Relates to the communist movement in Germany.

299. RAKOVSKII, KHRISTIAN GEORGIEVICH, 1873-1941.
Memoirs (in Bulgarian), n.d. "Avtobiografia" (Autobiography). 10 p.
Typescript (photocopy).
Bulgarian-Russian revolutionary; chairman, Council of People's Commissars of the Ukraine, 1919-1923; Soviet ambassador to Great Britain, 1923-1925, and to France, 1925-1927. Relates to socialist activities in the Balkans and to the Russian Revolution.

300. RAMPLEE-SMITH, WINIFRED V., COLLECTOR.
W. V. Ramplee-Smith collection on the Russian Revolution (in

Russian and English), 1915-1917. 1 ms. box, 1 folder, 1 envelope.
   Pamphlets, leaflets, clippings, and postcards relating to the February 1917 Revolution in Russia. Includes fragments of burned records of the tsarist secret police (Okhrana), which W. V. Ramplee-Smith surreptitiously removed from the Okhrana's St. Petersburg office files, then being burned by Bolshevik soldiers.
   Preliminary inventory.
   Gift, W. V. Ramplee-Smith, 1963. Subsequent increments.

301. RODICHEV, FEDOR IZMAILOVICH, 1854-1933.
   Memoirs (in Russian), 1924. "Vospominaniia F. I. Rodicheva o 1917 godu" (Reminiscences of F. I. Rodichev about 1917). 1 folder.
   Typescript.
   Leader of Russian Constitutional Democratic Party; member of all State Dumas; minister for Finnish affairs in the Provisional Government, 1917. Relates to events in Russia during the 1917 revolution. Includes a biographical sketch of F. I. Rodichev by his daughter, Alexandrine Rodichev, 1933.

302. ROGERS, LEIGHTON W.
   Memoir, n.d. "An Account of the March Revolution, 1917." 1 folder.
   Typescript.
   American official, Petrograd branch, National City Bank, 1917. Relates to the Russian revolution of February 1917.

303. RUSSIA. POSOL'STVO (FRANCE).
   Records (in Russian and French), 1917-1924. 36 1/2 ms. boxes.
   Russian embassy in France. Correspondence, reports, memoranda, and notes relating to relations between France and the Russian Provisional Government, the Russian Revolution, counter-revolutionary movements, the Paris Peace Conference, and Russian émigrés after the Revolution. Includes ca. 2 ms. boxes dealing specifically with the Ukraine, 1918-1922.
   Register.
   Gift, Vasilii Maklakov, 1926. Incremental gift, G. de Lastours, 1951.

304. RUSSIA. POSOL'STVO (U.S.).
   Records (mainly in Russian), ca. 1914-1933. 260 l. ft.
   Imperial Russian and Provisional Government embassies in the United States. Correspondence, telegrams, memoranda, reports, agreements, minutes, histories, financial records, lists, and printed matter relating to Russia's role in World War I, the Russian Revolution and Civil War, activities of the Russian Red Cross, Russian émigrés in foreign countries, and operations of the embassy office. Includes files of the Russian military attaché in the United States, the Russian financial agent in the U.S., and numerous Imperial Russian and Provisional Government embassies and

legations that closed after the Russian Revolution and Civil War. Gift, Serge Ughet, 1933.

305. RUSSIA (1917. PROVISIONAL GOVERNMENT). VSEROSSIISKOE UCHREDITEL´NOE SOBRANIE.
   Translation of proceedings, 1918. 1 vol.
   Typescript.
   All-Russian Constituent Assembly. Relates to the opening session of the assembly, January 5, 1918.

306. RUSSIA (1917-   R.S.F.S.R.). SOVET NARODNYKH KOMISSAROV.
   Appeal (in French), 1918. "Aux masses laborieuses de France, d´Angleterre, d´Amérique et du Japon" (To the laboring masses of France, England, America and Japan). 1 folder.
   Printed.
   Council of People´s Commissars. Calls upon the peoples of these countries to protest Allied intervention in Russia.

307. RUSSIA (1917-   R.S.F.S.R.). TSENTRAL´NAIA KOMISSIIA POMOSHCHI GOLODAIUSHCHIM.
   Translation of report, 1922. "Totals of the struggle against famine in 1921-22: Collection of articles and reports." 1 ms. box.
   Typescript.
   Central Famine Relief Committee of the Soviet government. Translated by the Historical Division, American Relief Administration, Russian Unit.

308. "THE RUSSIAN PUBLIC DEBT."
   Translation of study, 1923. 1 folder.
   Typescript (mimeographed).
   Relates to the financial situation of the Russian government. Study published in <u>Agence économique et financière</u> (August 2, 1923). Translated by S. Ughet.

309. RYSKULOV, T.
   Excerpts from a study (in Russian), 1925. <u>Revoliutsiia i korennoe naselenie Turkestana</u> (Revolution and the indigenous population of Turkestan). 1 folder.
   Typescript.
   Relates to the Russian Revolution in Turkestan, 1917-1919. Study published in Tashkent in 1925.

310. SOKOLNIKOV, GRIGORII IAKOVLEVICH, 1888-1939.
   Translation of study, 1931. <u>Soviet Policy in Public Finance, 1917-1928</u>. 1/2 ms. box.
   Typescript.
   Soviet commissar of finance, 1922-1926; deputy commissar of

foreign affairs and ambassador to Great Britain, 1929-1934. Translated by Elena Varneck. Translation published (Stanford, 1931).

311. SOKOLOV, BORIS FEDOROVICH, 1893-
Photographs, 1918-1920. 1 album.
Depicts scenes of daily life in Russia (primarily in Petrograd) during the Russian Revolution, including scenes of economic production under war communism, destroyed buildings, Soviet leaders and delegates to the Communist International, and examples of Soviet art. Includes holograph commentaries in French.

312. SOLSKI, WACŁAW, 1896-
Writings, n.d. 1 ms. box.
Polish novelist. Memoirs and a study relating to Bolshevik agitation in the Russian army during the Russian Revolution, the formation of Soviet policy in literature and other cultural affairs during the 1920s, and Soviet propaganda techniques. In Russian and English.
Purchase, W. Solski, 1983.

313. SPALDING, MERRILL TEN BROECK.
Papers (in English, Russian, French, and Flemish), 1922-1945. 1 1/2 ms. boxes, 1 card file box, 2 envelopes.
American historian. Correspondence, notes, clippings, and other printed matter relating to economic conditions and labor in Russia from 1917 to World War II. Includes newspaper and periodical issues published in Belgium immediately after its liberation in 1945 and reproductions of paintings at the Tretiakov State Gallery, Moscow.
Gift, M. T. B. Spalding. Incremental gift, Clara Spalding, 1978.

314. STANFIELD, BORIS, 1888-
Interview, 1976. 1 phonotape.
Russian-American journalist; reporter for Izvestiia. 1917-1920. Relates to the Revolution and Civil War in Russia. Interview conducted by Anatole Mazour at the Hoover Institution on War, Revolution and Peace, November 15-16, 1976.
Gift, B. Stanfield, 1976.

315. STINES, NORMAN CASWELL, JR., 1914-1980.
Papers, 1911-1968. 3 ms. boxes.
American diplomat; first secretary of embassy to the Soviet Union, 1950-1952. Letters, printed matter, and photographs relating to social conditions in Bolivia, Guatemala, Yugoslavia, and the Soviet Union and to U.S. Department of State loyalty investigations. Includes letters of the parents of N. C. Stines, Americans in Russia during the Russian Revolution.
Gift, estate of N. C. Stines, Jr., 1981.

316. "SVODKI O POLITICHESKOM I EKONOMICHESKOM POLOZHENII V SOVETSKOI ROSSII ZA 1922 GOD" (SUMMARIES OF THE POLITICAL AND ECONOMIC SITUATION IN SOVIET RUSSIA FOR 1922).
    Reports (in Russian), 1922. 1 folder.
    Typescript.

317. SWINNERTON, C. T.
    Letter, 1917. 1 folder.
    Typescript.
    American visitor to Russia. Relates to events in Petrograd during the Russian Revolution, March 12-27, 1917.
    Gift, Arthur Daily.

318. "TRINADTSAT' LET OKTIABRIA" (THIRTEEN YEARS OF OCTOBER).
    Study (in Russian), ca. 1930. 1 folder.
    Typescript (mimeographed).
    Relates to economic progress in the Soviet Union since the Russian Revolution.

319. U.S. CONSULATE, LENINGRAD.
    Dispatches, 1917. 1 vol.
    Typescript (carbon copy).
    Relates to events in Petrograd during the Russian Revolution, March 20-July 10, 1917.

320. URQUHART, LESLIE.
    Letter, 1917. 1 folder.
    Typescript.
    American living in Petrograd. Relates to the Russian Revolution and its prospective outcome as of May 1917.

321. VERNADSKY, GEORGE, 1887-1973.
    Miscellaneous papers (in English and Russian), 1935. 1/2 ms. box.
    Russian-American historian. Notes (handwritten and typewritten) for a projected social and economic history of Russia during the period 1917-1921 and a copy (typewritten in Russian, with translation) of a letter to A. F. Iziumov relating to the views of G. Vernadsky on serfdom in Russia.
    Gift, G. Vernadsky, 1935.

322. VERNADSKY, NINA.
    Memoirs (in Russian), n.d. 1/2 ms. box.
    Typescript.
    Russian teacher. Relates to the Russian Revolution and Civil War. Includes an incomplete translation.

323. VINOGRADOV, A. K.
   History, 1922. "The Fortunes of the Roumiantzow Museum." 1 vol.
   Typescript.
   Director, Rumiantsev Museum, Moscow. Relates to the museum and, especially, to its library. Includes photographs.

324. VIOLIN, IA. A.
   Study (in Russian), 1922. "Uzhasy goloda i liudoedstva v Rossii v 1921-22 gg." (The horrors of famine and cannibalism in Russia in 1921-1922). 1 vol.
   Typescript (carbon copy).

325. VLADIMIROV, IVAN ALEKSEEVICH, 1870-1947.
   Paintings, 1918-1923. 40 paintings.
   Russian artist. Depicts scenes of privation and revolutionary justice in Petrograd and elsewhere in Russia during the Russian Revolution and Civil War.
   Register.
   Purchase, I. A. Vladimirov, 1923.

326. WHITCOMB, JOHN M., COLLECTOR.
   Photographs, 1904-1939. 2 envelopes.
   Depicts communist leaders from various countries. Includes a number of photographs of delegates to congresses of the Communist International.
   Gift, J. M. Whitcomb, 1980.

327. ZAWODNY, JAY K.
   Interview transcripts, n.d. 1 folder, 2 microfilm reels.
   Typescript.
   Interviews, conducted by J. K. Zawodny, of former Soviet factory workers residing in the United States relating to labor conditions in the Soviet Union, 1919-1951.
   Gift, J. K. Zawodny, 1954.

ANTI-BOLSHEVIK PARTICIPANTS IN THE CIVIL WAR; ALLIED INTERVENTION

328. AKAEMOV, NIKOLAI.
History (in Russian), 1930. "Kaledinskie miatezhi" (The Kaledin rebellion). 1 folder.
Holograph.
Relates to the White Russian movement led by Aleksei Kaledin during the Russian Civil War.

329. AKINTIEVSKII, KONSTANTIN KONSTANTINOVICH, 1884-1962.
Memoirs (in Russian), n.d. 1/2 ms. box.
Typescript.
General, Imperial Russian Army. Relates to activities of the Imperial Russian Army during World War I and to the White Russian forces during the Russian Revolution and Civil War, 1914-1921. Includes an English translation.
Gift, Olga P. Zaitzevsky, 1971.

ALEKSEEV, MIKHAIL VASIL´EVICH, 1857-1918, see collection no. 170.

330. ANDERSON, ROY SCOTT, d. 1925.
Papers, 1920-1922. 1/2 ms. box.
American advisor to various officials of the Chinese government, 1903-1925. Letters and reports relating to the Chinese economy, Chinese foreign relations with Japan, Russia, and the United States, and historical and political events in China.
Gift, N. Peter Rathvon, 1965.

331. BAXTER, ROBERT I., COLLECTOR.
Map, n.d. 1 folder.
Hand drawn.
Represents the region around Archangel, Russia, indicating the route followed by a military expedition from Tiagra to Archangel, August-September 1918.
Gift, R. I. Baxter.

332. BAZAREVICH, VLADIMIR IOSIFOVICH.
Papers (in Russian), 1919-1926. 7 ms. boxes.
Russian military agent in Yugoslavia, 1919-1922. Correspondence, memoranda, instructions, orders, reports, and personnel lists relating to the Russian Civil War, White Russian military organization, prisoners of war, Russian refugees in Yugoslavia, and White Russian military activities in Gallipoli, Bulgaria, and Yugoslavia.

Register.
Deposit, I. A. Holmsen, 1928.

333. BENNIGSEN, EMMANUIL PAVLOVICH, GRAF, 1875-
Translations of papers, 1914-1919. 1/2 ms. box.
Typescript.
Colonel, Imperial Russian Army. Diary extracts, letters, and poems relating to Russian military activities during World War I and to activities of the White Army of General Denikin during the Russian Civil War. Includes an account of the February 1917 revolution by Grafinia Bennigsen.

BOREL´, VERA ALEKSEEVA de, see collection no. 175.

334. BULIUBASH, EVGENII GRIGOR´EVICH.
Papers (in Russian), 1954-1964. 1 ms. box.
General, Imperial Russian Army. Correspondence, clippings, printed matter, and photographs relating to Imperial Russian military forces before, during, and after the Russian Revolution and Civil War and to activities of the Russian émigré community in the United States.
Gift, Russian Historical Archive and Repository, 1974.

335. BUNIN, VIKTOR M., 1896-
Memoirs (in Russian), n.d. "Deviatyi val: vospominaniia uchastnika russkoi grazhdanskoi voiny 1918-1920 g.g." (The highest wave: Reminiscences of a participant in the Russian Civil War, 1918-1920). 1 vol.
Typescript (carbon copy).

336. BURLIN, P. G.
Writings (in Russian), 1941. 1 folder.
Typescript.
Imperial Russian Army officer. Study entitled "Kratkaia spravka o russkom kazachestve" (Brief note on the Russian Cossacks) and a report entitled "Proiskhozhdenie kazakov--Doklad" (Cossack parentage--A report) relating to Russian Cossack daily life and class and military structure.

337. BYKADOROV, I.
Papers (in Russian), 1919-1920. 1/2 ms. box.
General, Imperial Russian Army. Mandates, orders, and circulars relating to the Civil War in the south of Russia. Includes a list of the main events in the history of the Don Army prepared by I. Bykadorov.
Purchase, I. Bykadorov.

338. CARTER, LIEUTENANT.
   Letter, 1919. 1 vol.
   Holograph.
   British army officer. Relates to British military intervention against the Bolsheviks in northern Russia. Includes typewritten copy of original.

339. CHERIACHOUKIN, A. V.
   Papers (in Russian), 1918-1919. 1 folder.
   Ambassador of the Don Cossack Republic to the Ukraine during the Russian Civil War. Correspondence, reports, and dispatches relating to the activities of the anti-Bolshevik movements during the Russian Civil War and relations of the Don Cossack Republic with the Germans and with the Allied representatives in Odessa.
   Preliminary inventory.

340. CHERNOV, VIKTOR MIKHAILOVICH, 1873-1952.
   Writings (in Russian), n.d. 1/2 ms. box.
   Typescript.
   Leader of the Russian Partiia sotsialistov-revoliutsionerov (Socialist Revolutionary Party). Relates to activities of the Partiia sotsialistov-revoliutsionerov during the Russian Revolution.

341. COOPER, MERIAN C., 1894-1973.
   Papers, 1917-1958. 1 ms. box.
   Brigadier general, U.S. Air Force; pilot with the Kosciuszko Squadron in Poland, 1919-1921; chief of staff, China Air Task Force, 1942. Correspondence, memoranda, and memorabilia relating to the American Relief Administration and the U.S. Food Administration in Poland, the Kosciuszko Squadron during the Polish-Russian war of 1919-1921, General Douglas MacArthur, Lieutenant General Claire Chennault, U.S. defense policy, air power, and communist strategy.
   Gift, M. C. Cooper, 1958. Incremental gift, 1964.

342. DANILOFF, KARL B.
   Memoirs, 1978. "Revolutionary Odyssey of the White Rabbit." 85 p.
   Typescript (photocopy).
   White Russian soldier during the Russian Civil War. Relates to social conditions in tsarist Russia, the Russian Revolution, and Russian émigré life afterward.
   Gift, K. B. Daniloff, 1979.

343. DARLING, WILLIAM LAFAYETTE, 1856-1938.
   Diary, May-December 1917. 1 volume.
   Typescript.
   Member of the U.S. Advisory Commission of Railway Experts to Russia. Describes the condition of Russian railways and U.S. assistance to improve them.

344. DENIKINA, KSENIIA.
Chronology (in Russian), n.d. "Khronologiia sobytii vo vremia grazhdanskoi voiny v Rossii" (Chronology of events during the Civil War in Russia).
Typescript.
Relates to the southern and western fronts during the Russian Civil War.

345. DOBRYNIN, VASILII A.
Memoir (in Russian), 1923. "Oborona Mugani, 1918-1919: zapiski kavkazskago pogranichnika" (The defense of Mugan´, 1918-1919: Notes of a Caucasian frontier guard). 1 folder.
Typescript (photocopy).
Captain, Imperial Russian Army. Relates to the Russian Civil War in the region of Mugan´, Azerbaijan.
Gift, Vasili Romanov, 1980.

346. DRATSENKO, D. P.
Miscellaneous papers (in Russian), 1919-1920. 1 folder.
General, White Russian Army. Military reports, orders, and correspondence relating to the Russian Civil War in the Caucasus, political and military conditions in Georgia, and British foreign policy in Transcaucasia.
Preliminary inventory.

347. ELISEEV, FEDOR IVANOVICH, 1892-
Memoirs (in Russian and French), 1939-1945. 3 ms. boxes.
Holograph.
Colonel, Imperial Russian Army; lieutenant, French foreign legion. Relates to operations of the Kuban Cossack Divisions of the Imperial Russian Army, 1910-1916; the Russian Revolution and Civil War, 1917-1920; and operations of the French foreign legion in Indochina, 1943-1945.
Purchase, F. I. Eliseev, 1979.

348. EPSTEIN, FRITZ THEODOR, 1898-
Papers (in German), 1914-1948. 1 1/2 ms. box.
German-American historian. Writings, clippings, correspondence, and orders relating to Allied intervention in Russia during the Russian Revolution, the German military government of Strasbourg during World War I, the trial of Menshevik leaders in Russia in 1931, and the authenticity of the diaries of Joseph Goebbels. Includes an unpublished history entitled "Russland und die Weltpolitik, 1917-1920: Studien zur Geschichte der Interventionen in Russland" (Russia and world politics, 1917-1920: Studies on the history of the interventions in Russia).
Gift, F. T. Epstein, 1941. Subsequent increments.

349. ERGUSHOV, P.
   History (in Russian), 1938. "Kasaki i gortsy na Sunzhenskoi linii v 1917" (Cossacks and mountaineers on the Sunzhenskii Line in 1917). 1 folder.
   Typescript.
   Colonel, Imperial Russian Army. Relates to White Russian military activities during the Russian Revolution.

350. ERICKSON, DOUGLAS.
   Collection (in Russian), 1919-1963. 1/2 ms. box.
   Correspondence, lists, and bulletins relating to White Russian military activities during the Russian Revolution and to subsequent activities of émigré Imperial Russian Cavalry officers.

351. "ESTONIIA I POMOSHCH GOLODAIUSHCHIM" (ESTONIA AND AID TO THE STARVING).
   Essay (in Russian), 1921. 1 folder.
   Relates to civilian relief in Estonia at the end of World War I.

352. FEDICHKIN, DMITRI I.
   Papers (in Russian), 1918-1919. 1/2 ms. box.
   Colonel, Imperial Russian Army; commander in chief, Izhevsk People's Army, 1918. Writings, correspondence, and handbills relating to the Russian Civil War and the rebellion of workers and peasants in Izhevsk against the Bolsheviks, 1918.

353. FEDOROV, GEORGII.
   Memoirs (in Russian), n.d. "Iz vospominanii zalozhnika v Piatigorskom kontsentratsionnom lagere" (From the recollections of a prisoner in the Piatigorsk Concentration Camp). 1 vol.
   Typescript (carbon copy).
   Relates to the Russian Civil War in the Kuban region.

354. THE FROZEN WAR: AMERICA INTERVENES IN RUSSIA, 1918-1920.
   Motion picture film, 1973. 1 reel.
   Relates to American intervention during the Russian Revolution. Produced by Richard C. Raack.
   Purchase, R. C. Raack, 1980.

355. GESSEN, IOSIF VLADIMIROVICH, 1866-1943.
   Papers (in Russian and English), 1919-1920. 4 ms. boxes.
   Russian journalist and Constitutional Democratic Party leader. Reports, letters, and leaflets relating to the White Army in the Russian Civil War. Includes two translations of I. V. Gessen's memoirs, V dvukh vekakh (In two centuries), one entitled "Reminiscences," translated by E. Varneck, and a second entitled "Legality versus Autocracy," edited and annotated by Ladis K. D.

Kristof.
   Preliminary inventory.
   Purchase, I. V. Gessen, 1938.

356. GIRS, MIKHAIL NIKOLAEVICH, 1856-1932.
   Papers (in Russian), 1917-1926. 53 ms. boxes.
   White Russian diplomat; chief diplomatic representative of Baron Vrangel´ to the Allied Powers, 1920. Correspondence, reports, telegrams, and memoranda relating to the Russian Civil War, the Paris Peace Conference, and White Russian diplomatic relations. Includes a file on the American Relief Administration in Soviet Russia and dispatches from White Russian diplomats in Austria, the Baltic states, Belgium, Bulgaria, Czechoslovakia, Denmark, Egypt, Finland, Germany, Great Britain, Greece, Hungary, Italy, Japan, the Netherlands, Norway, Palestine, Persia, Poland, Romania, South America, Spain, Sweden, Switzerland, Turkey, the United States, and Yugoslavia.
      Preliminary inventory.
      Gift, Michel de Giers, 1926.

357. GNIESSEN, VLADIMIR F.
   Memoirs, n.d. "Through War and Revolution: Memoirs of a Russian Engineer." 1 ms. box.
   Typescript.
   Engineer and colonel, Imperial Russian Army. Relates to Russian military activities during World War I and White Russian military activities, especially in Turkestan, during the Russian Civil War.
   Gift, V. F. Gniessen, 1948.

358. GOLOVAN, SERGEI ALEXANDROVICH.
   Papers (in Russian), 1918-1921. 6 ms. boxes.
   White Russian military attaché to Switzerland. Correspondence, military orders, communiqués, and clippings relating to the Russian Civil War and White Russian military relations with Switzerland.
      Preliminary inventory.
      Gift, N. N. Golovin, 1928.

359. GOLOVIN, NIKOLAI N., 1875-1944.
   Papers (in Russian), 1912-1943. 16 ms. boxes.
   General, Imperial Russian Army. Correspondence, speeches and writings, and printed matter relating to Russian military activities during World War I, the Russian Civil War, and the Sino-Japanese War.
      Register.
      Gift, Michael Golovin, 1947.

360. GRAHAM, MALBONE WATSON, 1898-1965.
   Papers, 1914-1956. 15 1/2 ms. boxes, 2 card file boxes.
   American political scientist. Pamphlets, bulletins, writings,

memoranda, and clippings relating to the League of Nations and
to political conditions and diplomatic relations in Finland,
the Baltic States, and Eastern Europe from the Russian Revolution
to World War II. Includes the articles "The Ruthenian Question:
An Exposé," 1914; Aleksandr Shulgin, "Les problémes de l´Ukraine:
la question ethnique, la culture nationale, la vie économique, la
volonté du peuple," Paris, 1919; Ukrainian National Council, "Aux
nations civilisées: Appel des membres du Conseil national ukrainien
a l´étranger," Vienna, October 1919; Ukrainian National Council of
America, "The Cause of the Ukraine," Jersey City, N.J., n.d.; and
Eugen Petrushevich, "The Political Status of Eastern Galicia,"
Vienna, 1922.
   Preliminary inventory.
   Gift, Mrs. Gladys Graham, 1967.

GROUP OF ENGLISH SPEAKING COMMUNISTS, see collection no. 261.

361. GUBAREV, P. D.
   Report (in Russian), 1919. "Vremennoe polozhenie ob upravlenii
Terskim voiskom" (Temporary situation of the command of the Tersk
Forces). 1 folder.
   Typescript.
   Chairman, Main Circle, Tersk Forces. Relates to the Russian Civil
War in the Tersk area.

362. GUDELIS, PETRAS.
   History (in Lithuanian), 1975. "Joniskelio Apskrities Partizanai"
(Joniskelis County partisans). 1/2 ms. box.
   Typescript.
   Lieutenant major, Lithuanian Army. Relates to anti-Bolshevik
partisans in Joniskelis County, Lithuania, 1918-1919. Published as
<u>Joniskelio Apskrities Partizanai</u>, vol. 1 (Rome, 1975). Includes
correspondence between P. Gudelis and Zibuntas Miksys and between
Miksys and others, 1972-1975, relating to publication of the work.
   Gift, Z. Miksys, 1982.

363. HEIDEN, DIMITRI F., GRAF.
   Memoirs (in Russian), n.d. 1/2 ms. box.
   Typescript and holograph.
   Russian aristocrat. Relates to the involvement of Russia in
World War I and the Russian Revolution and Civil War.
   Register.
   Gift, Sophie Isakow, 1975.

364. HEROYS, BORIS VLADIMIR VICH.
   Papers (in Russian), 1917-1920. 8 ms. boxes.
   General, Imperial Russian Army; chief, Special Military Mission to
London sent by General Nikolai IUdenich, White Russian military
commander, during the Russian Civil War. Correspondence, reports,

communiqués, and printed matter relating to the Russian Revolution, anti-Bolshevik activities in northwest Russia, 1919-1920, and liaison between the White Russian forces and the British War Office.
   Preliminary inventory.
   Gift, B. V. Heroys, 1925.

365. HILL, GEORGE ALEXANDER, 1892-
   Papers, n.d. 1 folder.
   British secret service agent. Memoirs (typewritten) entitled "Reminiscences of Four Years with N. K. V. D." relating to Anglo-Soviet secret service relations during World War II and radio broadcast transcripts entitled "Go Spy the Land" relating to British intelligence activities in Russia, Turkey, and the Balkans, 1917-1918.
   May not be quoted without permission of G. A. Hill.
   Gift, G. A. Hill, 1968.

366. ISTORICHESKAIA KOMISSIIA MARKOVSKOGO ARTILLERIISKOGO DIVIZIONA.
   History (in Russian), 1931. "Istoriia Markovskoi artilleriiskoi brigady" (History of the Markovskii Artillery Brigade). 1 vol.
   Typescript (mimeographed).
   White Russian military unit. Relates to activities of the Markovskii Artillery Brigade during the Russian Civil War. Edited by Colonel Zholondkovskii, Lieutenant Colonel Shcharinskii and Captain Vinogradov.

367. IUDENICH, NIKOLAI NIKOLAEVICH, 1862-1933.
   Papers (in Russian), 1918-1920. 21 ms. boxes.
   General, Imperial Russian Army; commander, Northwestern White Russian armed forces, 1918-1920. Correspondence, memoranda, telegrams, reports, military documents, proclamations, maps, and printed matter relating to the campaigns of the Northwestern White Russian armed forces, communism in Russia, relations with the Allied Powers, and activities of White Russian representatives in Europe.
   Preliminary inventory.
   Gift, N. N. IUdenich, 1927.

368. IUNAKOV, N. L.
   Memoir (in Russian), 1927. "Moi posliednie miesiatsy v dieistvuiushchie armii: vospominaniia byvshago komanduiushchego armiei, oktiabr´-dekabr´ 1917 goda" (My last months in the active army: Reminiscences of a former army commander, October-December 1917). 1 vol.
   Holograph.

369. "IZ VOZZVANIIA K KAREL´SKOMU NASELENIIU KEMSKOGO UEZDA." (FROM THE APPEAL TO THE KARELIAN POPULACE OF THE KEMSK REGION).
   Appeal (in Russian), 1919. 1 folder.
   Typescript.

Relates to the Russian Civil War. Written by a group of White Russian leaders.

370. JENNISON, HARRY A.
　　Letter received, 1920. 1 folder.
　　Relates to conditions in Russia during the Russian Civil War. Written by a White Russian army colonel.
　　Gift, John W. Romine, 1973.

371. KALNINS, EDUARDS, 1876-1964.
　　Papers (in Latvian), 1919-1965. 1 ms. box.
　　General, Latvian army; chief of staff, 1919. Memoirs, correspondence, memorabilia, and printed matter relating to the establishment of Latvian independence and to post-World War II Latvian émigré affairs.
　　Gift, Edgar Anderson, 1982.

372. KHOSHEV, BORIS ALEKSANDROVICH, 1898-
　　Service record (in Russian), 1922. 1 folder.
　　Photocopy.
　　Captain, Imperial Russian Army. Relates to the military career of B. A. Khoshev before and during the Russian Revolution.
　　Gift, Nina Khoshev, 1980.

373. KLEMM, V., 1861-
　　Writings (in Russian and English), 1922-1926. 1 folder.
　　Holograph and typescript.
　　White Russian political leader during the Russian Civil War. Autobiographical sketch (typewritten), 1926; a history (handwritten in Russian) entitled "Ocherk revoliutsionnykh sobytii v russkoi srednei Azii" (Sketch of the Revolution in Russian Central Asia), 1922; and a translation (typewritten) of the above.
　　Gift, V. Klemm, 1926.

374. KORVIN-KROUKOVSKY, EUGENIE A.
　　Diary (in Russian), 1917-1918. 1 folder.
　　Typescript.
　　Relates to events in Petrograd during the Revolution of 1917 and to the escape of E. A. Korvin-Kroukovsky to the United States via the Far East, 1918.
　　Gift, E. A. Korvin-Kroukovsky, 1971.

375. KOUSSONSKII, PAVEL ALEKSEEVICH.
　　Papers (in Russian), 1918-1926. 12 ms. boxes.
　　Lieutenant general, White Russian army; staff officer under generals Denikin, Vrangel´, and Miller, 1918-1925. Correspondence, reports, telegrams, orders, circulars, proclamations, lists, maps, and charts relating to the general headquarters of the Volunteer

Army of the Armed Forces in South Russia; to the Caucasian, Crimean, and other campaigns of the Civil War; to the evacuation and resettlement of the army of General Vrangel´; and to Russian émigré military and political life in Europe.
   Register.
   Gift, I. A. Holmsen, 1928.

376. KRASNOV, PETR NIKOLAEVICH, 1869-1947.
   Letter (in Russian), 1937. 1 folder.
   Holograph.
   General, Imperial Russian Army; White Russian leader in the Russian Civil War. Relates to personal matters.

377. KRASSOVSKII, VITOL´D.
   Memoirs (in Russian), 1927. 1 folder.
   Typescript.
   Imperial Russian Army officer. Relates to Russian military activities during World War I and to White Russian military activities in southwestern Russia during the Russian Civil War.

378. KRYMSKOE KRAEVOE PRAVITEL´STVO.
   Miscellaneous records (in Russian), 1918-1919. 2 ms. boxes.
   Crimean Regional Government. Files of the president of the Council of Ministers, minister of foreign affairs, minister of justice, and minister of internal affairs relating to the relations of the Crimean Regional Government and the Constitutional Democratic Party with the Russian Volunteer Army and with the Allies.

379. KRZECZUNOWICZ, KORNEL.
   Study (in Polish), n.d. "Ostatnia kampania konna" (The last cavalry campaign). 1/2 ms. box.
   Typescript.
   Relates to Polish cavalry operations in the war against Russia, 1920.

380. KUTUKOV, LEONID NIKOLAEVICH, 1897-
   Papers (in Russian), 1914-1972. 2 ms. boxes, 1 album box.
   Russian author and journalist. Correspondence, writings, reports, clippings, and printed matter relating to conditions in Russia and Russian military campaigns during World War I and the Russian Civil War, the Moscow Household Troops Regiment and other Russian military units, and Russian émigré activities in France after the Civil War.
   Preliminary inventory.
   Gift, L. N. Kutukov, 1980.

381. KUTZEVALOV, BONIFACE SEMENOVICH.
   Study (in Russian), n.d. "Ubiistvo General Romanovskago" (The assassination of General Romanovskii). 1 folder.

Holograph.
Captain, Imperial Russian Army. Relates to the assassination of the White Russian military leader Ivan Pavlovich Romanovskii in the Russian embassy in Constantinople, 1920.
Gift, B. S. Kutzevalov, 1932.

382. LAMPE, ALEKSEI ALEKSANDROVICH von, 1885-1960.
Papers (mainly in Russian), 1917-1926. 10 ms. boxes.
General, Imperial Russian Army; Russian military agent in Germany, 1922-1926; Russian military representative to Hungary, 1921-1926. Correspondence, reports, memoranda, orders, newsletters, clippings, leaflets, maps, pamphlets, and printed matter relating to operations of the offices of the Russian military agent in Germany and the Russian military representative to Hungary, Russian counter-revolutionary activities, political events in Russia, and activities of Russian civilians and military personnel in Europe. Includes the office files of the delegation of the Russian Society of the Red Cross for Relief to Prisoners of War, 1919-1922.
Register.
Purchase, Nikolai Golovin, 1928.

383. LEIKHTENBERG, NIKOLAI NIKOLAEVICH, GERTSOG fon.
Diary (in Russian), 1918. 1 folder, 1 envelope.
Holograph (photocopy).
Relates to the activities of White Russian forces under General Krasnov in southern Russia during the Russian Civil War.
Gift, Marvin Lyons, 1966.

384. LEVITSKY, EUGENE L.
Writings (in Russian), n.d. 1 folder.
Typescript (photocopy).
Imperial Russian Army officer. History, entitled "Ataka" (Attack), relating to the operations of the 2d Ufim Cavalry Division during the Russian Civil War in May 1919 and memoirs, entitled "Fevral´skie dni" (February days), relating to Russian military operations, 1916-1917, and to the Russian Revolution.
Gift, E. L. Levitsky, 1974.

385. LODYGENSKY, GEORGES.
Writings (in French), n.d. 1/2 ms. box.
Russian physician. Memoirs, entitled "Une carriere médicale mouvementée" (A turbulent medical career), relating to medical practice in Russia during World War I, the Russian Revolution, and Civil War, 1908-1923, and a history, entitled "Face au communisme--le mouvement anticommuniste internationale de 1923-1950" (In the face of communism--The Anticommunist International from 1923 to 1950), relating to the operations of the International Anticommunist Entente.
Gift, G. Lodygensky, 1975.

386. LUKOMSKII, ALEKSANDR SERGEEVICH, d. 1939.
    Papers (in Russian), 1914-1939. 4 ms. boxes, 1 envelope.
    General, Imperial Russian Army; White Russian military leader under generals Kornilov and Denikin, 1917-1919. Correspondence, memoranda, reports, writings, notes, and printed matter relating to Russian military operations during World War I and to the Russian Civil War.
    Register.
    Gift, Sophie Isakow, 1975.

387. MAKHNO, NESTOR IVANOVICH, 1889-1935.
    Memoirs (in Russian), 1932. Pechal´nye stranitsy russkoi revoliutsii (Sad pages of the Russian Revolution). 1 folder.
    Printed.
    Anarchist leader. Relates to the role of the anarchists in the Russian Civil War. Published serially in the Chicago Rassvet.

388. MARKOV, ANATOLII.
    Study (in Russian), n.d. "Entsiklopediia belago dvizheniia: vozhdi, partizany, fronty, pokhody i narodnyia vozstaniia protiv sovetov v Rossii" (Encyclopedia of the White Movement: Leaders, partisans, fronts, marches and popular uprisings against the soviets in Russia). 4 vols.
    Typescript.
    Relates to White Russian activities during the Russian Civil War and after, 1917-1958. Includes biographical sketches.

389. MARTOV, IULII OSIPOVICH, 1873-1923.
    Writings (in Russian), 1920. "Oborona revoliutsii i sotsial-demokratiia: sbornik statei" (Defense of the Revolution and social democracy: Collected articles). 1 vol.
    Typescript.
    Russian Menshevik leader. Relates to the Russian Revolution and Civil War.

390. MARTYNOV, ZAKHAR NIKIFOROVICH.
    Papers (in Russian), 1914-1977. 1 ms. box.
    Imperial Russian soldier in the convoy of His Imperial Majesty Emperor Nicholas II. Correspondence, writings, reminiscences, printed matter, clippings, and photographs relating to the Imperial Russian Army, Russia´s role in World War I, the Russian Revolution and Civil War, and anticommunist movements in the United States. Includes a cigarette case from the desk of Tsar Alexander III, a dagger presented to Tsarevich Aleksei Nikolaevich when he was made ataman of the Cossacks, and the St. George´s Cross awarded to Z. N. Martynov for his military service.
    Gift, Z. N. Martynov, 1977.

391. MEYER, HENRY CORD, 1913-
   Papers (in German and English), 1916-1963. 1 ms. box, 2 phonorecords.
   American historian. Correspondence, reports, conference papers, notes, speech, memorandum, and printed matter relating to miscellaneous aspects of twentieth-century European (especially German) history and to the ideas of the German nationalist writer, Paul Rohrbach. Includes material on the German occupation of the Ukraine in 1918.
   Preliminary inventory.
   Gift, H. C. Meyer, 1969.

392. MILLER, EVGENII KARLOVICH, 1867-1937.
   Papers (in Russian), 1917-1924. 12 ms. boxes.
   General, Imperial Russian Army; representative of General Vrangel´ in Paris during the Russian Civil War. Correspondence, reports, and military orders relating to White Russian military and diplomatic activities during the Russian Civil War.
   Preliminary inventory.
   Gift, N. N. Golovin, 1928.

393. MITKIEWICZ, LEON, 1896-1972.
   Papers (in Polish), 1918-1969. 8 1/2 ms. boxes.
   Colonel and chief of intelligence, Polish army; military attaché to Lithuania: Polish representative, Allied Combined Chiefs of Staff, 1943-1945. Diary, correspondence, writings, and printed matter relating to Polish foreign relations with Russia, Czechoslovakia, the Baltic States, and other countries, 1914-1944; the Warsaw uprising of August 1944; and World War II Allied diplomacy.
   Register.
   Gift, L. Mitkiewicz, 1965. Incremental gift, 1976.

394. "NAKAZ BOL´SHOGO I MALAGO VOISKOVOGO KRUGA VOISKA TERSKAGO" (ORDER OF THE LARGE AND SMALL MILITARY UNION OF THE TERSK UNIT).
   Memorandum (in Russian), 1919. 1 folder.
   Typescript.
   Relates to the bylaws of a White Russian officers´ association.

395. NIROD, FEODOR MAKSIMILIANOVICH, GRAF, 1871-
   Memoirs (in Russian), n.d. "Prozhitoe" (What I have lived through). 1 ms. box.
   Typescript and holograph.
   Imperial Russian Army officer. Relates to Russian military life, 1892-1917, including the Russo-Japanese War, Russian participation in World War I, and the Russian Revolution.
   Gift, Dimitri Shvetsoff, 1970.

396. NOSOVICH, ANATOLII.
   Writings (in Russian), n.d.   1 folder.
   Typescript (photocopy).
   General, Imperial Russian Army. Histories entitled "Ulany Ego Velichestva, 1876-1926: Imperator Aleksandr II; Imperator Nikolai II" (Uhlans of His Majesty, 1876-1926: Emperor Alexander II and Emperor Nicholas II) and "Leib gvardii ulanskii Ego Velichestva polk v velikuiu i grazhdanskuiu voinu: kratkoe proshloe polka v emigratsii" (Uhlan Household Troops of His Majesty's Regiment in the Great and Civil Wars: A brief history of the regiment in emigration).
   Gift, Marvin Lyons, 1971.

397. NOWAK, JAN.
   Sound recordings (in Polish), 1965.   14 phonorecords.
   Speeches, radio broadcasts, and reminiscences of Polish statesmen, diplomats, military officers, and émigrés, ca. 1918-1974, relating to major events in Polish twentieth-century history, especially the Polish-Soviet wars of 1918-1921 and the World War II period, and to Polish émigré activities. Recorded by the Polish Broadcasting Department of Radio Free Europe.
   Records 1-8 open. Records 9-10 closed until 1985. Records 11-12 closed until 1987. Records 13-14 closed until 2030.
   Preliminary inventory.
   Gift and deposit, Jan Nowak, 1967. Increment, May 1980.

398. OBSHCHESTVA FORMIROVANIIA BOEVYKH OTRIADOV.
   Proclamation (in Russian), 1920.   1 folder.
   Printed.
   Societies of Forming Combat Detachments, a White Russian organization. States regulations of the Obshchestva formirovaniia boevykh otriadov.

399. OBSHCHESTVA OB"EDINENIIA I VZAIMOPOMOSHCHI RUSSKIKH OFITSEROV I DOBROVOL'TSEV.
   Proclamation (in Russian), 1920.   1 folder.
   Printed.
   Societies of Unification and Mutual Assistance of Russian Officers and Volunteers, a White Russian organization. States basic regulations of the Obshchestva ob"edineniia i vzaimopomoshchi russkikh ofitserov i dobrovol'tsev.

400. ODINTSOV, GLEB NIKOLAEVICH.
   Papers (in Russian), 1928-1973.   3 ms. boxes, 1 oversize framed photograph.
   Colonel, Imperial Russian Army. Correspondence, writings, clippings, printed matter, documents, and photographs relating to the Imperial Russian Army, events in Russia before, during, and after the Russian Revolution and Civil War, the Romanov family, and

other Russian dignitaries and nobility.
Gift, G. N. Odintsov, 1975.

401. OIDERMAN, M.
History, n.d. "Estonian Independence." 1/2 ms. box.
Typescript.
Relates to the history of Estonia during the Russian Revolution and to the establishment of an independent Estonian state. Prepared under the auspices of the Estonian Foreign Office.

402. OZELS, OSKARS, 1889-1975.
Memoirs (in Latvian), n.d. "Pieredzejumi Riga Bermonta Dienas" (Experiences in Riga during Bermondt's campaign). 1 folder.
Typescript (photocopy).
Latvian engineer and educator. Relates to the Bermondt-Avalov campaign in Riga, October-November 1919, during the Russian Civil War.
Gift, Edgar Anderson, 1977.

403. PALEOLOGUE, SERGEI NIKOLAEVICH, 1887-
Papers (in Russian), 1920-1933. 34 ms. boxes.
Chairman, Board of the Government Plenipotentiary for the Settlement of Russian Refugees in Yugoslavia. Correspondence, reports, and memoranda relating to the activities of the board.

404. PALEY, OLGA VALERIANOVNA, 1865-
Memoirs, n.d. <u>Memories of Russia, 1916-1919.</u> 1/2 ms. box.
Holograph and typescript.
Morganatic wife of Grand Duke Pavel Aleksandrovich of Russia. Relates to the Russian Revolution and Civil War. Memoirs published.
Gift, Harper and Row, publishers, 1964.

405. PALITSYN, FEDOR FEDOROVICH, 1851-1923.
Memoirs (in Russian), 1918-1921. 1 ms. box.
Typescript.
General, Imperial Russian Army; chief of staff, 1905-1908. Memoirs entitled "Perezhitoe, 1916-1918" (My experience, 1916-1918), 1918, and "Zapiski Generala F. Palitsyna" (Notes of General F. Palitsyn), 1921, relating to Russian military activities during the Russian Civil War.

406. PANTIUKHOV, OLEG IVANOVICH, 1882-1974.
Papers (in Russian), 1904-1966. 1 ms. box.
Colonel, Imperial Russian Army. Correspondence, writings, reports, military documents, personnel lists, maps, printed matter, and photographs relating to Russian participation in World War I, the Russian Revolution, and activities of His Majesty's 1st Rifle

Household Troops Regiment during this period and after emigration.
Gift, Oleg Pantuhoff, Jr., 1982.

407. PASH, BORIS T.
Papers, 1918-1976. 1 ms. box, 4 envelopes, 3 albums, 62 reels of film.
Colonel, U.S. Army; military intelligence officer. Correspondence, memoranda, reports, orders, writings, photographs, films, and printed matter relating to the naval forces of General Nikolai IUdenich during the Russian Civil War; the Russian refugee camp in Wuensdorf, Germany in 1922; U.S. military intelligence service activities, including the Baja Peninsula mission to investigate the possible establishment of a Japanese base in Mexico in 1942 and the Alsos mission to determine the status of German nuclear development in 1944-1945; and to allegations made in 1975 about the involvement of B. T. Pash with Central Intelligence Agency assassination plots.
Gift, B. T. Pash, 1972. Incremental gift, 1976.

408. PETRUSHEVICH, IVAN, 1875-1950.
Papers, 1910-1941. 6 ms. boxes, 5 microfilm reels.
Ukrainian journalist. Diaries, correspondence, speeches, writings, memoranda, and clippings relating to the Ukraine during the Russian Revolution, Ukrainian territorial questions, the Western Ukrainian National Republic, the Polish-Ukrainian war, the cooperative movement in the Ukraine, the Carpathian Ukraine (ca. 1920-1930, 1 folder), and Ukrainians in Canada and the United States. Includes "Declaration du gouvernement de la République démocratique Ukrainienne," 1920; "Aspects of the Ukrainian Problem," lecture delivered at the University of California, Los Angeles, on May 17, 1935; "Some Aspects of the Ukrainian Problem As Seen in Historical Perspective," lecture delivered at the University of California, Los Angeles on May 3, 1935; and correspondence with M. Rudnitsky, V. Rebikoff, Baroness Procter, D. Chambashidze, Colonel Oulianin, Stephen Tomashivsky, Valentin O'Hara, Nadine Procter, and George Kurdyduk, 1919-1923.

409. POLAND. AMBASADA (U.S.).
Records (in Polish), 1918-1956. 118 ms. boxes.
Polish embassy in the United States. Reports, correspondence, bulletins, communiqués, memoranda, dispatches and instructions, speeches and writings, and printed matter relating to the establishment of the Republic of Poland; the Polish-Soviet war of 1920; Polish politics and foreign relations; national minorities in Poland; the territorial questions of Danzig, Memel, the Polish Corridor, and Galicia; the Polish emigration abroad; Poland during World War II; and the Polish government-in-exile in London.
Register.
Deposit, Jan Ciechanowski, 1945.

410. "POLTAVSKIIA EPARKHIAL´NYIA DIELA."
   Broadside (in Russian), June 1917. 1 folder.
   Printed.
   Relates to the situation of religion in Poltava, Ukraine during the Russian Revolution.

411. POPOVSKII, MARK ALEKSANDROVICH, <u>COLLECTOR</u>.
   Collection, 1919-1977. 16 microfilm reels.
   Microfilm of originals.
   Reminiscences, reports, correspondence, and other writings of members of the Tolstovtsy communes in the Soviet Union relating to the agrarian dissent movement of followers of Leo Tolstoy. In Russian.
   Preliminary inventory.
   Purchase, M. A. Popovskii, 1984.

412. POST, WILBUR E.
   History, 1918-1919. 1 vol.
   Typescript (carbon copy).
   Relates to the Russian Revolution and Civil War in the Caucasus region, Allied intervention in the area, and economic conditions in the Caucasus. Written by W. E. Post and Maurice Wertheim.

413. RERBERG, FEDOR PETROVICH, 1868-
   Memoirs (in Russian and French), 1922-1925. 1 ms. box.
   Holograph and typescript.
   Imperial Russian Army officer; chief of staff, X Corps, and chief of staff, Sevastopol´ Fortress, during World War I. Relates to the X Corps, the Sevastopol´ Fortress during World War I and the Russian Civil War, and White Russian and Allied military activities in the Crimea during the Russian Civil War.

414. "REVEL´SKAIA GAVAN´ I BOL´SHEVIKI" (REVEL HARBOR AND THE BOLSHEVIKS).
   Report (in Russian), 1921. 1 vol.
   Typescript (carbon copy).
   Relates to commerce conducted through the port of Tallinn, Estonia during the Russian Civil War.

415. RIGA, TREATY OF, 1920.
   Translation of preliminary peace treaty and armistice, 1920.
   1 folder.
   Typescript.
   Treaty between Poland and Russia, signed at Riga on October 11, 1920, halting the Russo-Polish war.

416. RUSSIA (1917-1922. CIVIL WAR GOVERNMENTS). DOBROVOL´CHESKAIA ARMIIA. GLAVNYI KAZNACHEI.

Account books (in Russian), n.d. 1 folder.
Treasury of the White Russian Volunteer Army. Relates to the financial operations for the Russian Volunteer Army.

417. RUSSIA (1917-1922. CIVIL WAR GOVERNMENTS). DONSKAIA ARMIIA.
Orders (in Russian), 1918-1920. 1 ms. box.
White Russian Don army. Relates to the Russian Civil War in the south of Russia.

418. RUSSIA (1917-1922. CIVIL WAR GOVERNMENTS). VOORUZHENNYE SILY IUGA ROSSII. NACHAL'NIK SNABZHENIIA.
Records (in Russian), 1916-1926. 6 ms. boxes.
Chief of supply, White Russian army. Correspondence, reports, receipts, and accounts relating to the payment of Russian soldiers in Bulgaria and Yugoslavia, financial subsidies to refugees, administration of refugee camp facilities, and the composition and distribution of units of the First Army Corps and the Don Corps.
Register.
Purchase, Ivan A. Holmsen, 1930.

419. RUSSIA (1917-1922. CIVIL WAR GOVERNMENTS). VOORUZHENNYE SILY IUGA ROSSII. SUDNOE OTDELENIE.
Records (in Russian and Bulgarian), 1918-1927. 9 ms. boxes.
Justice Department, White Russian army. Correspondence, reports, memoranda, orders, and affidavits relating to administration of military justice in the White Russian army, Russian émigrés in Bulgaria, the political situation in Bulgaria, and the composition and distribution of the First Army Corps and the Don Corps.
Register.
Purchase, Ivan A. Holmsen, 1930.

420. RUSSKAIA NARODNAIA ARMIIA (RUSSIAN PEOPLE'S ARMY).
Leaflet (in Russian), 1919. 1 folder.
Printed.
Relates to White Russian military activities during the Russian Civil War. Issued by White Russian forces in Azov.

421. RUSSKIIA VEDOMOSTI (RUSSIAN NEWS) (MOSCOW).
Translation of excerpts from articles, 1918. 1 folder.
Typescript.
Moscow newspaper. Relates to instances of religious persecution of the Russian Orthodox Church in Soviet Russia. Includes accounts of events at the Aleksandro-Nevskaia lavra and the All-Russian Church Congress in Moscow, January-February 1918.

422. SAVINKOV, BORIS VIKTOROVICH, 1879-1925.
Writings (in Russian and English), 1920-1924. 1 folder.
Russian Socialist Revolutionary Party leader. Letter (typewritten

in Russian) to Baron Petr Vrangel´, White Russian military commander, 1920, relating to White Russian military activities; and translation (typewritten) of the testimony of B. Savinkov at his trial for counterrevolutionary activities, 1924.

423. SCHAKOVSKOY, WLADIMIR, PRINCE, 1904-1972.
 Memoirs (in French), 1947. "Russie" (Russia). 206 p. Typescript (photocopy).
 Russian aristocrat. Relates to conditions in Russia during the Russian Revolution and Civil War.
 Gift, Princess Schakovskoy, 1981.

424. SCHAUMAN, GEORG CARL AUGUST, 1870-1930.
 Writings (in Swedish and French), 1920. 1 folder.
 Member of the parliament of Finland. Study (typewritten in Swedish) entitled "Kampen om Statsskicket i Finland 1918" (Struggles over the Constitution of Finland, 1918) and an untitled memorandum (handwritten and typewritten in French) relating to the Finnish revolution of 1917-1918 and to political conditions in Finland.

425. SCHNEIDER, LEO VICTOR, 1890-1963.
 Papers, 1928-1945. 1 folder.
 Russian-American physician; White Army surgeon during the Russian Revolution; U.S. Army surgeon during World War II. Writings, clippings, and miscellanea relating to the Russian Revolution and to U.S. military medicine during World War II.
 Gift, Alan Schneider, 1981.

426. SHALIKASHVILI, DIMITRI.
 Writings (in Russian), 1920-1960. 2 1/2 ms. boxes.
 Georgian diplomatic emissary to Turkey, 1920-1921; major, Polish army. Diary and memoirs relating to Georgian relations with Turkey, 1920-1921; Georgian refugee life in Turkey and Poland; the Polish army in the interwar period; its defeat in 1939; the Georgian legion in the German army during World War II; and Georgian prisoners in British prison camps at the end of the war. Includes English translations.
 Gift, Maria Shalikashvili, 1980.

427. SHCHERBACHEV, DMITRII GRIGOR´EVICH, 1855-1932.
 Papers (in Russian and French), 1914-1920. 8 ms. boxes.
 General, Imperial Russian Army. Correspondence, orders, reports, and printed matter relating to Russian prisoners of war in Germany during World War I and to counterrevolutionary movements during the Russian Revolution.
 Preliminary inventory.
 Gift, D. G. Shcherbachev, 1929.

428. SHEVELEV, KLAVDII VALENTINOVICH, 1881-
   Papers (in Russian), 1919-1948. 1 folder, 1 envelope.
   Photocopy.
   Rear admiral, Imperial Russian Navy. Birth certificate, White Russian Naval Ministry identification document, International Refugee Organization documents, and photographs relating to the naval career and émigré life of K. V. Shevelev.
   Gift, Yelena Andrejeff, 1976.

429. SHINKARENKO, NIKOLAI VSEVOLODOVICH, 1890-1968.
   Memoirs (in Russian), n.d. 7 pamphlet boxes (2 l. ft.).
   Typescript.
   Imperial Russian Army officer; brigadier general of the cavalry of the White Russian army; Spanish foreign legion officer. Relates to Russian cavalry operations in World War I, White Russian military operations in the Russian Civil War, Spanish military operations in Africa, and Francoist military operations in the Spanish Civil War. Includes copies of letters and photographs.
   Purchase, N. V. Shinkarenko, 1968.

430. SHREWSBURY, KENNETH O.
   Papers, 1919-1922. 1 ms. box.
   American volunteer in the Kosciuszko Squadron. Photographs, clippings, and miscellanea relating to the activities of volunteer American aviators who formed the Kosciuszko Squadron of the Polish army during the Polish-Russian war, 1919-1921.
   Gift, K. O. Shrewsbury, 1960.

431. SHVARTS, ALEKSEI VLADIMIROVICH fon, 1874-1953.
   Papers (in Russian), 1845-1955. 1 ms. box.
   General, Imperial Russian Army. Diary, correspondence, memoirs, writings, notes, and printed matter relating to Russian military campaigns in the Caucasus and Eastern Europe during World War I and the Russian Revolution.
   Purchase, Vera A. de Borel, 1981.

432. SHVETZOFF, DIMITRII ANDREEVICH, 1902-
   Memoir, n.d. "Captivity and Escape of Horseguardsman Dimitrii A. Shvetzoff in 1919-1920." 1 folder.
   Typescript (photocopy).
   Soldier, Imperial Russian Horse Guards. Relates to the activities of the Imperial Russian Horse Guard Regiment during the Russian Revolution and Civil War.
   Gift, D. A. Shvetzoff, 1972.

433. SKALSKII, VLADIMIR EVGENIEVICH.
   Memoir, n.d. 1 folder.
   Typescript (photocopy).

Imperial Russian Army officer. Relates to the escape of V. E. Skalskii from Bolshevik captivity, 1918.
Gift, Dmitrii Birkin, 1968.

434. "SOVIET-POLISH DISPUTE."
Study, ca. 1945. 157 p.
Typescript.
Relates to historical, political, and legal aspects of the boundary dispute between Poland and the Soviet Union, 1918-1945. Signed I.I.D.
Gift, estate of Witold S. Sworakowski, 1979.

435. STAFFORD, CLAYTON I.
Memoir, n.d. "Incident in the Crimea, 1920." 1 folder.
Typescript.
Sailor, U.S. Navy. Relates to a U.S. naval visit to the Crimea during the Russian Civil War, 1920.
Gift, C. I. Stafford, 1977.

436. STEINBERG, ISAAC NACHMAN, 1888-1957.
History, n.d. "The Events of July 1918." 1 vol.
Typescript.
Relates to the assassination of Count Wilhelm von Mirbach-Harff, German ambassador to Russia, in 1918.

437. STRUVE, PETR BERNGARDOVICH, 1870-1944.
Papers (mainly in Russian), 1890-1976. 22 ms. boxes, 1 envelope.
Russian journalist, historian, and politician; minister of foreign affairs in the Baron Petr Vrangel' government, 1919-1921. Correspondence, speeches and writings, reports, memoranda, essays, photographs, and printed matter relating to Russia in World War I, the Russian Revolution and Civil War, anti-Bolshevik movements, the Russian economy and industry, Russians in foreign countries, and conditions in the Soviet Union after the Revolution.
Register.
Purchase, Gleb P. Struve, 1979.

438. SUKACEV, LEV PAVLOVICH, 1895-1974.
Translation of memoirs, n.d. "Soldier Under Three Flags: The Personal Memoirs of Lev Pavlovich Sukacev." 1/2 ms. box.
Typescript (photocopy).
Lieutenant, Imperial Russian Army; major, Albanian Army; colonel, Italian army. Relates to Russian military activities during World War I and the Russian Civil War; Albanian military activities, 1924-1939; and Italian military activities during World War II. Original memoirs published in Novoe russkoe slovo, 1972.
Gift, Natalie Sukacev, 1976.

439. TIKHON, PATRIARCH OF MOSCOW AND ALL RUSSIA, 1865-1925.
Letter (in Russian), 1918, to the Council of People's Commissars.
1 folder.
Typewritten transcript.
Relates to the situation of religion in Russia. Includes a photocopy of a translation (typewritten) of the above by Peter Nicholas Kurguz, 1962.

440. TOMILOV, P. A.
History (in Russian), n.d. "Sievero-zapadnyi front grazhdanskoi voiny v Rossii 1919 goda" (The northwestern front of the Civil War in Russia, 1919). 1 ms. box.
Typescript.

441. TRELOAR, GEORGE D.
Diary, 1920. 1 item (9 p.)
Typed copy of original in possession of D. W. G. Treloar.
Major, British army. Relates to British liaison with White Russian forces in the Crimea during the Russian Revolution, September 22-November 11, 1920.
Gift, D. W. G. Treloar, 1983.

442. TSCHEBOTARIOFF, GREGORY PORPHYRIEWITCH, 1899-
Correspondence (in Russian and English), 1941-1975. 1 folder.
Typescript and holograph.
Lieutentant, Russian army, 1916-1921; subsequently émigré in the United States. Relates to the Don Cadet Corps during the Russian Revolution and to relations between the United States and Russia in 1941.
Gift, G. P. Tschebotarioff, 1968. Subsequent increments.

443. "ULANY EGO VELICHESTVA, 1876-1926" (HIS MAJESTY'S LANCERS, 1876-1926).
Commemorative history (in Russian), 1926. 1 folder.
Typescript (mimeographed).
Relates to the history of the Uhlan troops of the Imperial Russian Army.

444. U.S. COMMITTEE UPON THE ARBITRATION OF THE BOUNDARY BETWEEN TURKEY AND ARMENIA.
Report, ca. 1920. 2 vols.
Typescript (carbon copy).

445. U.S. MILITARY MISSION TO ARMENIA.
Photographs, 1919. 1 envelope.
Depicts U.S. Army officers in Armenia and conditions in Armenia

at the end of World War I.
Preliminary inventory.
Gift, Eliot Grinnell Mears.

446. UPOVALOV, IVAN.
Translation of memoirs, 1922-1923. "How We Lost Our Liberty." 1 folder.
Typescript.
Russian Menshevik. Relates to the Russian Civil War in the areas of Votkinsk and Izhevsk, Russia in 1918. Original memoirs, entitled "Kak my poteriali svobodu" and "Rabochee vosstanie protiv sovetskoi vlasti," published in Zaria (Berlin), 1922-1923. Translated by Elena Varneck.

447. VAKSMUT, A. P.
Memoir (in Russian), n.d. "Konets Kaspiiskoi flotilii vremeni grazhdanskoi voiny pod komandoi Generala Denikina" (The end of the Caspian Flotilla during the Civil War under the command of General Denikin). 1 folder.
Holograph.
Captain, White Russian navy.

448. VESSELAGO, GEORGE M., 1892-
Papers (in Russian), 1904-1970. 8 ms. boxes, 1 envelope.
Lieutenant commander, Imperial Russian Navy. Correspondence, writings, printed matter, clippings, and photographs relating to Russian naval operations during World War I and the Russian Revolution and Civil War.
Register.
Gift, Vasili Romanov, 1975.

449. VINAVER, ROSE GEORGIEVNA.
Memoirs (in Russian), 1944. 1 vol.
Typescript.
Wife of Maxim Moiseevich Vinaver, a leader of the Russian Constitutional Democratic Party and foreign minister of the Crimean regional government, 1918-1919. Relates to political conditions in Russia, the Russian Revolution, and the Crimean regional government.

450. VITKOVSKII, VLADIMIR K.
Memoir (in Russian), 1933. "Konstantinopol'skii pokhod: iz vospominanii o Gallipoli" (The Constantinople march: From the reminiscences about Gallipoli). 1 folder.
Typescript (mimeographed).
Lieutenant general, Imperial Russian Army. Relates to the evacuation of White Russian troops at the end of the Russian Civil War.

451. VRANGEL', MARIIA D.
    Papers (in Russian), 1919-1924. ca. 42 linear ft.
    Mother of General P. N. Vrangel', commander of the White Russian forces in southern Russia. Correspondence, writings, pamphlets, periodicals, newspapers, photographs, clippings, and printed matter relating to the life and military career of P. N. Vrangel', the anti-Bolshevik campaigns of the Armed Forces of Southern Russia, the Russian Revolution and Civil War, communism in Russia, and the activities of Russian refugees in foreign countries.
    Preliminary inventory.
    Deposit, M. D. Vrangel', 1932.

452. VRANGEL', PETR NIKOLAEVICH, BARON, 1878-1928.
    Papers (in Russian), 1916-1923. 94 1/2 ms. boxes, 18 1/2 l. ft.
    Commander in chief, White Russian Volunteer Army, 1920. Correspondence, memoranda, reports, military orders, dispatches, printed matter, and photographs relating to the Russian Revolution and Civil War, the operations of the Volunteer Army and the Armed Forces of Southern Russia, evacuation of White Russian military personnel and civilians from the Crimea in 1920, and the resettlement of Russian refugees, first in Constantinople, and subsequently in various European countries.
    Preliminary inventory.
    Deposit, P. N. Vrangel', 1926. Incremental deposit, 1929.

453. VYRYPAEV, V. I.
    Memoir (in Russian), n.d. "Vladimir Oskarovich Kappel': vospominaniia uchastnika beloi bor'by" (Vladimir Oskarovich Kappel': Memoirs of a participant in the White struggle). 1/2 ms. box.
    Typescript.
    Soldier, White Russian army. Relates to the Russian Civil War and the activities of the Volunteer Army detachments under the command of V. O. Kappel'. Includes partial translation.

454. ZVEGINTSOV, NIKOLAI.
    Papers (in Russian), 1920-1922. 1 ms. box.
    Imperial Russian Navy officer. Correspondence, writings, and memoranda relating to activities of the White Russian military forces during the Russian Civil War.
    Register.
    Gift, Vasili Romanov, 1975.

SIBERIA

455. ANDRUSHKEVICH, NIKOLAI ALEKSANDROVICH.
Writings (in Russian), 1931-1936. 1/2 ms. box.
Holograph.
Histories entitled "Posledniaia Rossiia" (The last Russia), 1931, and "Prokliatyi korabl´" (The damned ship), 1936, relating to the Russian Civil War in Vladivostok and the Far East, 1919-1922, and to travels in Eastern Europe, the Near East, and Asia.
Gift, N. A. Andrushkevich, 1936.

456. ANICHKOV, VLADIMIR PETROVICH.
Memoirs (in Russian), n.d. "Vospominaniia" (Reminiscences).
1 1/2 ms. boxes.
Typescript.
Manager of the Volga Kama Bank and head of the Alapaevsk District. Relates to the Russian Revolution and Civil War in Siberia, 1917-1922. Includes a typescript translation (photocopy) by his daughter, Nathalie Nicolai.
Gift, Nathalie Nicolai, 1975. Incremental gift, 1977.

457. ANNENKOV, BORIS VLADIMIROVICH, 1890-1927.
Orders (in Russian), 1920. 1 folder.
Holograph.
Cossack ataman and White Russian military leader. Orders (in Russian) of the 1st Assault Mounted Battery of the partisan detachment of B. Annenkov relating to the Russian Civil War.

458. ANTONENKO, V. P.
History (in Russian), ca. 1922. "Kratkaia istoriia smieny pravitel´stv vo Vladivostokie s 31 ianvaria 1920 g. do evakuatsii oktiabria 1922 g." (Brief history of the changeover of government in Vladivostok from January 31, 1920 until the evacuation of October 1922). 1 vol.
Typescript (carbon copy).

459. BARRETT, WILLIAM S.
Diary, 1918-1920. "America in Russia, or the Diary of a Russian Wolfhound." 1 folder.
Typescript.
Captain, U.S. Army. Relates to the U.S. intervention in Siberia during the Russian Revolution.

460. BERK, STEPHEN M.
History, n.d. "The Coup d´Etat of Admiral Kolchak: The Counter-

revolution in Siberia and East Russia, 1917-1918." 1/2 ms. box.
Typescript.
American historian. Relates to activities of anti-Bolshevik forces in Siberia during the period from October 1917 to November 1918.
Deposit, S. M. Berk, 1972.

461. BOGDANOV, A., 1872-
Writings (in Russian), 1923-1930. 1/2 ms. box.
Holograph.
Relates to travels in Russia, Siberia, and Manchuria, gold-diggers in the Amur Republic of Zheltuga, and the Russian Revolution and Civil War in Siberia.

462. BOLDYREV, VASILII GEORGIEVICH, 1875-
Translation of excerpts from memoirs, n.d. Direktoriia, Kolchak interventy: vospominaniia (The Directory, Kolchak, intervention: Recollections). 1/2 ms. box.
Typescript.
General, Imperial Russian Army; White Russian military leader. Relates to the Russian Civil War in the Siberian Far East, activities of anti-Bolshevik forces, and Allied intervention in Siberia.

463. BREITIGAM, GERALD B.
Fictionalized history, 1923. "The Retreat of the Hundred Thousand: An Article-Novelette." 201 p. (1/2 ms. box).
Typescript.
American journalist. Relates to activities of the Czechoslovak legion during the Russian Civil War. Published in Adventure Magazine.
Additional copy, increment, 1981.

464. BUDBERG, ALEKSEI PAVLOVICH, BARON, 1869-1945.
Papers (in Russian), 1919-1920. 1 ms. box.
Lieutenant general, Imperial Russian Army. Memoirs and diaries relating to Russian military activities during World War I and to White Russian military activities in Siberia during the Russian Civil War.

465. BUGBEE, FRED WILLIAM, 1876-1932.
Correspondence, 1919-1921. 1 folder.
Photocopy.
Colonel, U.S. Army; commanding officer, 31st Infantry Regiment, and base and line of communications, American Expeditionary Forces in Vladivostok, 1919-1920. Excerpts from letters from F. W. Bugbee to his wife, 1919-1920, and a letter from General William S. Graves

to F. W. Bugbee, 1921, relating to American intervention and the Russian Civil War in Siberia.
Gift, Faith Bugbee Vogel, 1979.

466. CESKA DRUZINA.
Records (in English, Czech, and Russian), 1918-1920. 1 folder.
Czechoslovak legion in Russia. Orders, leaflets, and writings relating to the activities of the legion during the Russian Civil War. Includes a history of the legion, entitled "The Operations of the Czechoslovak Army in Russia in the Years 1917-1920."

467. DAVIES, E. ALFRED.
Diary, 1919. 1 folder.
U.S. Army officer. Relates to the evacuation of the American Expeditionary Forces in Siberia from Omsk to Irkutsk, September 4-October 4, 1919.
Gift, Bessie Eddy Lyon, 1974.

468. DOTSENKO, PAUL.
Writings, 1954-1979. 1/2 ms. box.
Member of Russian Socialist Revolutionary Party. Relates to Russian Revolution in Siberia. Includes a memoir, "The Struggle for a Democracy in Siberia: Reminiscences of a Contemporary;" a memorandum, "Kommuny" (The Communes), in Russian with English translation; and a speech, "The Fight for Freedom in Siberia: Its Successes and Failures."

469. EDISON, J.
Photographs, 1918-1921. 5 envelopes.
Depicts demonstrations, military personnel, railways, and scenery in northern China and southeastern Siberia.
Gift, J. Edison, 1957.

470. ELACHICH, S. A.
Memoirs (in Russian), 1934. "Obryvki vospominanii" (Scraps of reminiscences). 1 vol.
Typescript (carbon copy).
White Russian leader. Relates to the Russian Revolution, the Omsk government of Admiral Aleksandr Kolchak, and the Czechoslovak legion in Siberia.

471. EMERSON, GEORGE H.
Papers, 1918-1919. 1/2 ms. box, 1 envelope.
Colonel, U.S. Army; commanding officer, Russian Railway Service Corps. Correspondence, reports, maps, photographs, and clippings relating to the activities of the Russian Railway Service Corps, the political situation in Russia during the Russian Civil War, and the Czechoslovak legion in Siberia.

472. FAR EASTERN REPUBLIC COLLECTION, 1917-1921. 1 ms. box.
    Memoranda and copies of proclamations and correspondence relating to the creation of the Far Eastern Republic and to Japanese intervention in Siberia. Includes a mimeographed copy of the constitution of the republic and a memorandum from the Far Eastern Republic Special Trade Delegation to the United States government.

473. FAULSTICH, EDITH M., d. 1972, COLLECTOR.
    Collection, 1918-1975. 19 ms. boxes, 1 envelope.
    Diaries, letters, and reminiscences of members of the American Expeditionary Force in Siberia and reports, notes, printed matter, and photographs relating to American military activities in Siberia during the Russian Revolution.
    Preliminary inventory.
    Gift, Fred Faulstich, 1979.

474. FERGUSON, ALAN.
    Correspondence, 1938-1939, with William Sidney Graves. 1 folder.
    Holographs (photocopy).
    American soldier: member, 31st Infantry Regiment, in Siberia, 1918-1919. Relates to the history of the American Expeditionary Forces in Siberia.
    Gift, A. Ferguson, 1978.

475. GRAVES, WILLIAM SIDNEY, 1865-1940.
    Papers, 1914-1932. 3 ms. boxes.
    Major general, U.S. Army; commanding general, American Expeditionary Force in Siberia, 1918-1920. Correspondence, reports, monographs, and photographs relating to the Allied intervention in Siberia, 1918-1919.
    Preliminary inventory.
    Gift, Mrs. W. R. Orton, 1960.

476. GRAYSON, WALTER A.
    Papers, 1918-1920. 1/2 ms. box, 3 envelopes.
    First Lieutenant, U.S. Army; served with Amerian Expeditionary Force in Siberia, 1918-1920. Military intelligence studies, photographs, clippings, and memorabilia relating to activities of the U.S. 27th Infantry Regiment in Siberia, 1918-1920.
    Gift, W. A. Grayson, 1974. Incremental gift, 1977.

477. GUINS, GEORGE C., 1887-
    Papers (in Russian), 1918-1921. 1 ms. box, 1 envelope.
    Russian educator; White Russian political leader during the Russian Civil War. Correspondence, writings, reports, and declarations relating to the Russian Revolution and Civil War in the Siberian Far East, the activities of the anti-Bolshevik forces

in Siberia, and the Japanese intervention. Includes the article "Tri gody revoliutsii v Ukrainie" (Three years of revolution in the Ukraine), n.d., typescript, 15 p.

478. HAMMON, W. P., 1854-1938.
Papers, 1915-1930. 3 ms. boxes.
American businessman; associated with Yuba Manufacturing Company, San Francisco. Correspondence, reports, contracts, shipping lists, specifications for dredging equipment, annotated maps, and photographs relating to mining operations in China, Siberia, Korea, Malaya, and Poland.
Preliminary inventory.
Gift, W. P. Hammon, Jr., 1972. Subsequent increments.

479. HARRIS, ERNEST LLOYD, 1870-1946.
Papers, 1918-1921. 6 ms. boxes.
American consular official: consul general, Irkutsk, Siberia, 1918-1921. Reports, memoranda, and correspondence relating to the Russian Civil War in Siberia, the Czechoslovak legion, political and economic conditions in Siberia, and United States policy in Siberia.
Register.
Gift, Mrs. E. L. Harris, 1955.

480. HARRIS, GLADYS, COLLECTOR.
Photographs, 1919. 1 envelope.
Depicts the headquarters of the American Expeditionary Forces in Siberia and officers of the Japanese and Czechoslovak forces in Vladivostok.
Gift, G. Harris, 1978.

481. HOSKIN, HARRY L., 1887-
Papers, 1917-1973. 1/2 ms. box, 7 envelopes.
American officer, Russian Railway Service Corps, 1917-1920. Correspondence, clippings, reports, affidavits, court proceedings, and photographs relating to activities of the Russian Railway Service Corps in Siberia and to subsequent legal disputes regarding the military or civilian status of members of the corps.
Gift, H. L. Hoskin, 1976.

482. HOSKINS, EMMETT A.
Memoirs, 1970. "In the Service of the United States Navy, May 26, 1917-August 6, 1919." 1 folder.
Typescript.
Sailor, U.S. Navy. Relates to American naval operations in the Far East and Siberia.
Gift, E. A. Hoskins, 1974.

483. IAREMENKO, A. N.
   Translation of extracts from a memoir, n.d. "Diary of a Communist." 1 vol.
   Typescript.
   Russian Communist. Relates to the Russian Civil War in Siberia, 1918-1920. Translation of "Dnievnik kommunista," published in Revoliutsiia na Dal´nem vostoke (Revolution in the Far East) (Moscow, 1923).

484. IVANOV, VSEVOLOD NIKANOROVICH.
   Translation of extracts from study, n.d. "Manchuria and Manchukuo, 1932: Observations and Prognoses." 1 folder.
   Typescript.
   Relates to the Chinese Eastern Railway, 1898-1930. Translation by Elena Varneck of excerpts from "Manchuria i Manchugo, 1932: nabliudeniia i prognozy."

485. JANIN, PIERRE THIEBAUT CHARLES MAURICE, 1862-
   Extracts from a diary (in French), 1918-1920. 1 folder.
   Typewritten transcript.
   General, French army; commander of Czechoslovak and other Allied forces in Siberia, 1918-1920. Relates to Allied intervention in the Russian Civil War. Extracts published in Le Monde slave, 1924-1925.

486. JOHNSON, BENJAMIN O., 1878-
   Papers, 1917-1923. 1 ms. box.
   Photocopy.
   American engineer; colonel, Russian Railway Service Corps, 1917-1923; president pro tempore, Inter-Allied Technical Board, 1920-1921. Correspondence, reports, memoranda, diplomatic dispatches and instructions, and printed matter relating to the Russian Railway Service Corps in Siberia, the Inter-Allied Technical Board, and the Trans-Siberian Railroad during World War I and the Russian Civil War.
   Preliminary inventory.
   Gift, William B. Bishop, 1973.

487. JOHNSON, WILLIAM H.
   Papers, 1917-1919. 1 folder, 2 envelopes.
   American soldier assigned to the 31st Infantry Regiment during World War I. Diary, correspondence, and photographs relating to activities of the 31st Infantry Regiment in Siberia.
   Gift, Margaret C. Johnson, 1974.

488. KAPNIST, LIEUTENANT.
   Papers (in Russian, French and Czech), 1919-1920. 1 folder.
   White Russian army officer. Orders, telegrams, and correspondence relating to the liaison work of Lieutenant Kapnist with General

Pierre Janin, French army officer and commander of Czechoslovak and other Allied troops in Siberia during the Russian Civil War.

489. KHORVAT, DMITRII LEONIDOVICH, 1858-1937.
Memoirs, n.d. 1 vol.
Typescript (carbon copy).
Lieutenant general, Imperial Russian Army. Relates to Imperial Russian administration of the Chinese Eastern Railway and to White Russian military activities in the Far East during the Russian Civil War.

490. KHRABROFF, NICHOLAS, 1869-1940.
Memoir, 1926. "Providence or Chance? Reminiscences." 62 p.
Typescript (photocopy)
General, Imperial Russian Army. Relates to the Russian Civil War in Siberia, 1919-1920.
Gift, Thetford (Vermont) Historical Society, 1980.

491. KITITSYN, CAPTAIN.
Order (in Russian), 1920. 1 folder.
Typescript (mimeographed).
White Russian navy officer. Relates to White Russian naval activities at Vladivostok.

492. KOLCHAK, ALEKSANDR VASIL´EVICH, 1873-1920.
Correspondence, May 26 to June 4, 1919. 1 vol.
Typescript (mimeographed copy).
Correspondence between the heads of government of the Allied and Associated Powers and Admiral Aleksandr Kolchak, White Russian leader during the Russian Civil War. Relates to conditions for Allied support of the forces of Admiral Kolchak.

493. KOLOBOV, MIKHAIL VIKTOROVICH.
Memoirs (in Russian), n.d. "Bor´ba s bol´shevikami na Dal´nem vostokie (Khorvat, Kolchak, Semenov, Merkulovy, Diterikhs): vospominaniia uchastnika" (Struggle with the Bolsheviks in the Far East: Reminiscences of a participant). 1 vol.
Typescript (carbon copy).
General; chief of staff to the White Russian commander, General Dmitrii Khorvat. Relates to White Russian military activities in Siberia during the Russian Civil War.

494. KRIUKOV, BORIS ALEKSANDROVICH, 1898-
Papers (in Russian), 1917-1923. 4 ms. boxes, 9 envelopes.
White Russian army and marine corps officer. Memoranda, military and naval intelligence reports, civil, naval and military orders, correspondence, and photographs relating to the Russian Revolution and Civil War in the Siberian Far East, especially operations of the

Amur Flotilla (Red) and the Siberian Flotilla (White).
Register.
Gift, B. A. Kriukov, 1934.

495. KUHN, SYLVESTER E.
Papers, 1920-1976. 1 folder.
Private, U.S. Army; soldier in the 31st Infantry Regiment in Siberia, 1918-1920. Correspondence, reminiscences, and photocopies of documents relating to the American Expeditionary Forces in Siberia during the Russian Revolution and especially to the Posolskaia incident.
Gift, S. E. Kuhn, 1978.

496. LONGUEVAN, JOSEPH B., COLLECTOR.
J. B. Longuevan collection on Siberia, 1918-1920. 1 folder.
Reminiscences, letters, and printed matter relating to activities of the U.S. 31st Infantry in Siberia and to the Russian Revolution in Siberia.
Gift, George Masury and J. B. Longuevan, 1974.

497. MCDONNELL, GEOFFREY.
Papers, 1918-1919. 1 scrapbook.
Lieutenant Colonel, Canadian Army. Photographs, correspondence, and memorabilia relating to the activities of the Canadian and other Allied expeditionary forces in Siberia.
Gift, A. W. Hazelton.

498. MARITIME PROVINCE, SIBERIA. KOMISSIIA PO OBSLEDOVANIIU OBSTOIATEL´STV SOBYTII 4-6 APRELIA VO VLADIVOSTOKE.
Report (in Russian), ca. 1920. "Doklad Vremennomu pravitel´stvu, Primorskoi oblastnoi zemskoi uprave, Komissii po obsledovaniiu obstoiatel´stv sobytii 4-6 aprelia vo Vladivostoke." 1 vol.
Typescript (carbon copy).
Commission for the Investigation of the Circumstances of the Events of April 4-6 in Vladivostok. Relates to activities of Japanese troops in the Maritime Province of Siberia during the Russian Civil War.

499. MASARYK, TOMAS GARRIGUE, PRES., CZECHOSLOVAKIA, 1850-1937.
Proclamation (in Czech), 1919. 1 vol.
Photographic reproduction of typescript.
Issued by Tomás G. Masaryk, president of Czechoslovakia, to the Czechoslovak army in Siberia.

500. MORAVSKII, VALERIAN IVANOVICH, 1884-1940.
Papers (in Russian), 1917-1934. 20 ms. boxes.
White Russian political leader in Siberia during the Russian Civil War. Correspondence, reports, proclamations, and photographs

relating to White Russian political activities in the Far East, the first and second anti-Bolshevik Siberian governments, 1918-1922, and the Council of Plenipotentiary Representatives of Organizations of Autonomous Siberia.
Preliminary inventory.
Purchase, 1948.

501. MURRAY, A. C.
Report, 1920. 1 folder.
Typescript.
Member of the Inter-Allied Railway Commission in Russia. Relates to the operations of the Trans-Siberian Railroad between Omsk and Irkutsk during the Russian Revolution, 1919-1920.

502. NEWSPAPER ENTERPRISE ASSOCIATION.
Miscellaneous records, 1919-1921. 1/2 ms. box.
American news service with headquarters in Cleveland, Ohio. Correspondence, dispatches, memoranda, and clippings relating to the political, economic, and diplomatic situation in China and to Japanese activities in Siberia and China. Consists mainly of communications from Jack Mason, Far Eastern Bureau correspondent, to Alfred O. Anderson, president, Newspaper Enterprise Association.
Gift, Western Reserve Historical Society, 1983.

503. NILUS, EVGENII KHRISTIANOVICH, 1880-
History (in Russian), 1923. "Istoricheskii obzor Kitaiskoi vostochnoi zhelieznoi dorogi, 1896-1923 g.g." (Historical survey of the Chinese Eastern Railway, 1896-1923). 4 vols.
Printed and typescript.
Commissioned by the Board of Directors of the Chinese Eastern Railway, Harbin.

504. OSTROUKHOV, P., COLLECTOR.
Newspaper articles (in Russian), 1918-1920. 1 folder.
Typewritten transcript.
Relates to the Russian Civil War in Siberia. Articles published in Siberian newspapers.

505. OVCHINNIKOV, ANTON ZAKHAROVICH.
Memoirs (in Russian), 1932. 1 vol.
Holograph.
Red Army soldier. Relates to guerrilla warfare in the Russian Far East, 1918-1920.

506. PARES, Sir BERNARD, 1867-1949.
Miscellaneous papers, 1919. 1/2 ms. box.
British historian. Correspondence, notes, memoranda, and diary

relating to political conditions in western Siberia during the Russian Civil War.

507. PARTRIDGE, STANLEY N.
Papers, 1918-1945. 1 ms. box.
Colonel, U.S. Army; served with the American Expeditionary Force in Siberia. Photographs, postcards, and letters relating to conditions in Siberia, China, and Japan, 1918-1920, and United States military facilities in New Guinea and the Philippines, 1943-1945.
Gift, Mrs. S. N. Partridge, 1967.

508. PERTSOV, V. A.
Translation of diary extracts, 1919. 1 vol.
Typescript (carbon copy).
White Russian military aviation cadet, 1919. Relates to the evacuation of White Russian military personnel from Kurgan in western Siberia to Spassk, near Vladivostok, July-August 1919.

509. PERTZOFF, CONSTANTIN A., 1899-
Letter, 1932, to Harold H. Fisher. 1 vol.
Typescript (photocopy).
White Russian soldier in the Russian Civil War. Relates to the question of Allied responsibility for the downfall of Admiral Aleksandr Kolchak during the Russian Civil War.

510. PETROV, ARKADII NIKOLAEVICH.
Two certificates, 1918. 1 folder.
Typescript.
Issued by the White Russian Omsk government in Siberia. Relates to the appointment of Arkadii Petrov to official positions under the Omsk government. In Russian.

511. POGREBETSKII, ALEKSANDR I.
Translation, by Elena Varneck, entitled "Monetary Circulation and Currencies of the Russian Far East During the Revolution and Civil War," Harbin, 1924. 1 folder.
Typescript.
Excerpts from a book by A. I. Pogrebetskii entitled _Denezhnoe obrashchenie i denezhnye znaki Dalnego vostoka za period voiny i revoliutsii_.

512. PUCHKOV, F. A.
Translation of history, n.d. "The Icy March." 1 vol.
Typescript.
Relates to White Russian military activities in Siberia during the Russian Civil War. Original published under the title "Vos´maia Kamskaia strelkovaia diviziia v sibirskom ledianom pokhode" in

Vestnik Obshchestva russkikh veteranov velikoi voiny. Translated, with commentary, by Elena Varneck.

513. PURINGTON, CHESTER WELLS.
 Report, 1921. 1 folder.
 Typewritten transcript.
 American mining engineer. Relates to political and economic conditions in eastern Siberia and to Japanese intervention in that area during the period 1918-1921. Report submitted to the U.S. State Department and U.S. Army Military Intelligence Division.

514. REYNOLDS, ELLIOTT H.
 Letters to Helen B. Sutleff, 1918-1919. 1 folder.
 Holograph.
 Private, U.S. Army. Relates to activities of the American Expeditionary Force in Siberia.

515. RUSSIA (1917-1922. CIVIL WAR GOVERNMENTS). VREMENNOE SIBIRSKOE PRAVITEL´STVO.
 Miscellaneous records (in English and Russian), 1918-1919. 1 folder.
 Provisional Government of Autonomous Siberia. Proclamations, memoranda, and reports. Includes some issuances of the U.S. Army forces in Siberia relating to the Provisional Government and to the Civil War in Siberia.
 Gift, Dimitri Panteleev.

516. SAKHAROV, KONSTANTIN VIACHESLAVOVICH, 1881-
 Letter to Major General W. S. Graves, Berlin, 1933. 10 l.
 Typescript (carbon copy).

517. SALNAIS, VOLDEMARS, 1886-1948.
 Papers (mainly in Latvian), 1918-1945. 1 1/2 ms. boxes, 2 envelopes.
 Latvian diplomat; delegate to the League of Nations, 1921-1934; minister to Sweden, Norway, and Denmark, 1937-1940. Correspondence, reports, clippings, printed matter, and photographs relating to Latvian independence movements, foreign relations, women´s organizations, Latvians in Siberia, the Latvian National Council in Siberia (Vladivostok), and the Office of the Latvian Representative in the Far East and Siberia. Includes some materials collected by Milda Salnais.
 Register.
 Gift, Lilija Salnais, 1975.

518. SAVINTSEV, LIEUTENANT.
 Diary (in Russian), 1920-1921. 1 folder.
 Typescript.

White Russian army officer. Relates to the Russian Civil War in Siberia, August 1920-January 1921.

519. SEMENOV, GRIGORII MIKHAILOVICH, 1890-1945.
Memoirs (in Russian), ca. 1937. "Istoriia moei bor´by s bol´shevikami" (History of my struggle with the Bolsheviks). 1 folder.
Typescript (photocopy).
Cossack ataman; White Russian military leader in Siberia during the Russian Civil War. Includes photocopy of a biographical sketch (typewritten in Russian) of G. Semenov, ca. 1937.

520. SEREBRENNIKOV, IVAN INNOKENTIEVICH, 1882-
Papers (in Russian), 1906-1948. 25 ms. boxes, 29 albums, 11 envelopes.
Russian journalist; official, Siberian government, Omsk, 1917-1918. Diaries, correspondence, writings, photographs, clippings, and notebooks relating to the Russian Civil War in Siberia, Russian émigrés in the Far East, and Chinese history and culture.
Register.
Consult archivist for access.
Purchase, I. I. Serebrennikov, 1951.

521. SHAPIRO-LAVROVA, NADEZHDA L.
Memoir (in Russian) n.d. 1 folder.
Typescript.
Resident of Blagoveshchensk, Siberia. Relates to the Russian Civil War in the Blagoveshchensk area and to the trial of A. N. Alekseevskii, a Socialist Revolutionary, by the Bolsheviks in Blagoveshchensk in 1918. Includes a translation (typewritten) of the memoir by Elena Varneck.

522. SHCHEPIKHIN, SERGEI AFANASEVICH.
Papers (in Russian), 1919-1920. 1 ms. box.
General and chief of staff, White Russian army, 1919-1920. Diaries and writings relating to the retreat of the Russian volunteer armies toward Siberia, the government of Grigorii Semenov, Japanese intervention in the Siberian Far East, and the military activities of the Ural Cossacks against the Bolsheviks.
Purchase, S. A. Shchepikhin, 1933.

523. SMITH, JACK A.
Study, 1950. "White Russian Emigrants and the Japanese Army in the Far East." 1 folder.
Typescript.
Relates to White Russian military activities and Japanese intervention in Siberia during the Russian Civil War.
Gift, Fritz Epstein, 1970.

524. SPRIGG, RODNEY SEARLE, 1894-
   Papers, 1918-1980. 1/2 ms. box, 7 envelopes.
   Captain, U.S. Army; commanding officer, Replacement Battalion, Vladivostok, Siberia, 1918-1919. Memoirs, correspondence, writings, bulletins, clippings, and photographs relating to American military activities in Siberia during the Russian Revolution.
   Gift, R. S. Sprigg, 1980.

525. STEINFELDT, ERIC, COLLECTOR.
   Photographs, 1918. 1 envelope.
   Depicts scenes at Vladivostok, the Allied intervention, and the Czechoslovak legion.
   Gift, E. Steinfeldt.

526. STEPANOV, ALEKSANDR STEPANOVICH.
   Outline of projected memoirs (in Russian), 1932. 1 folder.
   Typescript.
   White Russian army officer. Relates to secret military organizations in Siberia, 1918-1920.

527. STEVENS, JOHN FRANK, 1853-1943.
   Papers, 1917-1931. 1/2 ms. box.
   American civil engineer; chairman, U.S. Advisory Commission of Railway Experts to Russia, 1917; president, Technical Board, Inter-Allied Railway Commission for the Supervision of the Siberian and Chinese Eastern Railways, 1919-1922. Memoirs and correspondence relating to railroads in Siberia and Manchuria during the Russian Revolution and to Allied intervention in the Russian Revolution.

528. STROBRIDGE, WILLIAM S.
   History, n.d. "Golden Gate to Golden Horn: Camp Fremont, California, and the American Expedition to Siberia of 1918." 70 p.
   Mimeographed.
   Colonel, U. S. Army. Relates to the training of the 8th Division of the U.S. Army at Camp Fremont, California prior to its departure for Siberia during the Russian Revolution.
   Gift, John K. Caldwell, 1981.

529. SYCHEV, E.
   Report (in Russian), n.d. "Vozstanie v Irkutske" (Uprising in Irkutsk). 1 folder.
   Typescript.
   General, White Russian army. Relates to the uprising in Irkutsk and the liquidation of the rule of Admiral Aleksandr Kolchak in the region of Irkutsk in the period from December 23, 1919 to January 5, 1920.

530. U.S. ARMY. A.E.F., 1917-1920.
   Miscellaneous records, 1917-1920. 4 ms. boxes.
   Intelligence reports, news summaries, bulletins, orders, instructions, memoranda, proclamations, and miscellany relating to military operations of the American Expeditionary Forces in France and Siberia during World War I and the Russian Revolution.
   Preliminary inventory.

531. USTRIALOV, NIKOLAI VASIL´EVICH, 1890-
   Papers (in Russian), 1920-1934. 1 ms. box.
   Russian historian. Correspondence and writings relating to the Russian Revolution, the White governments in Omsk, 1918-1919, and Eurasianism.

532. VARNECK, ELENA.
   Papers, n.d. 5 cu. ft. boxes.
   Russian-American historian. Research notes, drafts of writings, and translations relating to a proposed publication entitled "Revolution and Civil War in Siberia and the Far East" pertaining to events of the Russian Revolution and Civil War in Siberia.

533. VARSKA, A. S.
   Series of articles (in Russian), 1938. "Krovavye dni na Amure" (Bloody days on the Amur). 1 folder.
   Printed.
   Relates to the Russian Civil War in Blagoveshchensk, 1918. Published in Russkoe obozrenie (Chicago), March 1938. Written by A. S. Varska under the pseudonym A. Ravich.

534. VOLOGODSKII, PETR VASIL´EVICH.
   Papers (in Russian and English). 1918-1925. 1/2 ms. box.
   Prime minister, White Russian Omsk government, 1918-1919.
   Diaries, resolutions, reports, and translations of diary excerpts relating to the Omsk government, the Russian Civil War in Siberia, and economic conditions in Siberia.

535. VOROTOVOV, COLONEL.
   Memoirs (in Russian), n.d. 1 folder.
   Holograph.
   White Russian army officer. Memoirs entitled "2-i Orenburgskii kazachii polk v 1918-1920 g.g." (The 2nd Orenburg Cossack Regiment in 1918-1920) and "V Zabaikal´ie i na Primorskom frontie v 1920-21 g.g." (In the Zabaikal and on the maritime front in 1920-21) relating to the Russian Civil War.

536. WASHINGTON, HAROLD GEORGE, 1892-1961?, COLLECTOR.
   Miscellany, 1918-1920. 1 ms. box.
   Depicts social conditions, railroads, and Allied troops in

Siberia and Manchuria during the Russian Revolution. Includes some postcards of buildings and war damage in France.
Gift, estate of H. G. Washington, 1961.

537. WHITEHEAD, JAMES H., COLLECTOR.
J. H. Whitehead collection on Siberia, 1918-1920. 2 albums, 1 envelope.
Depicts activities of members of the American Expeditionary Force in Siberia and the Russian Railway Service Corps; General William S. Graves; Czech, Slovak, and Russian military forces; and the living quarters of Tsar Nicholas II at Ekaterinburg.
Gift, J. H. Whitehead, 1974.

538. YELSKY, ISADORE, 1896-1958.
Photographs, ca. 1918-1920. 3 envelopes.
Soldier, U.S. Army; member, American Expeditionary Force in Siberia. Depicts American and other foreign troops in Siberia during the Russian Revolution, scenes of the Russian Civil War in Siberia, and American troops and scenes of everyday life in the Philippines.
Gift, Shirley Shulman, 1982.

539. ZAVARIN, KONSTANTIN NIKOLAEVICH.
History (in Russian), n.d. "Rechnaia boevaia flotiliia na reke Kame v 1919 godu" (The fighting river flotilla on the Kama in 1919). 1/2 ms. box.
Typescript.
Relates to the river warfare campaigns and tactics of the White Russian forces on the Kama River in Siberia during the Russian Civil War, 1918-1919. Written by K. N. Zavarin and Mikhail Smirnov.
Purchase, Natalie N. Zavarin, 1977.

MONGOLIA

540. GENKIN, E.
   Translation of report, 1924. "A Few Words about Mongolia."
   1 folder.
   Typescript.
   Relates to the development of the communist movement in Mongolia. Original report published in Tretii s"ezd Mongolskoi narodnoi partii (Third Congress of the Mongolian People's Party), 1924.

541. GOLUBEV.
   History (in Russian), 1926. 1 vol.
   Typescript.
   Relates to White Russian military activities in Mongolia during the Russian Civil War and particularly to Baron Roman Ungern-Shternberg.

542. HITOON, SERGE E.
   Memoir, 1936. "From Aral Sea to the Western Turkestan." 1 vol.
   Typescript.
   White Russian army officer. Relates to the Russian Civil War in Mongolia.

543. KNIAZEV, N. N.
   Translation, n.d. "The Legendary Baron (From Reminiscences About Lieutenant-General Baron Ungern)." 1 vol., 1 negative microfilm reel.
   Typescript.
   Relates to Baron Roman Ungern-Shternberg, White Russian military leader in Mongolia during the Russian Revolution. Translation of "Legendarnyi baron," published in Luch Azii, 1937.

544. LAVRENT'EV, K. I.
   Memoir (in Russian), 1925. "Urginskiia sobytiia 1921 goda" (Events in Urga in 1921). 1 folder.
   Typescript.
   White Russian. Relates to White Russian activities in Mongolia during the Russian Revolution.

545. LAVROV, SERGEI.
   Memoir (in Russian), 1942. "Sobytiia v Mongolii-Khalkhie, 1920-1921 godakh--voenno-istoricheskii ocherk--vospominaniia" (Events in Mongolia-Khalkha, 1920-1921--A military-historical essay--Reminiscences). 1 folder.
   Holograph.
   Major, Imperial Russian Army. Relates to Baron Roman Ungern-

Shternberg and White Russian military activities in Mongolia, 1920-1921.
   Deposit, S. Lavrov, 1948.

546. OTORCHI, ULAN.
   Memoir (in Russian) 1928. "Ozero Tolbo: vospominaniia o nachalnom period mongol'skoi revoliutsii" (Lake Tolbo: Recollections from the initial period of the Mongolian revolution).
   1 folder.
   Typescript.
   Mongolian Communist. Relates to the communist movement in Mongolia during the Russian Revolution.

547. PERSHIN, DIMITRII PETROVICH.
   Papers (in Russian), 1916-1936. 2 1/2 ms. boxes.
   White Russian diplomat. Correspondence, diaries, writings, notes, and clippings relating to White Russian and Soviet activities in Mongolia during the Russian Revolution and the Russian émigré population during the Russian Civil War and subsequent years. Includes a memoir (handwritten) entitled "Baron Ungern, Urga i Altan-Bulak: zapiski ochevidtsa o smutnom vremeni vo vneshnei (khakhaskoi) Mongolii v pervoi treti XX-go veka" (Baron Ungern, Urga and Altan-Bulak: An eyewitness account of the troubled times in Outer (Khalkha) Mongolia during the first third of the twentieth century) relating to counterrevolutionary events in Mongolia during the Russian Revolution and a translation (typewritten) by Elena Varneck of the memoir.

548. RIABUKHIN, N. M.
   Translation of memoir, n.d. "The Story of Baron Ungern-Sternberg." 1 vol.
   Russian staff physician to Baron Roman Ungern-Shternberg. Relates to activities of White Russian military forces under Baron Ungern-Shternberg in Mongolia during the Russian Civil War.

549. SOKOLNITSKII, V.
   Translation of memoir, n.d. "Kaigorodovshchina" (Kaigorodoviana).
   1 folder.
   Typescript.
   Colonel, White Russian army. Relates to the activities of Aleksandr Petrovich Kaigorodov, Cossack ataman and White Russian military leader in Mongolia during the Russian Civil War, 1919-1921.

550. UNGERN-SHTERNBERG (ROMAN FEDOROVICH, BARON) COLLECTION, 1921.
   1 folder.
   Copy (typewritten) of a pamphlet entitled "Letters Captured from Baron Ungern in Mongolia" reprinting correspondence of Baron Roman Fedorovich Ungern-Shternberg (1887-1921), White Russian military

leader, and translation (typewritten) by Elena Varneck of a military order issued by Baron Ungern-Shternberg relating to White Russian activities in Mongolia during the Russian Revolution.

551. VOLKOV, BORIS.
    Writings (in Russian), 1921-1931. 1/2 ms. box.
    Typescript.
    White Russian army officer. Relates to the Russian Civil War in Siberia and Mongolia, the career of the White Russian commander Baron Ungern-Shternberg, the capture of Troitskosavsk, and the massacre of officers on the Khor River. Includes a translation (typewritten) by Elena Varneck of one manuscript.
    Gift, B. Volkov, 1936.

RELIEF AGENCIES

552. AXENTIEFF, N.
    Memorandum, n.d. 1 folder.
    Typescript.
    Relates to relief needs of Russian refugees living in exile. Sent to Herbert Hoover during or immediately after the Russian Civil War.

553. BABB, NANCY, 1884-1948.
    Papers, 1917-1925. 1 ms. box.
    American Relief Administration and American Friends Service Committee relief worker in Russia, 1917-1925. Correspondence, reports, and memoranda relating to American Relief Administration and American Friends Service Committee work in Russia.
    Gift, Elizabeth Baker.

554. BANE, SUDA LORENA, 1886-1952.
    Documentary history, 1943. Organization of American Relief in Europe, 1918-1919. 1/2 ms. box.
    Galley proofs (annotated).
    Relates to World War I relief activities of the American Relief Administration and U.S. Food Administration. Edited by S. L. Bane and Ralph Haswell Lutz. Published by Stanford University Press, 1943.

555. BARBER, ALVIN B.
    Papers, 1919-1922. 5 ms. boxes.
    American Relief Administration worker; European Technical Advisor for Poland, 1919-1922. Correspondence, reports, and memoranda relating to Polish railways; coal, oil, and timber resources; Danzig, Upper Silesia, and the Ukraine.
    Gift, A. B. Barber, 1959.

556. BARRINGER, THOMAS C.
    Papers, 1922-1925. 2 ms. boxes.
    District supervisor, American Relief Administration in Russia, 1921-1923. Correspondence, reports, memoranda, photographs, and clippings relating to relief operations of the American Relief Administration in two famine areas in Russia.
    Gift, T. C. Barringer, 1956.

557. BEKEART, LAURA HELENE.
    Study, n.d. "The A.R.A.: Herbert Hoover and Russian Relief."
    1 folder.
    Typescript.
    Gift, L. H. Bekeart, 1965.

558. BLAND, RAYMOND L.
   Papers, 1919-1941. 3 ms. boxes, 3 envelopes, 3 medals.
   Statistician, American Relief Administration, 1919-1924; member, President's Committee on War Relief Agencies, 1941. Correspondence, reports, memoranda, financial records, and printed matter relating to the work of the American Relief Administration in Europe and Russia, 1919-1924, and the President's Committee on War Relief Agencies, 1941.
   Register.
   Gift, R. L. Bland, 1968. Incremental gift, Mrs. R. L. Bland, 1973.

559. BRAMHALL, BURLE, COLLECTOR.
   B. Bramhall collection on the Petrograd Children's Colony (in Russian), 1973-1976. 1/2 ms. box.
   American Red Cross business manager in Siberia, 1919-1920. Reminiscences of several of the 781 Russian children known as the "Petrograd Children's Colony," who were sent by their parents from Moscow and Petrograd in 1918 because of wartime shortages, were stranded in the Ural Mountains, evacuated from the war zones via Vladivostok by the American Red Cross, and restored to their families in 1920 following a global ocean voyage. Includes a description of the reunion of American Red Cross staff members and members of the Petrograd Children's Colony in Leningrad, 1973.
   Gift, B. Bramhall, 1977.

560. BUNGEY, GRACE BELLE REAMES.
   Papers, 1918-1981. 1 scrapbook.
   American Red Cross worker in Siberia, 1919-1920. Photographs, memorabilia, and miscellany relating to Red Cross relief work in Siberia during the Russian Revolution and subsequent travels and personal matters.
   Gift, G. B. Bungey, 1981.

561. CAMPBELL, HANNAH BRAIN, 1880-
   Memoirs, 1945. 1 folder.
   Typescript.
   American Red Cross worker in Siberia, 1917-1920. Memoir entitled "Adventure in Siberia," as told to Sarah E. Mathews, relating to activities of the American Red Cross in the eastern part of Russia, 1917-1920; and memoir entitled "Children's Ark" relating to the return of Russian children by the American Red Cross to their parents in Russia in 1920.
   Gift, S. E. Mathews, 1973.

562. CARROLL, PHILIP H., 1885-1941.
   Papers, 1917-1939. 1 ms. box.

Captain, U.S. Army, 1917-1920; American Relief Administration (A.R.A.) worker in Germany and Russia, 1920-1922. Memoranda, outlines of procedures, organization and personnel charts, preliminary programs, routine charts, and specimen forms relating to activities of the U.S. 348th Field Artillery in France and Germany, 1917-1920, of the A.R.A. in Hamburg, Germany, 1920-1921, and of the A.R.A. Russian Unit Supply Division in Moscow, 1921-1922. Includes correspondence with Herbert Hoover, 1934-1939, relating to U.S. politics.
Gift, P. H. Carroll, 1941.

563. CHILDS, JAMES RIVES, 1893-
Memoirs, n.d. 1/2 ms. box.
Typescript.
American diplomat; American Relief Administration worker in Russia, 1921-1923; chargé d'affairs in Morocco, 1941-1945; ambassador to Saudi Arabia, 1946-1950; ambassador to Ethiopia, 1951-1953. Relates to relief work and social conditions in Russia, U.S. foreign relations with Balkan and Near Eastern countries, diplomacy regarding Morocco in World War II, and the role of Iran in world politics, especially in relation to Russia.

564. CLARK, MARMADUKE R., d. 1964.
Papers, 1918-1920. 1 ms. box, 9 envelopes.
Senior secretary, Young Men's Christian Association; with the American Expeditionary Force in Siberia. Correspondence, memoranda, writings, newspaper clippings, memorabilia, and photographs relating to Y.M.C.A. activities in Siberia, political developments during the last stages of the Russian Civil War, and the Allied intervention.
Gift, Robert L. Clark, 1976.

565. COLTON, ETHAN THEODORE, 1872-
Papers, 1918-1952. 7 ms. boxes.
American relief worker with the European Student Relief and the Young Men's Christian Association in Russia. Correspondence, reports, manuscripts of writings, and clippings relating to European Student Relief activities in Russia and other European countries, 1920-1925; and to social conditions, the educational system, and the status of religion in Russia in the 1920s and 1930s. Includes the memoirs of E. T. Colton and 13 antireligious Soviet posters.
Gift, E. T. Colton.

566. DAVIS, BENJAMIN B.
Papers, 1919-1920. 1/2 ms. box, 2 envelopes.
American Red Cross worker in Siberia, 1919-1920. Correspondence, writings, diary, reports, pamphlets, postcards, and photographs relating to American Red Cross activities in Siberia, primarily in Vladivostok.

567. DAVIS, ROBERT E.
   Reports, 1917-1919. 1 folder.
   Typescript.
   Major, U.S. Army; American Red Cross worker in Kuban area, Russia. Relates to the work of the American Red Cross and the political and military situation in south Russia, 1917-1919. Addressed to Colonel Robert E. Olds, American Red Cross commissioner in Europe.
   Gift, Earl Talbot, 1973.

568. DUNCAN, WILLIAM YOUNG.
   Papers, 1918-1920. 1/2 ms. box.
   Photocopy.
   American clergyman; Young Men's Christian Association chaplain with the Czechoslovak legion in Siberia, 1917-1920. Diary and letters relating to the Russian Revolution and Civil War and the Allied intervention in Siberia, 1918-1920.
   Quotations may not be published without permission of Donald G. Duncan, during his lifetime. Any publication using the collection as a source must carry acknowledgment. A copy of any such publication must be provided to D. G. Duncan free of charge.
   Gift, D. G. Duncan, 1976.

569. EGBERT, EDWARD H., d. 1939.
   Papers, 1914-1921. 1 ms. box.
   Chief surgeon, American Red Cross detachment in Russia, during World War I; executive secretary, Catherine Breshkovsky Russian Relief Fund. Correspondence, notes, clippings, printed matter, and photographs relating to the Russian Revolution, relief work in Russia, and Ekaterina Breshko-Breshkovskaia. Includes correspondence with E. Breshko-Breshkovskaia and Herbert Hoover.
   Preliminary inventory.
   Gift, Margaret Durand, 1960.

570. FISHER, HAROLD HENRY, 1890-1975.
   Papers, 1917-1974. 32 ms. boxes, 4 card file boxes (2/3 l. ft.), 5 envelopes, 1 album.
   American historian; Director, Hoover Institution on War, Revolution and Peace, 1943-1952. Clippings, printed matter, notes, correspondence, pamphlets, articles, microfilm, and photographs relating to the Soviet Union, the San Francisco conference organizing the United Nations, the Civil War in Spain, Herbert Hoover and the American Relief Administration, and the history of Finland.
   Register.
   Gift, H. H. Fisher.

571. FLEMING, HAROLD M., 1900-
   Papers, 1922-1923. 1 ms. box.

American Relief Administration worker in Russia. Correspondence, writings, maps, and clippings relating to the American Relief Administration in Russia, economic conditions, and political and social developments in Russia after the Revolution.
Gift, H. M. Fleming, 1956.

572. FULLER, ADALINE W., 1888-
Papers, 1919-1920. 1 folder.
American Relief Administration worker in Poland, 1919-1920. Correspondence and memoranda relating to work of the American Relief Administration in France, Belgium, Poland, and Russia. Includes letters from Clemens Pirquet and George B. Baker.
Gift, A. W. Fuller, 1972.

573. GASKILL, C. A.
Diary, June 1-16, 1920. 1 folder.
Typescript.
Colonel, member of the American Relief Administration and technical adviser to Poland, 1919-1921. Relates to conditions in the Ukraine during the Russian Civil War.
Gift, C. A. Gaskill, 1943.

574. GIBSON, HUGH SIMMONS, 1883-1954.
Papers, 1903-1954. 81 ms. boxes, 11 cu. ft. boxes, 12 l. ft.
American diplomat; ambassador to Poland, 1919-1924; ambassador to Switzerland, 1924-1927; ambassador to Belgium, 1927-1933 and 1937-1938; ambassador to Brazil, 1933-1937. Diaries, writings, correspondence, reports, minutes of meetings, and printed matter relating to U.S. foreign relations, international disarmament negotiations, the League of Nations, and relief work in Europe during World Wars I and II.
Preliminary inventory.
Gift, Michael Gibson, 1956.

575. GOLDER, FRANK ALFRED, 1877-1929.
Papers (in English and Russian), 1812-1930. 40 ms. boxes, 1 envelope.
American historian; American Relief Administration worker in Russia. Correspondence, diaries, memoranda, articles, pamphlets, and photographs relating to Russian history in the late nineteenth and early twentieth centuries, the Russian American Company in Alaska, the Russian Revolution, and American Relief Administration work in Russia. Includes articles, ca. 1 ms. box, by F. A. Golder dealing with the Ukraine, 1918, with emphasis on his A.R.A. work.
Preliminary inventory.
Gift, Thomas and Henrietta Eliot and H. M. Hart.

576. GOODYEAR, A. CONGER.
Papers, 1919. 3 ms. boxes.

President of the U.S. American Relief Administration Coal Commission. Correspondence, memoranda, reports, maps, photographs, clippings, and printed matter relating to coal production and distribution in Silesia, Bohemia, Galicia, and Serbia; political and economic conditions in Poland; and the partition of Silesia.
Gift, A. Conger Goodyear, 1956. Increment, 1957.

577. GRANT, DONALD, 1889-
Writings, 1920-1935. 1 folder.
British author and lecturer; director, European Student Relief, 1920-1925. Notes, diary entries, letter extracts, and a pamphlet relating to social conditions and relief work in Russia and Eastern and Central Europe, 1920-1922, and to the economic and social policy of the socialist municipal government in Vienna, 1919-1934.
Gift, Joseph Jones, 1977. Gift, D. Grant, 1978.

578. GREEN, JOSEPH COY, 1887-
Papers, 1914-1957. 21 ms. boxes, 2 envelopes.
American diplomat; chief of inspection, Commission for Relief in Belgium, 1915-1917; director for Romania and the Near East, American Relief Administration, 1918-1919. Diary, correspondence, writings, reports, pamphlets, clippings, maps, and printed matter relating to the Commission for Relief in Belgium, American Relief Administration activities in Romania and Transcaucasia, and the Herbert Hoover-for-President campaign in 1920.
Register.
Gift, J. C. Green, 1956. Subsequent increments.

579. HALL, CHARLES L.
Papers, 1922-1923. 1 folder, 1 envelope.
Major, U.S. Army; American Relief Administration worker in Russia. Photographs and memorabilia relating to famine conditions and American Relief Administration work in Orenburg and Samara, Russia.
Gift, C. L. Hall, 1964.

580. HAMILTON, MINARD, 1891-1976.
Papers, 1913-1930. 1 ms. box.
Captain, U.S. Army; executive officer, American Relief Administration operations in the Baltic States, 1919. Diary and correspondence relating to activities of the 313th Machine Gun Battalion in France during World War I, food distribution by the American Relief Administration in the Baltic States, and civil aviation in China, 1929-1930.
Gift, Albert H. Hamilton, 1977.

581. HENDERSON, LOY WESLEY, 1892-
Memoirs, n.d. 3 ms. boxes.
Typescript (photocopy).
American diplomat; secretary of embassy to the Soviet Union, 1934-

1938; assistant chief, Division of European Affairs, U.S. Department of State, 1938-1942; director, Near Eastern and African Affairs, U.S. Department of State, 1945-1948; and ambassador to India, 1948-1951. Relates to American Red Cross relief work in Russia and the Baltic States, 1919-1920, and in Germany, 1920-1921, and to U.S. foreign policy and U.S. relations with Ireland and the Soviet Union between the two world wars.
   Closed during the lifetime of L. W. Henderson.
   Gift, L. W. Henderson, 1977.

582. HILTON, RONALD, 1911-
   Miscellaneous papers, 1922-1980. 1 folder.
   American educator; editor, World Affairs Report, 1970-   .
Correspondence and miscellaneous research material used for the article by R. Hilton, "Bread: A Pretext for Soviet Defamation of Presidents Hoover and Carter," World Affairs Report (March 1980), relating to Soviet historiography on Herbert Hoover and American food relief to Russia.
   Gift, R. Hilton, 1980.

583. HOLDEN, FRANK HARVEY.
   Miscellaneous papers, 1919-1923. 1 folder, 1 envelope.
   American Relief Administration worker in France and Russia, 1919-1923. Letter written by F. H. Holden in Moscow in 1923, relating to Russian operations of the American Relief Administration and photographs of the German cruiser Wolf, its crew, and ships encountered and sunk by it during its raiding cruise in World War I, 1916-1917.
   Gift, F. H. Holden, 1956. Incremental gift, Miriam Miller, 1977.

584. HOOVER, HERBERT CLARK, 1874-1964.
   Papers, 1897-1969. 306 ms. boxes, 90 envelopes, 1 album, 1 microfilm reel, 18 motion pictures, 31 phonotapes, 10 phonorecords.
   President of the United States, 1929-1933. Appointment calendars, correspondence, office files, speeches and writings, analyses of newspaper editorials, printed matter, photographs, motion pictures, sound recordings, and other material relating to the administration of relief during and after the two world wars (see subject file under American Relief Administration for material on Russia), Hoover's relationship with Woodrow Wilson, U.S. politics and government, and the philosophy and public service contributions of Herbert Hoover. Includes photocopies of selected files from his Presidential and Commerce Department papers, which are located at the Herbert Hoover Presidential Library, West Branch, Iowa.
   Register published by Hoover Institution Press.
   Gift, Herbert Hoover, 1962. Subsequent increments.

585. HOOVER INSTITUTION ON WAR, REVOLUTION AND PEACE. SUPREME ECONOMIC COUNCIL AND AMERICAN RELIEF ADMINISTRATION DOCUMENTS PROJECT.

Records, 1930-1937. 21 ms. boxes, 45 vols.
Project for compilation of selected Supreme Economic Council and American Relief Administration documents. Typed copies of minutes of meetings, reports, correspondence, press releases, and clippings relating to economic policies of the Supreme Economic Council and its predecessor, the Supreme Council of Supply and Relief, and to relief activities of the American Relief Administration in Europe and Russia.
Preliminary inventory.

586. JACOBS, JOHN F. de.
Memoir, 1925. "The American Relief Administration and My Crime." 1 vol.
Typescript.
Interpreter for the American Relief Administration in Russia. Relates to the arrest of J. F. de Jacobs by Soviet authorities.

587. JENNY, ARNOLD E., 1895-1978.
Papers, 1917-1953. 4 1/2 ms. boxes, 2 envelopes.
Young Men's Christian Association worker in Siberia, 1919-1920, and in Germany, 1945-1946. Correspondence, diary, reports, memoranda, and printed matter relating to relief work in Siberia during the Russian Revolution and among displaced persons in Germany at the end of World War II.
Register.
Gift, A. E. Jenny, 1973.

588. KOLUPAEV, EUGENIA RITTER.
Memoir notes, 1919. 1 folder.
Holograph.
American Red Cross translator, Kiev, Ukraine. Relates to events in Kiev during the Russian Civil War, 1917-1919.
Gift, Stephen G. Kolupaev, 1979.

589. LAPTEFF, ALEXIS V.
Papers, 1921-1971. 1 folder, 1 envelope.
American Relief Administration worker in the Ufa-Urals District of Russia, 1921-1923. Memoirs, reports, and photographs relating to relief work in the Ufa-Urals District.
Preliminary inventory.
Gift, A. V. Lapteff, 1971.

590. LAWRENCE, EVA.
Papers, 1919-1920. 1/2 ms. box, 1 album.
American Red Cross worker in Siberia, 1919-1920. Diary and photographs relating to Red Cross work in Siberia during the Russian Revolution.
Gift, William H. Hastings, 1982.

591. LEWIS, ROGER L., d. 1936.
   Papers, 1917-1919. 1/2 ms. box, 1 envelope.
   American journalist and Red Cross worker in Russia. Reports, notes, correspondence, printed matter, clippings, photographs, and memorabilia relating to operations of the American Red Cross in Archangel, Russia.
   Gift, Helen Wells, 1964.

592. LYKES, GIBBES.
   Papers, 1919-1923. 2 ms. boxes.
   Captain, U.S. Army; supervisor, Ukrainian District, Russian unit, American Relief Administration. Reports, dispatches, correspondence, and photographs relating to relief work in the Ukraine and to political conditions in Hungary during the Hungarian revolution.
   Gift, William F. G. Lykes, 1957.

593. LYON, BESSIE EDDY.
   Papers, 1918-1920. 1 folder.
   Stenographer, American Red Cross Commission in Siberia, 1918-1920. Letters and reports relating to activities of the American Red Cross Commission in Siberia and the political and military conditions in Siberia during the Russian Civil War.
   Gift, B. E. Lyon, 1974.

594. MCCORMICK, CHAUNCEY, 1884-1954.
   Papers, 1917-1954. 1 ms. box, 1 roll of posters, 3 phonorecords.
   Member, U.S. Food Aministration Mission to Poland, 1919. Reports, correspondence, orders, printed matter, phonograph records, photographs, and posters relating to relief work in Poland and political and economic conditions in Poland at the end of World War I.
   Gift, Mrs. C. McCormick, 1957.

595. MCLEAN, KATHERINE S.
   Papers, 1918-1920. 1 folder, 1 envelope.
   Young Women's Christian Association worker at Camp Fremont and Camp Kearny, California, 1918-1919. Memoranda, clippings, photographs, and miscellanea relating to Y.W.C.A. work among American soldiers stationed at Camps Fremont and Kearny and soldiers of the Czechoslovak legion evacuated to these camps from Siberia.

596. MATHEWS, SARAH E., 1880-
   Papers, 1918-1920. 1 folder, 1 album, 1 envelope.
   American Red Cross worker in Siberia, 1918-1920.
   Memoirs, diary, reports, clippings, and photographs relating to the disposition of the remains of Tsar Nicholas II and his family,

social and political conditions in Siberia, and relief work of the American Red Cross in Siberia during the Russian Civil War.
Gift, S. E. Mathews, 1971. Incremental gift, 1975.

597. MITCHELL, ANNA V. S.
Papers, 1920-1944. 6 ms. boxes, 9 envelopes, 4 medals.
American relief worker. Correspondence, memoranda, reports, clippings, memorabilia, and photographs relating to World War I relief work in France, 1915-1920, and relief work with Russian refugees in Istanbul, 1921-1936.
Register.
Gift, John Davis Hatch, 1967. Incremental gift, 1975.

598. MORAN, HUGH ANDERSON, 1881-
Papers, 1916-1933. 2 ms. boxes.
American clergyman; Young Men's Christian Association worker in Siberia and China, 1909-1918. Correspondence, writings, clippings, maps, posters, and photographs relating to the Russian Civil War, political and economic conditions in Siberia and Manchuria, and relief work in Siberia and Manchuria, especially in the prisoner of war camps, during the Russian Civil War.
Preliminary inventory.

599. MURPHY, MERLE FARMER.
Memoir, n.d. "Record of a Russian Year, 1921-1922: Daily Life in Soviet Russia." 1 folder.
Typescript.
American Relief Administration worker in Russia, 1921-1922.
Relates to social and economic conditions in Russia.

600. O'BRIEN, CHARLES A.
Papers, 1918-1923. 1/2 ms. box, 1 scrapbook.
American Red Cross worker in Siberia, 1919-1920. Diary, notes, photographs, postcards, clippings and memorabilia relating to American Red Cross activities in Siberia and the Russian Civil War and Allied intervention in Siberia.
Gift, John McGinty, 1978.

601. ORBISON, THOMAS JAMES, 1866-1938.
Papers, 1919-1922. 2 ms. boxes.
Chief, Latvian Mission, American Relief Administration European Children's Fund, 1919-1920. Diaries, writings, photographs, and memorabilia relating to relief work in Latvia at the end of World War I.
Preliminary inventory.

602. PICKETT, CARRIE.
Papers, 1919-1921. 1/2 ms. box, 1 envelope.

American Red Cross nurse in Siberia and Poland, 1919-1921. Letters, reports, citations, photographs, and memorabilia relating to the activities of the American Red Cross in Siberia and Poland. Includes an account of various operations of the Czechoslovak legion in Siberia.
   Gift, Grace Bungey, 1973.

603. PIRNIE, MALCOLM.
   Papers, 1917-1918. 1/2 ms. box, 1 envelope, 1 album.
   American Red Cross worker in Russia, 1917. Diary transcripts, correspondence, photographs, clippings, and miscellanea relating to Red Cross relief work in Russia and to conditions in Russia during the Russian Revolution.
   Gift, Mrs. M. Pirnie, 1958.

604. POLISH GREY SAMARITANS.
   Records, 1918-1965. 3 ms. boxes.
   Organization of Polish-American women relief workers. Memoirs, reports, correspondence, printed matter, photographs, and memorabilia relating to relief activities carried out in Poland at the end of World War I and to conditions in Poland at that time. Includes memoirs by Martha Gedgowd and Amy Pryor Tapping, members of the Polish Grey Samaritans.
   Gift, Martha Gedgowd and Amy Pryor Tapping, 1957. Subsequent increments.

605. RED CROSS. U.S. AMERICAN NATIONAL RED CROSS.
   Records, 1917-1921. 217 ms. boxes, 38 vols., 2 scrapbooks.
   American charitable organization. Correspondence, memoranda, reports, financial records, and photographs relating to relief work in Europe, the Middle East, China, and Siberia during and immediately following World War I. Includes the records of its Commission to Russia concerning the Ukraine, 1918-1919--ca. 2 ms. boxes (boxes 177-178).
   Preliminary inventory.
   Gift, American National Red Cross, 1923. Subsequent increments.

606. RICHARDSON, GARDNER.
   Papers, 1911-1924. 1/2 ms. box, 2 albums, 2 envelopes, 1 portfolio.
   Official of the Commission for Relief of Belgium and of the American Relief Administration in Austria. Photographs, resolutions, and letters of gratitude relating to relief work in Syria, Austria, and Odessa, Russia, and to the University of Vienna Children's Clinic. Includes 21 photos of A.R.A. activities in Odessa.
   Gift, G. Richardson.

607. RINGLAND, ARTHUR C.
Papers, 1921-1960. 1 folder.
American Relief Administration worker in Czechoslovakia, 1921-1922. Memoranda and printed matter relating to League of Nations cooperation with American Relief Administration activities in Russia, the attitude of Aleksandr Kerenskii in 1921 toward American Relief Administration activities in Russia, and subsequent Soviet attitudes toward American Relief Administration activities in Russia.
Gift, A. C. Ringland, 1959. Subsequent increments.

608. RODGERS, MARVIN.
Thesis, 1966. "Herbert Hoover and American Relief: A Study of the Relationship between Hoover's American Relief Program and Bolshevism in Europe in 1919." 1 folder.
Typescript (photocopy).
M.A. thesis, Fresno State College.
Gift, M. Rodgers, 1966.

609. ROSENBLUTH, ROBERT.
Reports, 1919. 1 folder.
Typescript.
American Relief Administration worker in Russia, 1919. Reports entitled "General Resumé, Russian Situation" and "Memorandum on Russian Affairs" relating to political and economic conditions and relief needs in Russia.

610. SABINE, EDWARD G., COLLECTOR.
Photographs, ca. 1921-1923. 1/2 ms. box.
Depicts famine victims and American Relief Administration relief activities in the Samara region of Russia.
Gift, John Speaks, 1961.

611. SCIPIO, LYNN A., 1876-   , COLLECTOR.
Photographs, 1920-1922. 1 album.
Depicts educational and relief work of the Young Men's Christian Associations among Russian, Armenian, and other refugees in Constantinople, Turkey.
Gift, Sydney N. Fisher, 1979.

612. SMITH, HENRY BANCROFT, 1884-
Papers, 1919-1928. 28 ms. boxes, 1 cu. ft. box.
U.S. Grain Corporation agent, technical advisor to Poland, and commercial attaché to Poland, 1919-1923; special representative, U.S. Department of Commerce, 1923-1928. Diaries, correspondence, reports, memoranda, financial records, printed matter, and photographs relating to American food relief in Europe, economic

reconstruction in Poland, and agricultural market conditions in Europe.
   Gift, H. B. Smith, 1957.

613. SMITH, JESSICA.
   Reports, 1923. 1 folder.
   Typescript.
   Quaker relief worker in Russia. Relates to famine conditions in the Bashkir area of the Soviet Union.

614. STEPHENS, FREDERICK DORSEY, 1891-
   Papers, 1909-1945. 1 ms. box.
   American relief worker in World Wars I and II. Correspondence, photographs, printed matter, and miscellanea relating to relief activities of the Commission for Relief in Belgium, 1914-1916, of the American Relief Administration in Russia, 1921-1922, and of the Finnish Relief Fund, 1939-1940.
   Gift, F. D. Stephens, 1957.

615. STORY, RUSSELL MCCULLOCH, 1883-1942.
   Papers, 1917-1921. 1/2 ms. box, 1 envelope, 6 boxes of slides (2 l. ft.).
   War work secretary, Young Men's Christian Association in Russia, 1917-1918. Letters, photographs, and glass slides relating to relief work in Russia, conditions in Moscow and elsewhere in Russia during the Russian Revolution, and the Czechoslovak legion, and depicting scenes in Japan, Russia, and Western Europe.
   Preliminary inventory.
   Gift, Gertrude A. Story, 1957. Gift, Katherine S. French, 1972.

616. TURROU, LEON G.
   Memorandum, 1926. "An Unwritten Chapter." 1 folder.
   Typescript.
   American Relief Administration worker in Russia. Relates to a meeting in 1922 between L. G. Turrou and Feliks Dzerzhinskii, Soviet Cheka director and commissar of transport, regarding transport of American Relief Administration supplies.

617. U.S. AMERICAN RELIEF ADMINISTRATION. RUSSIAN OPERATIONS, 1921-1923.
   Records, 1919-1925. 336 ms. boxes.
   U.S. Government agency to provide relief in Europe after World War I (unofficial agency after June 28, 1919, incorporated May 27, 1921) and unofficial agency to provide relief in Soviet Russia between August 1921 and June 1923. Correspondence, telegrams, memoranda, reports, agreements, minutes, histories, financial records, lists, press summaries, and photographs relating to relief operations, food and public health problems, agriculture, economic conditions, transportation and communications, and political and

social developments in Soviet Russia.
Register.
Gift, American Relief Administration, 1923.

618. VAIL, EDWIN H.
Letters, 1922-1924. 1 folder.
Typescript.
Relief worker in Russia. Relates to social and economic conditions
in Russia and to Quaker relief work in Russia.

619. VALKEAPAEAE, P. J.
Report (in English and Finnish), 1918-1919. 1 folder.
Printed.
Report entitled "Selostus Toiminnastaan Elintarpeiden Hankkimiseksi Amerikasta Suomeen Vuosina 1918-1919" (Report on American food relief activities in Finland for the year 1918-1919) by P. J. Valkeapaeae, 1919, and first issue of the Finland Sentinel, organ of the Finland Constitutional League of America, July 4, 1918, relating to Finnish independence.

620. WACHHOLD, ALLEN.
Thesis, 1978. "Frank A. Golder: An Adventure in Life and History." 196 p.
Typescript (photocopy).
American historian. Relates to the role of historian Frank A. Golder in developing the library and archival holdings of the Hoover Institution on War, Revolution and Peace. M.A. thesis, San Jose State University.
Gift, Charles Burdick, 1982.

621. WALLEN, E. CARL, 1889-1961.
Papers, 1918-1923. 1 ms. box.
American photographer. Photographs depicting relief work in the Caucasus, Turkey, and other areas of the Near East at the end of World War I. Includes a few papers of Mary Jane Steel (Mrs. E. C. Wallen) relating to her service as a Red Cross nurse in the Near East at this time and a photograph of President Warren G. Harding in 1923.
Gift, Barney Gould, 1975.

622. WILLIS, EDWARD FREDERICK, 1904-
Papers, 1917-1977. 5 1/2 ms. boxes, 1 card file box, 2 microfilm reels.
American historian. Writings, notes, memoranda clippings, hearing testimony, printed matter, and microfilm relating to Herbert Hoover, World War I relief operations, the blockade of Germany at the end of World War I, and the Bonus March on Washington in 1932. Includes

"Herbert Hoover and the Russian Prisoners of World War I."
Typescript.

623. WILSON, SAMUEL GRAHAM.
Letter to Ella W. Stewart, 1916. 1 folder.
Holograph.
Relief worker in Armenia. Relates to relief work in Armenia during World War I.

624. WOLFE, HENRY CUTLER, 1898-1976.
Papers, 1921-1923. 1 folder, 1 envelope.
American Relief Administration worker in Russia. Printed matter, identification card, medals, and photographs relating to conditions in the Samara Province of Russia and operations of the American Relief Administration.
Gift, Mrs. H. C. Wolfe, 1977.

625. YOUNG MEN'S CHRISTIAN ASSOCIATIONS.
Miscellaneous records, 1917-1920. 68 ms. boxes, 5 folios, 79 envelopes, 40 albums.
International social and charitable organization. Clippings, printed matter, posters, and photographs relating to the activities of the Young Men's Christian Associations in the United States and Europe during World War I. Includes material on Russia, Russian liaison, and Russian work, particularly in Siberia (box 57); Russian posters (box 67); and photographs/glass plates of Siberia, Russia, and Russian POWs in Austria (envelopes HHHHH-JJJJJ, PPPPP, and QQQQQ).
Register.
Gift, World Alliance of Young Men's Christian Associations, 1933.

626. ZNAMIECKI, ALEXANDER.
Memoir, 1954. "Hoover's Aid to Poland." 1 folder.
Typescript.
Member, U.S. Food Administration Mission to Poland. Relates to Herbert Hoover and U.S. Food Administration relief work in Poland at the end of World War I.
Gift, A. Znamiecki, 1957.

EMIGRE ACTIVITIES

627. AMERICAN SLAV CONGRESS.
Issuances, 1942. 1/2 ms. box.
Antifascist organization of American Slavs. Program, press releases, speeches, resolutions, and pamphlets issued at the founding congress in Detroit relating to American Slav contributions to the U.S. and Allied war effort.

628. ARKHANGEL´SKII, ALEKSEI PETROVICH.
Papers (in Russian), 1918-1956. 5 ms. boxes, 1 oversize box.
General, Imperial Russian Army; chairman, Russkii obshchevoinskii soiuz. Correspondence, reports, memoranda, writings, military records, printed matter, and photographs relating to Russian émigré affairs, Russian nationalism, monarchism and anticommunism, and Russian military activities in World War I and the Russian Revolution. Includes records of the Russkii obshchevoinskii soiuz.
Closed until January 1988.
Gift, V. V. Orekhov, 1982.

629. BALYKOV, V. P.
Speech (in Russian), 1935. 1 folder.
Typescript.
Representative of the Russkaia fashistskaia partiia (Russian Fascist Party) in Japan. Calls for patriotic unity among Russians in the struggle against Bolshevism in Russia.

630. BOGOIAVLENSKY, NIKOLAI VASIL´EVICH.
Correspondence (in Russian), 1928-1937. 1 folder.
Russian émigré in the United States. Relates to foreign relations between the United States and Russia and to political activities of Russian immigrants in the United States.
Gift, Gleb Bogoiavlensky, 1946.

631. BOTKINE, SERGE, COLLECTOR.
Collection, 1918-1932. 11 ms. boxes.
Correspondence, reports, memoranda, interview summaries, notes, and printed matter relating to Russian émigrés in Berlin, elsewhere in Germany, and in other European countries after the Russian Revolution and to the claim of one Anastasiia Nikolaevna Chaikovskaia to be Grand Duchess Anastasia of Russia. Mainly in Russian.
Preliminary inventory.
Gift, S. Botkine, 1930.

632. BREESE, ALEXANDER, 1889-1976.
Papers, 1915-1944. 1/2 ms. box.

Russian-American meteorologist; assistant meteorologist, Meteorological Physics Section, U.S. Weather Bureau, 1942-1944. Correspondence, passports, certificates, letters of recommendation, and printed matter relating to meteorology.

633. BREESE, MARIE ANNENKOV.
Memoirs, n.d. "Another Look at Russia." 2 folders.
Typescript.
Member of the Russian nobility; émigré in the United States after Russian Revolution. Relates to the history of the Annenkov family, the Russian Revolution and Civil War, and émigré life in the United States, 1922-1943.
Gift, Gordon W. Hewes, 1975.

634. CHASOVOI (SENTINEL).
Records (in Russian), 1898-1981. 3 ms. boxes, 1 oversize box.
Russian émigré periodical published in Paris. Correspondence, serial issues, clippings, brochures, histories, other writings, and photographs relating to Russian émigré affairs, Russian nationalism, monarchism, and anticommunism, and events in the Soviet Union since World War I.
Closed until January 1988.
Gift, V. V. Orekhov, 1982.

635. CHUHNOV, NICHOLAS.
Open letter (in Russian), 1951, to Harry S. Truman, president of the United States. 1 folder.
Typescript (mimeographed).
Editor of The Banner of Russia (New York). Objects to a comparison of Iosif Stalin and Emperor Alexander I made by President Truman. Includes a translation of the letter (printed).

636. DAY, GEORGE MARTIN.
Papers, 1922-1937. 1/2 ms. box.
Professor of sociology, Occidental College, Los Angeles. Writings, correspondence, and questionnaires relating to social conditions, education, and religion in the Soviet Union and to the adjustment to American society of Russians living in the Los Angeles area in 1930.

637. "EGERSKII VESTNIK" (EGERSKII [REGIMENT] HERALD).
Bulletins (in Russian), 1925-1932. 1 folder.
Typescript (mimeographed).
Relates to the history of the Imperial Russian Army regiment, Leib-gvardii Egerskii polk, especially during the Russian Civil War, and to activities of veterans of the regiment. Issued by a regimental veterans association.
Gift, Russian Historical Archive and Repository, 1974.

638. ERASMUS-FEIT FAMILY.
   Papers (in Russian), 1895-1956. 3 ms. boxes.
   Family of Baron Erasmus-Feit, Imperial Russian Army officer. Correspondence, scrapbooks, memorabilia, printed matter, and photographs relating to the daily lives of Russian émigrés in China and the United States and family matters.
   Gift, Mr. and Mrs. Ogden Scoville, 1977.

639. "FINLIANDETS" (MEMBER OF THE FINLAND REGIMENT).
   Bulletins (in Russian), 1963-1972. 1/2 ms. box.
   Typescript (mimeographed).
   Organ of the Society of the Household Troops of the Finland Regiment, an organization of veterans of this regiment of the Imperial Russian Army. Relates to activities of members.
   Gift, Nicholas T. Yakunin, 1974.

640. GOODFELLOW, MILLARD PRESTON, 1892-1973.
   Papers, 1942-1967. 5 ms. boxes, 2 envelopes.
   Colonel, U.S. Army; deputy director, Office of Strategic Services, 1942-1946; political adviser to the U.S. commanding general in Korea, 1946. Correspondence, reports, printed matter, and phonotapes relating to Office of Strategic Services operations in North Africa and the Far East during World War II, and to postwar reconstruction in Korea. Includes correspondence of Ilia and Beatrice Tolstoy, 1942-1943.
   Register.
   Gift, M. P. Goodfellow, 1969.

641. GRIMM, DAVID DAVIDOVICH, 1864-
   Papers (in Russian), 1919-1934. 4 ms. boxes.
   Russian educator; rector, Petersburg University, 1899-1910; assistant minister of education, Russian Provisional Government, 1917. Correspondence, memoranda, press reports, printed and other material relating to the Russian émigré community in Finland and other parts of Europe and to the Russian Civil War.
   Register.
   Purchase, Nikita Struve, 1976.

642. HERTMANOWICZ, JOSEPH JOHN.
   Papers, 1916-1941. 1/2 ms. box.
   Official, Lithuanian Council of Chicago. Writings and speeches, memoranda, and resolutions relating to the history, economy, and foreign policy of Lithuania and to appeals from Lithuanian-American organizations to the U.S. government urging recognition of the independence of Lithuania.
   Preliminary inventory.
   Gift, J. J. Hermanowicz.

643. ILIN, I. S., COLLECTOR.
Newspaper clippings (in Russian), 1931-1932. 1 oversize package (1/2 l. ft.).
Relates to Japanese military activities in Manchuria. From Russian-language newspapers in China.
Gift, I. S. Ilin.

644. KARMILOF, OLGA, 1897-
Memoirs, n.d. "Story of My Life." 98 p.
Mimeograph.
Russian émigré to China, Argentina, and the United States, successively. Relates to social conditions in Russia, the Russian Revolution, and Russian émigré life, especially in China.
Gift, O. Karmilof, 1982.

645. KASTCHENKO, MARIE, 1902-
Memoirs, n.d. "A World Destroyed: Memoirs." 298 p.
Typescript (Photocopy).
Daughter of a Ukrainian landowner. Relates to social conditions in the Ukraine prior to and during the Russian Revolution and to Ukrainian refugee life in Poland.
May not be quoted without permission of M. Kastchenko.
Gift, M. Kastchenko, 1980.

646. KHARBINSKII KOMITET POMOSHCHI RUSSKIM BEZHENTSAM.
Miscellanea (in Russian), 1927-1928. 1 folder.
Harbin Committee of Aid to Russian Refugees. Correspondence, pamphlets, brochures, and financial reports relating to assistance provided to Russian refugees by the Harbin Committee and affiliated organizations.

647. KOMOR, PAUL.
Extracts from a letter, received 1951, from an unidentified White Russian émigré in Shanghai. 1 folder.
Typescript.
Relates to political and economic conditions in China.

648. KONSTITUTSIONNO-DEMOKRATICHESKAIA PARTIIA.
Miscellaneous records (in Russian and French), 1920-1924. 2 ms. boxes.
Constitutional Democratic Party of Russia. Minutes of meetings, resolutions, reports, and correspondence relating to the Russian Revolution and to activities of the Konstitutsionno-demokraticheskaia partiia in exile.
Preliminary inventory.

649. LANDESEN, ARTHUR C.
Papers (in Russian), 1926-1933. 3 ms. boxes.

White Russian consular agent in San Francisco, 1926-1933.
Correspondence, memoranda, and miscellanea relating to White Russian consular activities in San Francisco.
Preliminary inventory.
Gift, A. C. Landesen.

650. LITHUANIAN NATIONAL COUNCIL IN AMERICA.
Miscellaneous records, 1918-1925. 1/2 ms. box.
Typewritten transcripts.
Organization of Lithuanian-Americans. Correspondence, resolutions, and reports relating to the movements to secure Lithuanian independence and U.S. recognition of Lithuania.
Gift, Malbone T. Graham.

651. MARTYNOV, GENERAL.
Study (in Russian), 1925. "Soobrazheniia ob ustroistvie, obuchenii i upotreblenii budushchei russkoi kavalerii" (Considerations on the organization, training, and utilization of the future Russian cavalry). 1 folder.
Typescript (mimeographed).
Lieutenant general, Imperial Russian Army.

652. MURAV´EVA, EKATERINA IVANOVNA.
Papers (in Russian), 1914-1948. 6 ms. boxes.
Russian refugee in France. Correspondence, memoirs, and notes relating to the Russian Revolution and political events in Russia and abroad. Correspondents include V. A. Maklakov, P. N. Miliukov, Vera Figner, and other leading political figures.
Preliminary inventory.
Deposit, E. I. Murav´eva, 1949.

653. NIKOLAIEFF, ALEXANDER MIKHAILOVITCH, 1876-
Series of articles, 1933-1935. "Japan´s Conquest of Manchuria and Jehol." 1 folder.
Proof sheets.
Colonel, Imperial Russian Army. Relates to Japanese military activities in Manchuria. Published in the Canadian Defense Quarterly.

654. OB"EDINENIE RUSSKIKH V MAROKKO.
Records (in Russian), 1930-1965. 2 ms. boxes.
Russian émigré organization. Correspondence, memoranda, reports, lists, and financial records relating to activities of the Russian émigré community and the Russian Orthodox Church in Morocco, primarily in Casablanca.

655. POLITICHESKII OB"EDINENNYI KOMITET.
Miscellany (in Russian), 1921. 1 folder.

Russian émigré organization. Memorandum (mimeographed) relating to the program of the Politicheskii ob"edinennyi komitet and bulletins (typewritten) relating to the Politicheskii ob"edinennyi komitet and to political developments in Russia.

656. PRIANISHNIKOV, BORIS V.
Miscellaneous papers (in Russian and English), 1940-1957. 1/2 ms. box.
Russian-American author and journalist. Writings, clippings, and printed matter relating to Russian émigré anticommunist movements, the Narodno-trudovoi soiuz organization, the White movement during the Russian Revolution, and Russian displaced persons after World War II.

657. ROSSIISKOE NATSIONAL´NOE OB"EDINENIE.
Records (in Russian), 1929-1981. 6 ms. boxes, 1 oversize box.
Russian émigré organization in Belgium. Reports, statutes, bylaws, minutes, leaflets, bulletins, radio broadcast transcripts, programs, studies, placards, clippings, and photographs relating to Russian émigré affairs, Russian nationalism, monarchism and anti-communism, and conditions in the Soviet Union.
Closed until January 1988.
Gift, V. V. Orekhov, 1982.

658. ROSTOVTSEFF, FEDOR.
Papers (in Russian), n.d. 2 ms. boxes.
Russian émigré teacher in France. Writings, reports, notes and outlines for lectures, clippings, memorabilia, and syllabi for courses in Russian high schools in Paris relating to Russian history from 1850 to 1940, French history, and logic.
Gift, F. Rostovtseff.

659. RUSSIAN NATIONAL COMMITTEE.
Appeal, 1921. 1 folder.
Printed.
Organization of Russian émigrés. Relates to the policy of the Great Powers toward the communist government of Russia. Addressed to the Washington Naval Conference.

660. SAFONOV, LUDMILA, 1897-
Memoirs, ca. 1974. "Only My Memories." 1/2 ms. box.
Typescript (photocopy).
Russian émigré in the United States. Relates to life in Russia from 1900 to 1919, immigration through the Far East and arrival in the United States, and work with displaced persons in Europe during World War II.
Gift, L. Safonov, 1975.

661. SAVIN, PETR PANTELEIMONOVICH.
   Papers (in Russian), n.d. 1/2 ms. box.
   Captain, Imperial Russian Army. Photocopy of writing entitled "Gibel´ Generala Millera" (The demise of General Miller) relating to the death of White Russian military leader E. K. Miller and correspondence and printed matter relating to the writing and to Russian émigré anticommunist activities, 1917-1968.
   Gift, P. P. Savin, 1975.

662. SHKURO, ANDREI GRIGOR´EVICH, 1887-1947.
   Letter (in Russian) to Grand Duke Andrei Vladimirovich, 1932. 1 folder.
   Typescript (mimeographed).
   General, White Russian army. Relates to Russian émigré politics.

663. SOVET OPPOZITSII MAN´CHZHURII I DAL´NIAGO VOSTOKA.
   Pamphlet (in Russian), 1927. "Rossiia dlia russkikh" (Russia for Russians). 1 folder.
   Printed.
   Russian fascist émigré organization in the Far East. Relates to the program of the organization.

664. TCHERNIGOVETZ, NIKOLAI.
   Essay (in Russian), ca. 1976. "Pisateliu Solzhenitsynu ot immigranta staroi revoliutsii" (To author Solzhenitsyn from an immigrant of the Old Revolution). 1 folder.
   Typescript.
   Russian émigré in the United States. Criticizes Aleksandr Solzhenitsyn for antimonarchist views and presents a personal evaluation of events in Russia from 1917-1976.
   Gift, N. Tchernigovetz, 1976.

665. TSURIKOV, N.
   Appeal (in Russian), n.d. "Svoim i chuzhym: o tragedii 22 sentiabria" (To ours and others: About the tragedy of September 22). 1 folder.
   Typescript (mimeographed).
   Member, Russkii obshchevoinskii soiuz, a Russian émigré association. Relates to circumstances surrounding the disappearance of generals E. K. Miller and N. Skoblin and calls for anti-Bolshevik unity among Russian émigrés.

666. U.S. FEDERAL SECURITY AGENCY.
   Radio broadcast series, 1939. "Americans All: Immigrants All." 24 phonorecords.
   Relates to the immigration of various nationalities and ethnic groups to the United States.
   Preliminary inventory.
   Gift, F. Curtis May, 1972.

667. VICTOR, GEORGE.
   Memoirs, n.d. "Odyssey from Russia." 1 folder.
   Transcript (mimeographed).
   Relates to the emigration of G. Victor from Russia via Turkey and Western Europe to the United States around the time of the Russian Civil War.

668. VLADIMIR KIRILLOVICH, GRAND DUKE OF RUSSIA, 1917-
   Appeal, 1952. "An Appeal to the Free World." 1 folder.
   Printed (photocopy).
   Relates to communism in Russia. Published in Nasha strana (Buenos Aires).

669. VOITSEKHOVSKII, SERGEI L´VOVICH, 1900-
   Papers (mainly in Russian), 1924-1977. 10 ms. boxes.
   Russian historian. Correspondence, memoranda, writings, printed matter, and photographs relating to Russian history after 1917, Russians and Russian anti-communist movements in foreign countries, the Romanov dynasty, Soviet espionage within Russian émigré circles, and Grand Duke Vladimir Kirillovich.
   Box 2 and part of Box 3 closed until 1990. Part of Box 3 closed until 1985.
   Gift, S. L. Voitsekhovskii, 1979.

670. VON ARNOLD, ANTONINA R.
   Study, 1937. "A Brief Study of the Russian Students in the University of California." 1 folder.
   Typescript.
   American social worker. Relates to the adjustment of Russian émigré students at the University of California, Berkeley, to American university life.

671. VON MOHRENSCHILDT, DIMITRI SERGIUS, 1902-
   Papers, 1917-1970. 1/2 ms. box, 1 envelope.
   American historian; editor, Russian Review. Correspondence, writings, printed matter, and photographs relating to acquisition of Russian historical materials and the Russian Orthodox Church in the United States. Includes letters from Sergei A. Von Mohrenschildt, Russian military historian and father of D. S. Von Mohrenschildt, describing political and economic conditions in Poland under Soviet and Lithuanian occupation, 1939-1940.
   Register.
   Gift, D. S. Von Mohrenschildt, 1971. Incremental gift, 1976.

672. WIASEMSKY, SERGE, PRINCE.
   Translations of miscellaneous papers, 1923-1924. 1 folder.
   Typescript.

Leader of the Russian National Progressive Party in England. Renunciation by S. Wiasemsky of landholdings in Russia, resolutions by the Russian National Progressive Party, and a memorandum on the dynasties of Russia.

673. YURCHENKO, IVAN.
Writings (in Russian), n.d. 25 ms. boxes.
Holograph.
Russian émigré in the United States. Relates to various aspects of philosophy, religion, and the sciences.
Preliminary inventory.
Gift, I. Yurchenko, 1972.

674. ZAKHARTCHENKO, CONSTANTINE L., 1900–
Papers, 1920-1976. 1 ms. box.
Russian émigré; aeronautical engineering designer; assistant chief engineer, Shiuchow Aircraft Works, Kwantung, China, 1934-1943. Correspondence, certificates, airplane designs, blueprints, technical and financial reports, telegrams, contracts, and photographs relating to engineering and military aspects of Chinese aviation.
Gift, C. L. Zakhartchenko, 1977.

675. ZEBRAK, NICHOLAS A.
Papers (in Russian), 1920-1931. 1 ms. box.
Chief of police, Russian Concession, Tientsin; advisor to the local Chinese administration. Correspondence, clippings, and pamphlets relating to Russian émigrés, police administration, and welfare and veterans' organizations in China.

676. ZUBETS, VLADIMIR ALEKSANDROVICH.
Memoir (in Russian), 1933. "Na sluzhbie v kitaiskoi armii" (Service in the Chinese army). 1/2 ms. box.
Typescript.
Russian émigré officer in the Chinese army. Relates to Russians in the Chinese army in the 1920's. Includes a summary of the contents in English (by Elena Varneck) and photographs.

INDEX

Collection identification numbers (not page numbers) are used throughout this index.

A.E.F., see U.S. Army. A.E.F., 1917-1920
A.R.A., see U.S. American Relief Administration
"The A.R.A.: Herbert Hoover and American Relief," 557
Abramoff, Fedor collection, see Russia (1917-1922. Civil War governments). Vooruzhennye sily iuga Rossii. Nachal´nik snabzheniia; Russia (1917-1922. Civil War governments). Vooruzhennye sily iuga Rossii. Sudnoe otdielenie
"An Account of the March Revolution, 1917," 302
Adams, Arthur E., 241
Advisory Commission of Railway Experts to Russia, see U.S. Advisory Commission of Railway Experts to Russia
Advocates, 143
Aebersold, 139
Aerenthal, Aloys Leopold Baptist Lexa von, Graf, 1854-1912, 20
Aeronautics, Military--China, 674
Agabekov, Georgii Sergeevich, 289
Agence économique et financière (August 2, 1923), 308
Agence télégraphique de Petrograd, 169
Agents provocateurs, 124, 133, 138, 139, 140
Agrarian question, 44, 50, 94, 145, 211
Agribusiness, 44, 50, 94
Agricultural economics, 44, 50, 94
Agricultural policy, 44, 145, 211
Agricultural production economics, 44, 50, 94
Agriculture, 78, 211, 249; Bessarabia, 62; Lithuania, 43
Agriculture and state, 44, 145; Germany, 211
Agriculture--Economic aspects, 44, 50; Armenia, 94
Agronomy, see Agriculture
Air attachés, see Military attachés
Air pilots, Military--Poland, 430
Airplanes--Design and construction, 674
Airplanes, Military--Pilots--Poland, 430
Akaëmov, Nikolai, 328
Akintievskii, Konstantin Konstantinovich, 1884-1962, 329
Aksakov, Konstantin Sergeevich, 1817-1860, 32
Aksel´rod, Pavel Borisovich, 1850-1928, 133, 139
Aksent´ev, N., see Axentieff, N.
Alapaevsk district, 456
"The Alapaevsk Tragedy: The Murder of the Russian Grand Dukes By the Bolsheviks," 93
Alaska--Discovery and exploration, 575
"Album of the Masquerade Ball at the Winter Palace in February 1903," 119
Aldanov, Mark, Tri goda, Berlin, Moscow, London, ms., 1941, 133
Aleksandr I, II, and III, see Alexander I, II, and III
Aleksandra Fedorovna, see Alexandra, Empress Consort of Nicholas II

Aleksandro-Nevskaia lavra, 421
Aleksandrovskii komitet o ranenykh, 154
Alekseev, F., 12
Alekseev, Mikhail Vasil´evich, 1857-1918, 170, 175
Alekseevskii, Aleksandr Nikolaevich, 521
Aleksinskii, G. A., 133
Alexander I, Emperor of Russia, 1777-1825, 133
Alexander II, Emperor of Russia, 1818-1881, 21, 105
Alexander III, Emperor of Russia, 1845-1894, 54, 84, 87
Alexander Nevskii Monastery, 421
Alexandra, Empress Consort of Nicholas II, Emperor of
    Russia, 1872-1918, 12, 101
Alexandra, Queen Consort of Edward VII, King of Great Britain,
    1844-1925, 59
All-Russian Church Congress, Moscow, Jan.-Feb. 1918, 421. See also
    Orthodox Eastern Church, Russian
All-Russian Executive Committee of the Railroad Union, 133, 291
All-Union Mendeleev Congress on Theoretical and Applied Chemistry,
    St. Petersburg, 1911, 12
Allied and Associated Powers (1914-1920). Supreme Economic Council,
    585; Supreme War Council. American Section, 257
Allied intervention in the Civil War, see Russia--History--Allied
    intervention, 1918-1920
Altengrabow (Prison camp), Germany, see Lager Altengrabow, Germany
Ammende, Edgar, 260
"America in Russia, or The Diary of a Russian Wolfhound," 459
American... See also headings beginning with "United States"
American art, 125
American Committee for the Encouragement of Democratic
    Government in Russia, 242
"The American Congress and the Russian Revolution, March 1917 to
    February 1918," 266
American diplomats, 29
American engineers in Russia, 37
American Expeditionary Forces, see U.S. Army. A.E.F., 1917-1920
American food relief, see Food relief, American
American foreign correspondents--Correspondence, reminiscences, etc.,
    287
American Friends Service Committee, 553, 617
American intervention in the Civil War, see Russia--History--Allied
    intervention, 1918-1920--American intervention
American Jewish Joint Distribution Committee, 617
American Mennonite Central Committee, 617
American National Red Cross, see Red Cross. U.S. American National
    Red Cross
American naval operations--World War, 1914-1918, see World War,
    1914-1918--Naval operations, American
American Relief Administration, see U.S. American Relief
    Administration
"The American Relief Administration and My Crime," 586
American Relief Administration Documents Project, see Hoover
    Institution on War, Revolution and Peace. Supreme Economic
    Council and American Relief Administration Documents Project
American Russian Institute, San Francisco, 12

American Slav Congress, 627
Amtorg Trading Corporation, New York, 478
Amur Flotilla, 494
Amur River and Valley--History--Fiction, 461
Amurskaia oblast´--History, 494
Amurskaia voennaia flotiliia, 494
Anarchism and anarchists, 133, 139, 262, 387
"Anarchism and Marxism in the Twentieth Century Revolution," 262
Anastasiia Nikolaevna, Grand Duchess of Russia, 1901-1918, 42, 631
Anderson, Alfred O., 502
Anderson, Anna, see under Anastasiia Nikolaevna, Grand Duchess of
    Russia, 1901-1918
Anderson, Edgar, 1920-   , 171, 371, 402
Anderson, Roy Scott, d. 1925, 330
Andreev, Leonid, 133
Andreev, N. N., 243
Andrei Vladimirovich, Grand Duke of Russia, 1879-   , 662
Andrejeff, Yelena, 428
Andrew, Prince, 52
Andrushkevich, Nikolai Aleksandrovich, 455
Anichkov, Vladimir Petrovich, 456
Annenkov, Boris Vladimirovich, 1890-1927, 457
"Antagonizm Azyi i Europy," 7
Anti-Bolshevik governments, see Russia (1917-1922. Civil War
    governments)
Anti-Bolshevik accounts of events of the Revolution and Civil War,
    see Russia--History--Revolution, 1917-1921--Anti-Bolshevik
    accounts and counterrevolutionary movements
Anti-communist movements, 133, 385, 388, 628, 634, 657, 661, 669;
    Europe, 437; Germany, 656; United States, 390
Anti-communist propaganda, 656
Anti-communist resistance, see Anti-communist movements
Antisemitism, 73. See also Jews
Antonenko, V. P., 458
"An Appeal to the Free World," 668
Appleton, Anne, 208
Arbitration, International, 155
Arbore, Z. K. Ralli-, 133
Archangel, 14, 246, 331, 591
Architecture, 117
Arkhangel´sk, see Archangel
Arkhangel´skii, Aleksei Petrovich, 628
Armed forces attachés, see Military attachés
Armed Forces of Southern Russia, see Russia (1917-1921. Civil War
    governments). Vooruzhennye sily iuga Rossii
Armenia--Agriculture--Economic aspects, 94; Boundaries--Turkey, 444;
    History, 578; Pictorial works, 445; Revolutionists, 133, 139
Armenia. Societé agricole arménienne, 94
Armenia--World War, 1914-1918, 623
Armenian question, 210
Armenians in Turkey--Pictorial works, 611
Army, 295
Army, Russian, see Russia. Armiia
Arnold, Antonina R. von, see Von Arnold, Antonina R.

Arrest, 289
Art, 25, 117; American, 125; analysis, interpretation, appreciation, 313, 325; and communism, 125; and socialism, 125
Arthur (Port)--Siege, 1904-1905, 162. See also Russo-Japanese War, 1904-1905
Asia--Description, 455; Study and teaching, 65
Asia, East--Description and travel, 29, 133
Asian pictorial collection, 1883-1948, 149
Asian studies, 65
Association of Russian Imperial Naval Officers in America, 105
Associations, institutions, etc.--Bookplates and stamps, 133
Astrakhan (guberniia), 133
"Ataka," 384
Atrocities of the Civil War, see Russia--History--Revolution, 1917-1921--Atrocities
Attachés, see Military attachés
Attorneys, 143
Austria--Foreign relations--Russia, 20; Politics and government, 133; Prisoners of war, 182
Austro-Hungarian Monarchy. Haus, Hof- und Staatsarchiv, 20; Legiony Polskie, 206; Ministerium des K. und K. Hauses und des Aeussern, 172
Autograph collection, 1
"Aux masses laborieuses de France, d´Angleterre, d´Amérique et du Japon," 306
Avalov, Pavel Mikhailovich, Kniaz´, 1884-   , 133, 402
Aviation, Military--China, 674
Aviators, Military--Poland, 430
Axelbank, Herman, 1900-1977, collector, 2
Axelbank, Jay, 2
Axelrod, Pavel Borisovich, 1850-1928, 133, 139
Axentieff, N., 552
Azef, Evno Fishelevich, 1869-1918, 124, 133, 139
Azerbaijan--History--Revolution, 1917-1921, 345; Mugan´, 345

Babb, Nancy, 1884-1948, 553
Badges of honor, 8, 68
Baian, I. I. Kolyshko-, 133
Baker, Elizabeth, 553
Bakhmetev, Boris Aleksandrovich, 286
Bakhmetev, Georgii, 66
Baku, British in, 412
Baku--Petroleum industry and trade, 412
Bakunin, Mikhail Aleksandrovich, 1814-1876, 133, 262
Balabanoff, Angelica, 133
Balabanova, Anzhelika, 133
Balk, A., 22, 118
Balkan Peninsula, Socialism in the, 299
Ball, Costume, St. Petersburg, 1903, 111, 119
"The Baltic Area in World Affairs, 1914-1920: A Military Political History," 171
Baltic provinces--World War, 1914-1918, 171, 209
Baltic Sea--Shipping, 414
Baltic states, 360; Boundaries, 209; Politics and government, 35,

171; World War, 1914-1918, 580
Balykov, V. P., 629
Bane, Suda Lorena, 1886-1952, 554
Banks and banking, 21
Bar (legal profession), 143
Baranov, M., 133
Baranova, F. F., 133
Baratoff, Eugenie, 173
Baratov, Nikolai Nikolaevich, 1864-1932, 173
Barber, Alvin B., 555
"Baron Ungern, Urga i Altan-Bulak," 547
Barrett, William S., 459
Barringer, Thomas C., 556
Barristers, 143
Bashkir region--History, 613
Basily, Lascelle Meserve de, 23, 70, 89
Basily, Nicolas Alexandrovich de, 1883-1963, 24, 91
Basily-Callimaki, Eva de, 1855-1913, 25
Bastunov, Vladimir J., collector, 146
Batiushin, N. S., 26
Battle of Tsushima, 1905, 158. See also Russo-Japanese War, 1904-1905
Baxter, Robert I., collector, 331
Bazarevich, Vladimir Iosifovich, 332
Bazarov, Pavel Aleksandrovich, 157
Bebutov, D. I., Kniaz´, 133
Bekeart, Laura Helene, 557
Belevskii, Lieutenant, see Bielevskii, Lieutenant, collector
Belogorskii, N., pseud., see Shinkarenko, Nikolai Vsevolodovich, 1890-1968
Benes, Eduard, 1884-1948, 244
Benjamin, Alfred, 245
Benkendorf´, Mariia Sergeevna, Grafinia, 115
Bennigsen, Emmanuil Pavlovich, Graf, 1875- , 333
Berberova, Nina N., 133
Berk, Stephen M., 460
Berkeley campus, University of California, 670
Berlin, Pavel A., 133
Berlinskoe obshchestvo pomoshchi politicheskim zakliuchennym v Sovetskoi Rossii, 133
Bermondt-Avalov, Pavel Mikhailovich, Kniaz´, 1884- , 133, 402
Bernatskii, Mikhail Vladimirovich, 1876- , collector, 174
Bessarabia 62, 197; Agriculture, 62; Territorial questions (World War I), 197
Biblioteka imeni Shevchenko, Lvov, 133
Bielevskii, Lieutenant, collector, 27
"Biezhentsy v Velikuiu voinu", 161
Binkley, Robert Cedric, 1897-1940, 222
Bint, Henri Jean, 14
Biography, Collected, 388
Birkin, Dmitrii, 433
Bishop, William B., 486
Bisk, I. S., 133
Blagoev, Dimitur, 1856-1924, 122, 184
Blagoevtsy (St. Petersburg group of social democrats), 133

Blagoveshchensk--History, 521, 533
Bland, Raymond L., 558
Bliumenfel´d, I. S., 133
Blums, Ivan, 292
Bogdanov, A., 1872-   , 461
Bogoiavlensky, Gleb, 630
Bogoiavlensky, Nikolai Vasil´evich, 630
Bogrov, D., 133
Boldyrev, Vasilii Georgievich, 1875-   , 462
Bolshevik posters, 11
"The Bolsheviks and the World War; the Origin of the Third
    International," 184
"Bolsheviks in the Ukraine (The Second Campaign, 1918-1919)," 241
Bolshevism, see Communism
Bolshevik Party, see Rossiiskaia sotsial-demokraticheskaia rabochaia
    partiia
Bol´shoi i malyi voiskovyi krug Voiska terskago, 394
Bonch-Bruevich, Vladimir Dmitrievich, 1873-1955, 2, 279
Bonds, 5
Book censorship, 133
Book trade--Bookplates and stamps, 133
Bookplates, 3, 133
Books--Censorship, 133
"Bor´ba s bol´shevikami na Dal´nem vostokie (Khorvat, Kolchak,
    Semenov, Merkulovy, Diterikhs): vospominaniia uchastnika," 493
Borel´, Vera Alekseeva de, 170, 175, 431
Botkine, Serge, collector, 79, 80, 81, 82, 83, 152, 631
Bourguina, Anna, 133, 246
Bourtzev, V. L., see Burtsev, Vladimir L´vovich, 1862-1942
Brailovskii, Anatolii, 133
Brain, Hannah, see Campbell, Hannah Brain, 1880-
Bramhall, Burle, collector, 559
Branden, Albrecht Paul Maerker, 1888-   , 176
Brandes, Annemarie Buschman-, 277
Brandt, Zoia G., 88
Bratstvo russkoi pravdy, 133
Breese, Alexander, 1889-1976, 632
Breese, Marie Annenkov, 633
Breitigam, Gerald B., 463
Breshko-Breshkovskaia, Ekaterina Konstantinovna, 1844-1934,
    123, 133, 139, 142, 569
Breshkovsky, Catherine, see Breshko-Breshkovskaia, Ekaterina
Breslau, Russian Consulate in, 79
Brest-Litovsk, Treaty of, Feb. 9, 1918 (Ukraine), 180
"A Brief Study of the Russian Students in the University of
    California," 670
British... See also headings beginning with "Great Britain"
British in Baku, 412; in the Crimea, 441
British intervention in the Civil War, see Russia--History--Allied
    intervention, 1918-1920--British intervention
Broeck Spalding, Merrill Ten, see Spalding, Merrill Ten Broeck
Broido, Eva L´vovna, 133
Brotherhood of Russian Truth, 133
Browder, Robert Paul, 264

Browne, Louis Edgar, 1891-1951, 247
Bruevich, Vladimir Dmitrievich Bonch-, 1873-1955, 2, 279
Brunelli, Paul, 150
Brunet, Court Councillor de, 28
Bryan, David Tennant, 18
Bryant, Louise, 2, 287
Bublikov, Aleksandr Aleksandrovich, 248
Budberg, Aleksei Pavlovich, Baron, 1869-1945, 464
Bugbee, Faith, 465
Bugbee, Fred William, 1876-1932, 465
Building design, 117
Bulgaria--Politics and government, 184, 419
Bulgaria, Socialism in, 122
Bulgarian Communist Party, 184
Bulgarian Review Center, 299
Bulgarska komunisticheska partiia, 184
Buliubash, Evgenii Grigor´evich, 334
Bund (Political party), 133, 139
Bungey, Grace Belle Reames, 560, 602
Bunin, I. A., 133
Bunin, Viktor M., 1896-   , 335
Bunyan, James, 1898-1977, 249
Burbank, Lyman B., 194
Burdick, Charles, 620
Burgina, Anna, see Bourguina, Anna
Burial grounds--France, 239
Burlin, P. G., 336
Burtsev, Vladimir L´vovich, 1862-1942, 124, 133, 139
Buschman-Brandes, Annemarie, 277
Business and government, 145
Byckoff, Michael M., collector, 4
Bykadorov, I., 337

Cabet, M. E., 133
Cadet Party, see Konstitutsionno-demokraticheskaia partiia
Caldwell, John Kenneth, 1881-   , 29, 480, 528
A Calendar of Soviet Treaties, 1917-1957, 265
California. Camp Fremont, 528, 595; Camp Kearny, 595; Fort Ross, 76; University, 670
California--World War, 1914-1918, 595
Callimaki, Eva de Basily-, see Basily-Callimaki, Eva de, 1855-1913
Camp Fremont, California, 528, 595
Camp Kearny, California, 595
Campbell, Hannah Brain, 1880-   , 561, 596
Canada. Army. Canadian Expeditionary Force (Russia)--Pictorial works, 497
Canada, Slavs in, 92
Canada, Ukrainians in, 408
Canadian Defense Quarterly, 653
Canadian Expeditionary Force (Russia)--Pictorial works, 497
"Captivity and Escape of Horseguardsman Dimitrii A. Shvetzoff in 1919-1921," 432
Carbonnel, François de, 1873-1957, 30
Carpathian Mountains--World War, 1914-1918, 205

"Une carrière médicale mouvementée", 385
Carroll, Philip H., 1885-1941, 562
Carter, Lieutenant, 338
Caspian Flotilla, 447
Caucasian army, see Russia. Armiia. Kavkazskaia armiia
Caucasus, 173, 345, 346, 375, 412, 431, 621; World War, 1914-1918, 173, 220, 621
Cavalry, see Russia. Armiia. Kavaleriia; Russia (1917-1922. Civil War governments). Armiia. Ufimskaia kavaleriiskaia diviziia
Cemeteries--France, 239
Censorship, 133
"Central and Eastern Europe," 177
Central Asia, Russian, see Soviet Central Asia
Central Europe--Politics and government, 177
Central Famine Relief Committee, see Russia (1917-   R.S.F.S.R.). TSentral'naia komissiia pomoshchi golodaiushchim
Ceská druzina, 463, 460, 466, 470, 471, 479, 480, 485, 488, 499, 509, 525, 568, 595, 602, 615
Chaikovskaia, Anastasiia Nikolaevna, see under Anastasiia Nikolaevna, Grand Duchess of Russia, 1901-1918
Chaikovskii, N. B., 133
Chainov, "Neobychainye, no istinnye prikliucheniia grafa Fedora Mikhailovicha Buturlina," 133
Charities, see Food relief; Russia--History--Revolution, 1917-1921-- Civilian relief; World War, 1914-1918--Civilian relief
Chasovoi (Sentinel), 634
Chebotarev, Grigorii Porfir'evich, see Tschebotarioff, Gregory Porphyriewitch, 1899-
Cheka, see Russia (1917-   R.S.F.S.R.). Chrezvychainaia komissiia po bor'be s kontr-revoliutsiei i sabotazhem
Chemists, 12, 49
Cheriachoukin, A. V., 339
Cherkasskii family, 31
Chernigovets, Nikolai, see Tchernigovetz, Nikolai
Chernov, Viktor Mikhailovich, 1873-1952, 133, 139, 340
Cherty i siluety proshlago: pravitel'stvo i obshchestvennost' v tsarstvovanie Nikolaia II, 40
Chichagov, Lieutenant General--photographs, 12
Chicherin, Georgii Vasil'evich, 1872-1936, 133, 139, 250, 287
Child health, 559, 561, 617
Child welfare, 559, 561, 617; Europe, 558
Children--Charities, 559, 561, 617; Protection, 559, 561, 617
Children's Colony, Petrograd, 559, 561
Childs, James Rives, 1893-   , 563
China--Aeronautics, Military, 674; Communism, 268; Economic conditions--1949-   , 647; Foreign relations--Russia, 330; History, 469, 520, 676; Politics and government, 647; Relations (general) with Russia, 268
China, Russians in, see Russians in China
China--Tientsin--Police administration, 675
Chinese Eastern Railway, 12, 330, 484, 489, 503. See also Railroads
Chkheidze, Nikolai Semenovich, 1864-1926, 133, 139
Chrezvychainaia komissiia po bor'be s kontr-revoliutsiei i

sabotazhem, see Russia (1917-   R.S.F.S.R.). Chrezvychainaia komissiia po bor'be s kontr-revoliutsiei i sabotazhem
Chrezvychainyi vserossiiskii zheleznodorozhnyi s"ezd, Petrograd, 1918, 291
Christianity, 88
Christoff, Peter K., collector, 32
Chuhnov, Nicholas, 635
Church and state, 1917-   , 276, 421, 439. See also Communism and religion
Ciechanowski, Jan, 409
Civil War, see Russia--History--Revolution, 1917-1921
Civilian relief, see Russia--History--Revolution, 1917-1921--Civilian relief; World War, 1914-1918--Civilian relief
Civilization, 7, 32
Clark, Marmaduke R., d. 1964, 564
Clark, Robert L., 564
Clendenen, Clarence Clements, 1899-   , 251
Coal--Galicia, 576. See also Mines and mineral resources
Coal oil, see Petroleum
Coins, 5, 99
Collective farms, 211
Colonies--North America, 14, 575
Colton, Ethan Theodore, 1872-   , 565
Columbia University. Research Program on the History of the Communist Party of the Soviet Union, 126, 136
Comintern, see Communist International
Commerce--Estonia, 414; Germany, 79, 80
Commercial policy, 53
Commission on Baltic Affairs, Paris Peace Conference, 1919, see Paris. Peace Conference, 1919. Commission on Baltic Affairs
Committee Upon the Arbitration of the Boundary Between Turkey and Armenia, see U.S. Committee Upon the Arbitration of the Boundary Between Turkey and Armenia
Communism. See also Rossiiskaia sotsial-demokraticheskaia rabochaia partiia; Socialism
Communism, 88, 128, 131, 133, 184, 227, 262, 276, 279, 289, 304, 356, 367, 451, 452, 668; international, 129, 134, 137, 262, 277, 281, 295, 299, 385, 608
Communism and art, 125; and culture, 312; and literature, 312; and religion, 277, 565. See also Church and state, 1917-
Communism and trade-unions, see Trade-unions and communism
Communism--China, 268; Georgia (Transcaucasia), 133; Germany, 298; Latvia, 133; Mongolia, 540, 546; United States, 252, 281
"Communism, Radicalism and the Arts," 125
Communist International, 184, 252, 256, 267, 277, 281, 326, 385
"The Communist International in Its Formative Stage, 1919-1920," 267
Communist Party of Bulgaria, 184
Communist Party of Latvia, 133
Communist Party of the Soviet Union, see under Rossiiskaia sotsial-demokraticheskaia rabochaia partiia
Communist Party of the Ukraine, 241
Communist propaganda, 261
Communist strategy, 341
Compulsory labor, 133, 249

Concessions, 478
Conference socialist internationale, Stockholm, 1917, 133, 297
Congress of Paris, 1856, 70
Congress on Theoretical and Applied Chemistry, St. Petersburg, 1911, 12
Conscript labor, 133, 249
Constantinoff, P. F., see Konstantinov, P. F.
Constituent Assembly, see Russia (1917. Provisional Government). Vserossiiskoe uchreditel'noe sobranie
Constitutional history, 188
Construction, 37, 117
Consular service, see Diplomatic and consular service
Consulates, see Diplomatic and consular service
Conventions (treaties), 180, 265, 415
"Conversation with a Chekist," 282
Convoy of His Imperial Majesty Emperor Nicholas II, 390
Cooper, Merian C., 1894-1973, 341
Cooperative societies, 411; Ukraine, 96, 408
Correspondents, Foreign, American--Correspondence, reminiscences, etc., 287
Cossacks, 133, 228, 336, 339, 347, 349, 522, 535. See also Don Cossacks, Province of the; Russia. Armiia. Cossacks; Russia (1918-1920). Armiia. Terskoe kazach'e voisko; Soiuz vol'nogo kazachestva
"Cossacks and Mountaineers on the Sunzhenskii Line in 1917," 349
Costume ball, St. Petersburg, 1903, 111, 119
Council of Ministers, see Russia. Sovet ministrov
Council of People's Commissars, see Russia (1917-   R.S.F.S.R.). Sovet narodnykh komissarov
Counterespionage, 139
Counterintelligence, 139
Counterrevolutionary movements in the Civil War, see Russia--History--Revolution, 1917-1921--Anti-Bolshevik accounts and counterrevolutionary movements
"The Coup d'Etat of Admiral Kolchak: The Counterrevolution in Siberia and East Russia, 1917-1918," 460
Courts and courtiers, 24, 26, 59, 120. See also Russia--Kings and rulers
Cozacks, see Cossacks
Crime and criminals, 289
Crimes, Political, 133, 139, 289
Crimea, British in the, 441
Crimea--History, 375, 378, 413, 435, 441, 449; Krymskoe kraevoe pravitel'stvo, see Krymskoe kraevoe pravitel'stvo
Crimean regional government, see Krymskoe kraevoe pravitel'stvo
Crimean War, 1853-1856--Peace, 70
Crimes, Military, 160, 419
Criminals, see Crime and criminals
Crops, see Agriculture
Crude oil, see Petroleum
Culture and communism, 312
Currency, 4, 5
Currency collection, n.d., 5
"Czar's List," 133

Czech and Slovak intervention in the Civil War, see Ceská druzina
Czech legion, see Ceská druzina
Czechoslovak legion, see Ceská druzina
Czechoslovakia--Foreign relations--Russia, 244

D., I. I., 434
Daily, Arthur, 317
Dal´nyi vostok (Siberia), see Far eastern region, Siberia
Dan, Fedor Il´ich, 1871-   , 389
Daniloff, Karl B., 342
Dardanelles campaign, 1915, 24
Darling, William Lafayette, 1856-1938, 343
Daschkow, Hilarion Woronzow-, see Woronzow-Daschkow, Hilarion, Graf, collector
Dashkov, Ilarion Vorontsov-, see Woronzow-Daschkow, Hilarion, Graf, collector
Dashnaktsutiun (Armenian revolutionary party), 133
Davies, E. Alfred, 467
Davis, Benjamin B., 566
Davis, Robert E., 567
Day, George Martin, 636
De Basily, see Basily
Debentures, 5
Deblin, Poland--Siege, 1914-1915, 431
De Borel´, Vera Alekseeva, see Borel´, Vera Alekseeva de
De Brunet, Court Councillor, see Brunet, Court Councillor de
Debts, Public, 248
De Carbonnel, Francois, see Carbonnel, Francois de, 1873-1957
Decorations, Military, 8, 68
De Fuhrman, P., see Fuhrman, P. de
De Giers, Mikhail Nikolaevich, see Girs, Mikhail Nikolaevich, 1856-1932
Deich, L. G., 133
De Jacobs, John F., see Jacobs, John F. de
De Lastours, G., 303
De L´Escaille, Mademoiselle, see L´Escaille, Mademoiselle de
Delevskii, IU., 133
Demetropoulos, Constantine, collector, 6
"Der demokratische Marxismus: zum vierzigsten Geburtstag der russischen Sozialdemokratie," 128
Denezhnoe obrashchenie i denezhnye znaki Dalnego vostoka za period voiny i revoliutsii, 511
Denikin, Anton Ivanovich, 1872-1947, 375, 447
Denikina, Kseniia, 71, 344
Denmark--Foreign relations--Russia, 213; Military attachés, Russian, in, 213
"The Department of State and the Russian Revolutions, March-November, 1917," 283
Detectives, see under Secret service
Detskaia koloniia, Petrograd, 559, 561
Deutsch, L. G., 133
"The Development of Soviet Orientalism", 65
"Deviatyi val: vospominaniia uchastnika russkoi grazhdanskoi voiny 1918-1920 g.g.," 335

Dialectical materialism, 277. See also Socialism
"Diary of a Communist," 483
"The Diary of a Russian Wolfhound," 459
"The Diary of General Balk," 118
Diplomatic and consular service, 28, 66, 79, 80, 81, 82, 83, 167, 213, 285, 286, 303, 304, 649. See also Diplomats; Military attachés
Diplomats, 24; American, 29; French, 114. See also Diplomatic and consular service; Military attachés
Direktoriia, Kolchak, interventy: vospominaniia, 462
Disarmament, 88
Dissenters, Religious, 411
Dmowski, Roman, 1864-1939, 177
Dnieperian cossacks, see Cossacks
"Dnievnik kommunista," 483
Dobrovol´cheskaia armiia, see Russia (1917-1922. Civil War Governments). Dobrovol´cheskaia armiia
Dobrynin, Vasilii A., 345
Doctors--Correspondence, reminiscences, etc., 288, 385, 425
Documentary History of American Industrial Society, 133
Defenses, National, 223
Dolgorouky, Barbara, Princess, 1885-   , 33
Dolgorukii, Aleksandr Aleksandrovich, 115
Dolgorukii, Vasilii Aleksandrovich, 115
Dom predvaritel´noe zakliuchenie, St. Petersburg, 133
Domanenko, General, 147
Don Cadet Corps, 442
Don Cossacks, Province of the, 178. See also Cossacks
Don (Province)--History, 328
Donskaia armiia, see Russia (1917-1922. Civil War governments). Donskaia armiia
Dorrian, Cecil, 253
Dostoevskii, Fedor Mikhailovich, 1821-1881, 51
Dotsenko, Paul, 468
"Douze fantomes revivent leur histoire," 38
"The Downfall of a Dynasty," 58
Dragomanov, M. P., 133
Draper, Theodore, 125
Dratsenko, D. P., 346
Dredges, 478
Dredging machinery, 478
Drenteln, Aleksandr Aleksandrovich, 282
Duma, 12, 77, 133
Duncan, D. G., 568
Duncan, William Young, 568
Dune, E. M., 133
Durand, Margaret, 569
Dutch travelers, 115
Dzerzhinskii, Feliks Edmundovich, 1877-1926, 275, 289, 616
Dzhems, J. M., 133
Dzvonkevich, Nikolai N., 142
Dzvonkevich-Vagner, Ekaterina N., see Vagner, Ekaterina Nikolaevna

East Asia--Description and travel, 29, 133; Fasciam, 663
East Europe--Description and travel, 455
East (Far East)--Description and travel, 29, 133
East (Far East), Russians in the, see Russians in the East (Far East)
East (Near East)--World War, 1914-1918--Campaigns, see World War, 1914-1918--Campaigns--Turkey and the Near East
East Prussia (Province)--World War, 1914-1918--Pictorial works, 224
Eastern Europe--Description and travel, 455
Eastern Orthodox Church, Russian, see Orthodox Eastern Church, Russian
Eastern question (Far East), 472
Economic and Financial Conference, Genoa, 1922, see Genoa. Economic and Financial Conference, 1922
Economic conditions, see Russia [or other country name]--Economic conditions
"Economic Conditions of Kuban Black Sea Region," 254
Economic policy, see Russia--Economic policy
Economic relations, Foreign, 258
Edison, J., 469
Education, 565, 636
"The Effects of the War upon the Central Government Institutions of Russia," 188
Egbert, Donald Drew, 1902-1973, 125
Egbert, Edward H., d. 1939, 569
"Egerskii Vestnik" (Egerskii [Regiment] Herald), 637
Eikons, 117
Eisenach-Saxe-Weimar--Foreign relations--Russia, 82
Eiserne Division, see Russia (1917-1922. Civil War governments). Severo-zapadnoe pravitel´stvo. Armiia. Eiserne Division
"Ekonomicheskoe polozhenie Sov. Rossii" (The economic situation of Soviet Russia), 255
Elachich, S. A., 470
Eliot, Henrietta, 575
Eliot, Thomas, 575
Eliseev, Fedor Ivanovich, 1892-   , 347
Ellis, Arthur, see Yelsky, Isador, 1896-1958
Elskii, Isadore, see Yelsky, Isadore, 1896-1958
Embassies, see Diplomatic and consular service
Emerson, George H., 471
Emigrants, 92, 112, 667
Emigration and immigration, 92, 112, 667. See also Refugees
Engineering, 37
Entente internationale anticommuniste, 385
"Entsiklopediia belago dvizheniia," 388
Entsiklopediia sovetskogo eksporta, 133
Enver Pasha, 133
Epstein, Fritz Theodor, 1898-   , 348, 523
Erasmus-Feit family, 638
Erenburg, I. L., 133
Ergushov, P., 349
Erickson, Douglas, 350
Ermakov, Petr Zacharovich, 34
Escaille, Mademoiselle de, see L´Escaille, Mademoiselle de
Espionage, 669. See also Secret service

Estonia--Commerce--Russia, 414; Exports, 414; Foreign
    relations--Russia, 401; History, 129, 401; World War,
    1914-1918, 351
"Estonian Independence," 401
"Estoniia i pomoshch golodaiushchim" (Estonia and aid to
    the starving), 351
Estrin, S. E., 133
Estrina, Liliia IAkovl., 133
Etter, Maria von, 151
Etterg, General--Photograph, 149
Eugenie, Princess, 59
Eurasian movement, 7, 531
Europe--Anti-communist movements, 437; Child welfare, 558; Food
    relief, American, 558, 565; History--1789-1815, 28;
    Reconstruction (1914-1939), 558
Europe, Central--Politics and government, 177
Europe, Eastern--Description and travel, 455
Europe, Russians in, 375, 452
European Student Relief. American Section, 565
European subject collection, 1889-1962, 35
European War, 1914-1918, see World War, 1914-1918
"The Events of July 1918," 436
Evreiskii mir (Berlin), 133
Ex libris, 3, 133
Ex-servicemen--Medical care, 154
Exchange of prisoners of war, see Prisoners of war
Executive Commission on Conferences of Members of the Constituent
    Assembly, 133
Exiles, see Emigration and immigration; Refugees
Exports--Estonia, 414; Germany, 79, 80
Extraordinary All-Russian Railroad Congress, Petrograd, 1918, 291

"Face au communism--le mouvement anticommuniste internationale
    de 1923-1950," 385
"Fakty," 215
Famines, 307, 324, 553, 556, 558, 562, 579, 613, 614, 617, 624;
    Pictorial works, 12, 575, 610. See also Food relief
Far East--Description and travel, 29, 133
Far Eastern question, 472
Far eastern region, Siberia--History, 2, 133, 455, 461, 462, 489,
    493, 494, 500, 505, 517, 532, 535
Far Eastern Republic, 249, 472, 511
Far Eastern Republic collection, 1917-1921, 472
Farming, see Agriculture
Fascism, 88; East Asia, 663
Faulstich, Edith M., d. 1972, collector, 473
Faulstich, Fred, 473
Features and Figures of the Past, 40
February Revolution, see Russia--History--March (February O.S.)
    Revolution, 1917
Fedichkin, Dmitri I., 352
Fedorov, Georgii, 353
Feit, A. IU., 133
Feit family, see Erasmus-Feit family

Ferguson, Alan, 474
Fermor, Elizabeth Stenbock-, 91
Fermor, Ivan Stenbock-, Graf, see Stenbock-Fermor, Ivan, Graf, 1897-   , collector
"Fevral´skie dni," 384
Fiat money, 4, 5
"The Fight for Freedom in Siberia: Its Successes and Failures," 468
Fighting, 295
Figner, Vera Nikolaevna, 1852-1942, 133, 139, 652
Films, see Moving-pictures
Finance, Public, 21, 47, 53, 290, 308, 310
Fine arts, 25, 117
Finland. Armeija, 205
Finland Constitutional League in America, 619
Finland--Foreign relations--United States, 263; History, 36, 570; History--Revolution, 1917-1918, 292, 360, 424, 619; Nationalism, 35
Finland. Oblastnoi komitet armii, flota i rabochikh Finliandii, see Oblastnoi komitet armii, flota i rabochikh Finliandii
Finland--Politics and government--1809-1917, 35; Politics and government, 1917-   , 360; Revolutionists, 139; Russians in, 641; World War, 1914-1918, 205, 619
Finland Sentinel, 619
"Finliandets" (Member of the Finland Regiment), 639
Finnish independence movement collection, see European subject collection, 1889-1962
Finnish Information Bureau, New York, 263, 272
Finnish subject collection, 1900-1946, 36
Fisher, Harold Henry, 1890-1975, 47, 509, 570
Fisher, Sydney N., 611
Fleming, Harold M., 1900-   , 571
Flug, V. E., 179
Fol´mar, Georg fon, 133
Fon-Fol´mar, Georg, 133
Fon Leikhtenberg, Nikolai Nikolaevich, Gertsog, see Leikhtenberg, Nikolai Nikolaevich, Gertsog fon
Fon Shvarts, A. V., see Shvarts, Aleksei Vladimirovich fon, 1874-1953
Fond pomoshchi nuzhdaiushchimsia rossiiskim literatoram i uchenym, 133
Fond vol´noi russkoi pressy, 133
Food aid programs, 307, 617. See also Famines
Food relief, 307, 617; American, 307, 556, 558, 563, 565, 582, 608, 616, 617, 624; American--Europe, 558, 565. See also Famines; Russia--History--Revolution, 1917-1921--Civilian relief; World War, 1914-1918--Civilian relief
Forced labor, 133, 249
Foreign affairs, see Russia [or other country name]--Foreign relations; International relations
Foreign commerce--Estonia, 414; Germany, 79, 80
Foreign correspondents, American--Correspondence, reminiscences, etc., 287
Foreign Delegation, Socialist Revolutionary Party, see Partiia sotsialistov-revoliutsionerov
Foreign economic relations, 258

Foreign intervention in the Civil War, see Russia--History--Allied intervention, 1918-1920
Foreign legion, French, 347
Foreign policy, see Russia [or other country name]--Foreign relations; International relations
Foreign population, 92, 112, 667
Foreign relations, see Russia [or other country name]--Foreign relations; International relations
Foreign service, see Diplomatic and consular service
Foreign trade--Estonia, 414; Germany, 79, 80
Foreign trade policy, 53
The Forming of the Communist International, 267
Fort Ross, California--Views, 76
"The Fortunes of the Roumiantzow Museum," 323
Foss, F. F., 37
France. See also entries beginning with "French"
France. Armée. Légion étrangère, 347; Armée--Officers--Correspondence, reminiscences, etc., 485
France--Cemeteries, 239; Diplomatic and consular service--Russia, 114; Foreign relations--Russia, 114, 285, 303; Military attachés, Russian, 153, 392; Mutiny, 256; Relations (military) with Russia, 153
France, Russians in, 229, 380, 652; Socialism in, 256
France--Study and teaching of the history of Russia, 658; World War, 1914-1918, 229; World War, 1939-1945, 133
Fredericks, General, 153
Free, Arthur M., collector, 180
Free Russian Press Union, 133
Freemasons, 133
Fremont (Army camp), California, 528, 595
French, Katherine S., 615
French communism--Translations of newspaper articles, 1919-1920, 256
French diplomats, 114
French foreign legion, 347
French Indochina--World War, 1939-1945, 347
French intervention in the Civil War, see Russia--History--Allied intervention, 1918-1920--French intervention
French leftist press--Newspaper articles, 256

French subject collection, 1665-1981, 256
Fried, Alfred Hermann, 1864-1921, 181
Friedlander, Ernst, 182
Friends, Society of, 618
Friends, Society of. American Friends Service Committee, 553, 617
"From Aral Sea to the Western Turkestan," 542
"From Nicholas II to Stalin: Half a Century of Foreign Politics," 63
The Frozen War: America Intervenes in Russia, 1918-1920, 354
Frumkin, Jacob G., 183
Fuhrman, P. de, 133
Fuller, Adaline W., 1888-   , 572
Fuller, Benjamin Apthorp Gould, 1879-   , 257
Furman, P. de, 133

Gairngrass, Alexander Alexeevich, 12

Gajda, Rudolf, 1892-   , 494
Galicia--Coal, 576; Politics and government, 100, 133
Gallipoli campaign, 1915, 24
Galvin, John A. T., collector, 158
Gankin, Olga Hess, 184
Gapon, Georgii Apollonovich, 1870-1906, 139
Garmidor-Baranov, M., 133
Garvi, Peter A., 1881-1944, 126, 133
Gaskill, C. A., 573
Gasztowtt, Anne, 30
Gautier, IU. V., 575
Gedgowd, Martha, 604
Gel'fand, Aleksandr, see Helphand, Alexander, 1867-1924
Gendarme office, 133
Gendarmes, see Police
"General Resumé, Russian Situation," 609
Geneva. Komitet pomoshchi politicheskim zakliuchennym, 133
Genkin, E., 540
Genoa. Economic and Financial Conference, 1922, 258
Georgia (Transcaucasia)--Communism, 133; History, 14, 105, 346, 426, 578; Maps, 105
Georgians in Poland, 426; in Turkey, 426
Georgievich, M., 185
Georgievskii, Georgii K., 133
Georgii Mikhailovich, Grand Duke of Russia, d. 1919, 186
German Army--World War I--Photographs, 239
German government subsidies to the Bolshevik Party, 133, 190, 227
"German Money to Lenin," 227
German Mennonites in Russia, 112
Germany. See also Prussia
Germany--Agriculture and state, 211; Anti-communist movements, 656; Commerce--Russia, 79, 80; Communism, 298; Exports, 79, 80; Foreign Relations--Russia, 57, 79, 80, 81, 82, 83; History--1918-1933, 391; History--Revolution, 1918, 240; Jews in, 53
Germany. Lager Altengrabow, see Lager Altengrabow, Germany
Germany. Oberste Heeresleitung, 187
Germany--Prisoners of war, 198, 214, 235, 427; Relations (military) with Russia, 152
Germany, Russians in, 631
Germany--World War, 1914-1918, 240
Germek, Joseph, 1893-   , 282
Germogen, episkop, 133
Gerngros, Aleksandr Alekseevich von--Photograph, 12
Gertsen, Aleksandr Ivanovich, 1812-1870, 32, 133
Gerua, Aleksandr, see Heroys, Alexandre
Gerua, Boris Vladimirovich, see Heroys, Boris Vladimirovich
Gessen, B., 259
Gessen, Iosif Vladimirovich, 1866-1943, 133, 355
"Gibel' Rigo-Shavel'skago otriada," 204
Gibson, Hugh Simmons, 1883-1954, 574
Gibson, Michael, 574
Giesche Spolka Akcyjna Company, Katowice, Poland, 478
Giers, Mikhail Nikolaevich, see Girs, Mikhail Nikloaevich, 1856-1932
Girs, Mikhail Nikolaevich, 1856-1932, 356

Glukhoozerskaia ferma, 78
Gniessen, Vladimir F., 357
"Go Spy the Land," 365
Gold mines and mining, 14; Mongolia, 14. See also Mines and mineral
    resources
Golder, Frank Alfred, 1877-1929, 575, 620
Golovan, Sergei Alexandrovich, 358
Golovin, Michael, 359
Golovin, Nikolai N., 1875-1944, 75, 164, 179, 223, 233, 358, 359,
    382, 392
Golovnin, Aleksandr Vasil´evich, 1821-1886, 48
Golubev, 541
Gómez Gorkin, Julián, 1901-   , 38
Goodfellow, Millard Preston, 1892-1973, 640
Goodyear, A. Conger, 576
Goremykin, Ivan Logginovich--Photograph, 12
Gor´kii, Maksim, 1868-1936, 133, 260, 617
Gor´kii, (Maksim) collection (in Russian and English), 1921, 260
Gorkin, Julián Gómez, see Gómez Gorkin, Julián, 1901-
Gorn, V. L., 133
Gorodetskii, Sergei, "Krasnyi Piter," 133
Gosudarstvennyi duma, 12, 77, 133
Gosudarstvennyi Rumiantsovskii muzei, 323
Got´e, IU. V., 1879-1943, 575
Gotz, Mikhail Rafailovich, 139
Goul, R. B., 133
Gould, Barney, 621
Government, see Russia [or other country name]--Politics and
    government
Government and business, 145
Government regulation of commerce, 53, 145
Graham, Gladys, 360
Graham, Malbone T., 650
Graham, Malbone Watson, 1898-1965, 360
Gramotin, Aleksandr Aleksandrovich, 39
Grant, Donald, 1889-   , 577
Graves, William Sidney, 1865-1940, 465, 474, 475, 516, 537
Graves--France, 239
Graveyards--France, 239
Grayson, Walter A., 476
Great Britain. See also headings beginning with British
Great Britain--Foreign relations--Russia, 346
Great Britain, Russians in, 672.
"The Great Dilemma," 245
Green, Joseph Coy, 1887-   , 578
Grigorovich, N. I.--Photograph, 12
Grimm, David Davidovich, 1864-   , 641
Gronskii, Pavel Pavlovich, 1883-1937, 188
Group of Assistance to the R.S.-D.R.P., 133
Group of English Speaking Communists, 261
Gruppa sodeistviia R.S.D.R.P., 133
Gruziia, see Georgia (Transcaucasia)
Gubarev, P. D., 361
Guchkov, Aleksandr Ivanovich, 133; Photograph, 12

Gudelis, Petras, 362
Guins, George C., 1887-   , 477
Gul', R. B., 133
Gulf of Riga, 236
Gulyga, Ivan Emel'ianovich, 1857-   , 189
Gurevich, Grigorii Evseevich, 133
Gurko, Vladimir Iosifovich, 1862-1927, 40
Gzel', A. A., 133

The Hague. International Peace Conference, 1899, 41
The Hague. International Peace Conference, 2d, 1907, 41
Hague International Peace Conference--Photographs, 1899-1907, 41
The Hague. Tribunal Arbitral, 1912, see Tribunal Arbitral, The
    Hague, 1912
Haimson, Leopold H., 145
Halbrook, Stephen P., 262
Hall, Charles L., 579
Halonen, George, 263
Hamilton, Albert H., 580
Hamilton, Minard, 1891-1976, 580
Hammon, W. P., 1854-1938, 478
Hand stamps, 133
Harbin Committee of Aid to Russian Refugees, see Kharbinskii komitet
    pomoshchi russkim bezhentsam
Harff, Wilhelm, Graf von Mirbach-, 1871-1918, 436
Harper and Row, publishers, 404
Harris, Ernest Lloyd, 1870-1946, 95, 479
Harris, Gladys, collector, 480
Hart, H. M., 575
Harvey, Peter A., see Garvi, Peter A., 1881-1944
Hastings, William H., 590
Hatch, John Davis, 597
Hazelton, A. W., 497
Health care, 617
Heiden, Dimitri F., Graf, 363
Helphand, Alexander, 1867-1924, 190
Henderson, Loy Wesley, 1892-   , 581
"Herbert Hoover and American Relief: A Study of the Relationship
    Between Hoover's American Relief Program and Bolshevism in
    Europe in 1919," 608
"Herbert Hoover and the Russian Prisoners of World War I," 622
Hermogen, episkop, 133
Heroys, Alexandre, 191
Heroys, Boris Vladimirovich, 364
Herron, George Davis, 1862-1925, 192
Hertmanowicz, Joseph John, 642
Hertzen, Aleksandr Ivanovich, 1812-1870, 32, 133
Herzen, Aleksandr Ivanovich, 1812-1870, 32, 133
Hesse--Foreign relations--Russia, 81
Hewes, Gordon W., 633
Hill, George Alexander, 1892-   , 365
Hilton, Ronald, 1911-   , 582
His Majesty's 1st Rifle Household Troops Regiment, 406
"The Historical Conditioning of Political Thought in Russia," 10

"Historical Investigation of the Church-State Conflict Caused by the Philosophy of Communism in Russia, 1917-1919," 276
Historiography, 15
"Historische Voraussetzungen des politischen Denkens in Russland," 10
History of Russia, see Russia--History
History, Political, 88, 295
Hitoon, Serge E., 542
Holden, Frank Harvey, 583
Holmsen, I. A., 332, 375, 418, 419
Hoover, Herbert Clark, 1874-1964, 8, 552, 557, 562, 570, 576, 578, 582, 584, 608, 617, 622, 626
Hoover Institution on War, Revolution and Peace, 620; Conference on One Hundred Years of Revolutionary Internationals, see One Hundred Years of Revolutionary Internationals, Conference; Russian Provisional Government Project, 264; Soviet Treaty Series Project, 265; Supreme Economic Council and American Relief Administration Documents Project, 585
Hoover, John Elwood, 1924-   , 266
"Hoover's Aid to Poland," 626
Horan, Brien Purcell, 42
Horvath, Dmitrii Leonidovich, see Khorvat, Dmitrii Leonidovich, 1858-1937.
Hoskin, Harry L., 1887-   , 481
Hoskins, Emmett A., 482
House Commission of Inquiry, see Paris. Peace Conference, 1919. U.S. Division of Territorial, Economic and Political Intelligence
House of Preliminary Detention, St. Petersburg, 133
"How We Lost Our Liberty," 446
Hulse, James W., 267
Hungary--History--Revolution, 1918-1919, 592
Hungary, Russians in, 87
Husbandry, see Agriculture
Huston, Jay Calvin, 268

I. I. D., 434
IAkutsk--History, 494
IAremenko, A. N., 483
Icons, 117
"The Icy March," 512
Ignat'ev, Graf, 133
Ikons, 117
Ilin, I. S., collector, 643
Iliodor, hieromonach, 2, 133
Immigrants, 92, 112, 667
Immigration, 92, 112, 667
Imperial Gendarme Office, 133
Imperial Russian Kirasir Household Troops Regiment, 14
Imperial Russian Household Troops Regiment of Her Majesty Mariia Fedorovna, 166, 400
Imports--Estonia, 414; Germany, 79, 80
"Imprisonment in Siberia," 182
"In the Service of the United States Navy, May 26, 1917-August 6, 1919," 482

"Incident in the Crimea," 435
Indochina, French--World War, 199-1945, 347
Industrial unions, see Trade-unions
Industries, see Russia [or other country name]--Industries
Industry and state, 145
Infantry, 179. See also Russia. Armiia. 5. pekhotnaia diviziia
"Infantry," 179
Ingerman, S. M., 133
The Inquiry (organization), see Paris. Peace Conference, 1919.
    U.S. Division of Territorial, Economic and Political
    Intelligence
Institutions, associations, etc.--Bookplates and stamps, 133
Insurrections, see Revolutions
Intellectual freedom, 133
Intelligence, Military, 365
Intelligence service, 139. See also Secret service
Inter-Allied Railway Commission for the Supervision of the Siberian
    and Chinese Eastern Railways, 1919-1922, 501, 527
Interdependence of nations, see Russia [or other country name]--
    Foreign relations; International relations
Internal line, 133
International, Third, see Communist International
International agreements, 180, 265, 415
International Anticommunist Entente, 385
International arbitration, 155
International Council of Women, 88
International Institute of Social History, 145
International Military Police, 12
International Peace Conference, The Hague, 1899, 41
International Peace Conference, 2d, The Hague, 1907, 41
International politics, 88, 295
International relations, 295. See also Russia [or other country
    name]--Foreign relations
International relief, see Russia--History--Revolution, 1917-1921--
    Civilian relief; World war, 1914-1918--Civilian relief
International Socialist Conference, Stockholm, 1917, 133, 297
International trade--Estonia, 414; Germany, 79, 80
Intervention by foreign powers in the Civil War, see Russia--
    History--Allied intervention, 1918-1920
Ipat´ev, Vladimir Nikolaevich, 1867-1952, 12, 49
Ipatieff, Vladimir Nikolaevich, 1867-1952, 12, 49
Iran--Relations (military) with Russia, 203
Irbe Strait, 236
Irina Aleksandrovna, Princess, 12
Irkutsk, 479, 529
Isabey, Jean Baptiste, 1767-1855, 25
Isakow, Sophie, 363, 386
Iskra, 133
Ispolnitel´naia komissiia soveshchaniia chlenov Uchreditel´nogo
    sobraniia, 133
Istoricheskaia komissiia Markovskogo artilleriiskogo diviziona, 366
"Istoricheskii obzor Kitaiskoi vostochnoi zhelieznoi dorogi,
    1896-1923 g.g.," 503
"Istoriia Markovskoi artilleriiskoi brigady," 366

"Istoriia moei bor´by s bol´shevikami," 519
"Istoriia ukrains´koi kooperatsii: korotkyi populiarnyi vyklad," 96
IUdelevskii, I. L., 133
IUdenich, Nikolai Nikolaevich, 1862-1933, 203, 364, 367, 407
IUnakov, N. L., 368
IUr´evskii, E., see Vol´skii, Nikolai Vladislavovich, 1879-1964
IUsupov, Feliks Feliksovich, Kniaz´, 12, 300
Ivanov, Sergei Andr., 133
Ivanov, Vsevolod Nikanorovich, 484
Ivanov-Razumnik, R., "Po tiur´mam na rodine," ms., 133
Ivanovich, St. (Portugeisia, S. O.), 133
"Iz utsielievshikh vospominanii," 67
"Iz vospominanii voennago iurista," 160
"Iz vospominanii zalozhnika v Piatigorskom kontsentratsionnom lagere," 353
"Iz vozzvaniia k karel´skomu naselneniiu Kemskogo uezda" (From the appeal to the Karelian populace of the Kemsk region), 369
Izhevsk--History, 352, 446
Iziumov, Aleksandr Filaretovich, 321
Izvestiia revoliutsionnoi nedeli (News of the revolutionary week), 269

Jacobs, John F. de, 586
Jacun, Konrad, 7
Jails, 127, 289
Jałowiecki, Mieczysław, 1886-   , 43
James, IA. M., 133
Janin, Pierre Thiébaut Charles Maurice, 1862-   , 485, 488
Japan--Foreign relations--Russia, 12, 165; History--Meiji period, 1868-1912--Pictorial works, 168; Military attachés, Russian, 164; Politics and government--20th century, 164; Relations (military) with Russia, 164
Japanese intervention in Maritime Province, Siberia, see Russia--History--Allied intervention, 1918-1920--Japanese intervention
Japanese intervention in Siberia, see Russia--History--Allied intervention, 1918-1920--Japanese intervention
"Japan´s Conquest of Manchuria and Jehol," 653
Jelacić, S. A., see Elachich, S. A.
Jennison, Harry A., 370
Jenny, Arnold E., 1895-1978, 587
Jewish Joint Distribution Committee, American, 617
Jews, 2, 53, 133, 139. See also Antisemitism
Jews in Germany, 53
Johnson, Benjamin O., 1878-   , 486
Johnson, Margaret C., 487
Johnson, William H., 487
Jones, Jefferson, collector, 159
Jones, Joseph, 577
"Joniskelio Apskrities Partizanai," 362
Joniskelis, Lithuania--History, 362
Jordan, David Starr, 1851-1931, 8, 270
Jordan, Jessie Knight, 270
Journalists, American--Correspondence, reminiscences, etc., 287
Jurists, 143

KGB, 51
"K studenchestvu: zadachi revoliutsionnoi molodezhi," 279
Kabet, M. E., 133
Kader, Boris M., collector, 127
Kadet Party, see Konstitutsionno-demokraticheskaia partiia
Kaigorodov, Aleksandr Petrovich, 549
"Kaigorodovshchina," 549
"Kak my poteriali svobodu," 446
Kaledin, Aleksei Maksimovich, 1861-1918, 328
"Kaledinskie miatezhi," 328
Kalnins, Eduards, 1876-1964, 371
Kama River, Siberia, 539
Kamchatskaia oblast'--History, 494
Kamermakher, M. 133
"Kampen om Sta\`sskicket i Finland 1918," 424
Kapnist, Lieutenant, 488
Kappel', Vladimir Oskarovich, 1881-1920, 14, 453
Karcz, George F., 1917-1970, 44
Karelia, 360; Economic conditions, 263; History, 263, 293, 369
Karelian Workers' Commune, 263
Karel'skaia trudovaia kommuna, 263
Karmilof, Olga, 1897-   , 644
Karpova, Olga, 236
Karpovich, Michael, 1888-1959, 273
Kartsev, 133
Kaspiiskaia flotiliia, 447
Kastchenko, Marie, 1902-   , 645
Katowice, Poland. Geische Spolka Akcyjna Company, 478
Kats, M., 133
Katz, M., 133
Kaul'bars, Aleksandr Vasil'evich, 1884-   , 193
Kautsky, Karl Johann, 1854-1938, 128
Kautsky, Karl, Jr., 128
Kavkazskaia armiia, see Russia. Armiia. Kavkazskaia armiia
Kayden, Eugene M., 271
Kazachestvo, see Cossacks
Kazan Cathedral, 119
Kazan demonstration, St. Petersburg, Dec. 6, 1876, 133
Kazanskii sobor, 119
"Kazanskii sobor 1811-1911, v Sanktpeterburge," 119
Kearny (army camp), California, 595
Kefali, M., 133
Kellock, Harold, 1879-   , 272
Kemsk region, 369
Kerenskii, Aleksandr Fedorovich, 1881-1970, 123, 139, 264, 273, 607
Keskűla, Aleksander, 1882-1963, 129
Kharbinskii komitet pomoshchi russkim bezhentsam, 646
Khodasevich, V. F., 133
Khomiakov, Aleksei Stepanovich, 1804-1860, 32
Khor River incident, 551
Khorvat, Dmitrii Leonidovich, 1858-1937, 489, 493
Khoshev, Boris Aleksandrovich, 1898-   , 372
Khoshev, Nina, 372

Khrabroff, Nicholas, 1869-1940, 490
"Khronologiia sobytii vo vremia grazhdanskoi voiny v Rossii," 344
Kiev--History, 588; Pictorial works, 12, 37
King, Gertrude, 194
Kings and rulers, 672. See also Russia--Court and courtiers
Kirasir Household Troops Regiment of Her Majesty Mariia Fedorovna, 166, 400
Kirasirskii Ego Velichestva polk, 14
Kireevskii, Ivan Vasil'evich, 1806-1856, 32
Kitaiskaia vostochnaia zheleznaia doroga, see Chinese Eastern Railway
Kititsyn, Captain, 491
Klemm, V., 1861-   , 373
Klimas, Petras, 1891-1969, 45
Klimov (pseud. of I. L. Erenburg), 133
Kniazev, N. N., 543
Kocoj, Henryk, 46
Kogan, S. M., see Semenov, Evgenii Petrovich, 1861-
Kokovtsov, Vladimir Nikolaevich, 1853-1942, 12, 47
Kolchak, Aleksandr Vasil'evich, 1873-1920, 89, 460, 462, 470, 492, 509, 523, 529
Kolchak Government, see Russia (1917-1922. Civil War governments). Vremennoe rossiiskoe pravitel'stvo (Kolchak)
Kollontai, Aleksandra Mikhailovna, 1872-1952, 139
Kolobov, Mikhail Viktorovich, 493
Kologrivov, Constantine Nikolaevich, 195
Kolupaev, Eugenia Ritter, 588
Kolupaev, Stephen G., 588
Kolyshko-Baian, I. I., 133
Komintern, see Communist International
Komissiia po obsledovaniiu obstoiatel'stv sobytii 4-6 aprelia vo Vladvostoke, see Maritime Province, Siberia. Komissiia po obsledovaniiu obstoiatel'stv sobytii 4-6 aprelia vo Vladivostoke
Komitet gosudarstvennoi bezopastnosti, 51
Komitet intellektual'noi pomoshchi politicheskim syl'nym i zakliuchennym, 133
Komitet pomoshchi politicheskim zakliuchennym, Geneva, 133
Kommunisticheskaia partiia Sovetskogo soiuza, see under Rossiiskaia sotsial-demokraticheskaia rabochaia partiia
Kommunisticheskaia partiia Ukrainy, 241
"Kommuny," 468
Komor, Paul, 647
Komunistychna partiia Ukrainy, 241
"Konets Kaspiiskoi flotilii vremeni grazhdanskoi voiny pod komandoi Generala Denikina," 447
Konokovich, General, 196
Konstantin Nikolaevich, Grand Duke of Russia, 1827-1892, 48
"Konstantinopol'skii pokhod: iz vospominanii o Gallipoli," 450
Konstantinov, P. F., 49
Konstitutsionno-demokraticheskaia partiia, 378, 648
Kontrabandisty (play), 133
Konvoi Ego Imperatorskogo Velichestva Gosudaria Imperatora Nikolaia II-go, 390

Kornilov, Lavr Georgievich, 1870-1918, 133, 170, 274
Kornilovskii polk, see Russia (1917-1922. Civil War governments).
    Dobrovol´cheskaia armiia. Kornilovskii polk
Korol´kov, M., 160
Korvin-Kroukovsky, Eugénie A., 374
Kościuszko Squadron, 430
Kosinskii, Vladimir Andreevich, 1866-1938, 50
Koslov (City), 288
Kossiakovskaia, Aleksandra Vladimirovna, 88
Koulomzin, Sophie, 61
Koussonskii, Pavel Alekseevich, 375
Kovalevskaia, Sof´ia, 133
Krajowa Agencja Wydawnicza, 275
Krasin, Leonid Borisovich, 139
Krasnaia armiia, see Russia (1917-   R.S.F.S.R.). Armiia
Krasnov, Petr Nikolaevich, 1869-1947, 376, 383
Krasnov, Vladislav Georgievich, see Krasnow, Wladislaw Georgievich,
    1937-
Krasnow, Wladislaw Georgievich, 1937-   , 51
Krassin, Leonid Borisovich, 139
Krassovskii, Vitol´d, 377
"Kratkaia istoriia smieny pravitel´stv vo Vladivostokie s 31 ianvaria
    1920 g. do evakuatsii oktiabria 1922 g.," 458
"Kratkaia spravka o russkom kazachestve," 336
"Kratkii otchet o dieiatel´nosti Voennago ministerstva za 1916 god,"
    223
Kravchinskii, Sergei Mikhailovich, 1852-1895, 130
Kremlin, Moscow--Pictorial works, 117
Kremnev, Nikolai, pseud., see Kutukov, Leonid Nikolaevich, 1897-
Krepost´ Ross, 76
Kriukov, Boris Aleksandrovich, 1898-   , 494
Krivoshein, Aleksandr Vasil´evich--Photograph, 12
"Krizis partii" (Party crisis), 131
Kronshtadt Rebellion, 1921, 133
Kronstadt Rebellion, 1921, 133
Kropotkin, Petr Alekseevich, Kniaz´, 1842-1921, 133, 139
Krotkov family, 108
Kroukovsky, Eugénie A. Korvin-, see Korvin-Kroukovsky, Eugénie A.
"Krovavye dni na Amure," 533
Krupenskii, Aleksandr Nikolaevich, 197
Krupskaia, Nadezhda Konstantinovna, 1869-1939, 139
Krymskoe kraevoe pravitel´stvo, 378
Krzeczunowicz, Kornel, 379
Kseniia Aleksandrovna, Grand Duchess of Russia, 52, 107
Kuban cossacks, see Cossacks
Kuban (District)--Economic conditions, 254
Kuban (Province)--History, 113, 353, 567
Kubansko-terskii plastunskii korpus, 189. See also Cossacks
Kubanskoe kazach´e voisko, 347. See also Cossacks
Kuharets, Valery, 203
Kuhn, Sylvester E., 495
Kulaev, Antonina Alexandrovna Maximova-, see Maximova-Kulaev,
    Antonina Alexandrovna
Kurgan (Settlement), 196

Kurguz, Peter Nicholas, 276, 439
Kuskova, Ekaterina Dmitrievna, 1869-   , 133, 652
Kutepov, Aleksandr Pavlovich, 1882-1930, 133, 665, 669
Kutukov, Leonid Nikolaevich, 1897-   , 380
Kutuzov, Mikhail Illarionovich, Svetleishii kniaz´ smolenskii, 1745-1813, 66
Kutzevalov, Boniface Semenovich, 381
Kwiatkowski, Antoni Wincenty, 1890-1970, 277

Labor and laboring classes, 37, 126, 145, 246, 313, 327; United States, 281
Labor, Compulsory, 133, 249
Labor, Forced, 133, 249
Labor unions, see Trade-unions
Lager Altengrabow, Germany, 198
Lampe, Aleksei Aleksandrovich von, 1885-1960, 382
Land question, 50, 145
Land tenure, 50, 145
Landesen, Arthur C., 649
Lansing, Robert, 1864-1928, 199
Lapteff, Alexis V., 589
Larsons, M. J., pseud., see Laserson, Maurice, 1880-
Laserson, Maurice, 1880-   , 53
Lastours, G. de, 303
Latin America, Slavs in, 92
Latvia--Communism, 133; Diplomatic and consular service, 517; History, 133; History--1918-1940, 371, 402, 517; Revolutionists, 139; World War, 1914-1918, 601
Latvian Communist Party, 133
Latvian intervention in Siberia, see Russia--History--Allied intervention, 1918-1920--Latvian intervention
Latvijas Komunistiska Partija, 133
Lavrent´ev, K. I., 544
Lavrov, P. L., 133
Lavrov, Sergei, 545
Lavrova, Nadezhda L. Shapiro-, see Shapiro-Lavrova, Nadezhda L.
Law, Industrial, 145
Law enforcement offficers, see Police
Lawrence, Eva, 590
Lawyers, 143
Lazarev, Mikhail Petrovich, 1788-1851, 156
"Lazarev of Mirny: Russia´s Greatest Admiral," 156
Lazarevich, I. I., 133
League of Nations, 607
Left SRs, 436. See also Partiia sotsialistov-revoliutsionerov
Left Socialist Revolutionary Party, 436. See also Partiia sotsialistov-revoliutsionerov
Legal profession, 143
"Legality versus Autocracy," 355
Legations, see Diplomatic and consular service
"The Legendary Baron," 543
LeGendre, William C., 200
Légion étrangère, France, 347
Legiony Polskie, 206

Leib-gvardii egerskii polk, 637
Leib-gvardii finliandskii polk, 639
Leib-gvardii kirasirskii Ego Velichestva polk, 14
Leib-gvardii kirasirskii Eia Velichestva polk, 166, 400
Leib-gvardii moskovskii polk, 380
Leib-gvardii 1. strelkovyi Ego Velichestva polk, 406
Leib-gvardii ulanskii Ego Velichestva polk, 396. See also Russia. Armiia. Kavaleriia
"Leib gvardii ulanskii Ego Velichestva polk v velikuiu grazhdanskuiu voinu," 396
Leikhtenberg, Nikolai Nikolaevich, Gertsog fon, 383
Leipzig, Russian Consulate in, 80
Leiteizen, G. D., 133
Leman, Rudolf, 1897-   , 278
Lemberg, see Lvov
Lenin, Vladimir Il'ich, 1870-1924, 2, 129, 139, 145, 262, 279, 314; and German money, 133, 190, 227
Leningrad, see Saint Petersburg
Leninism, see Communism
L'Escaille, Mademoiselle de, 54
Letopis' revoliutsii (Berlin), 133
"Letters Captured from Baron Ungern in Mongolia," 550
Leuchtenberg, Nikolai Nikolaevich, Herzog von, see Leikhtenberg, Nikolai Nikolaevich, Gertsog fon
Levental', N., 133
Leventhal, N., 133
Levi, Paul, 1883-1930, 298
Levitsky, Eugene L., 384
Lewis, Roger L., d. 1936, 591
Libraries--Bookplates and stamps, 133
Library of Congress, 199
Liebknecht, Karl Paul August Friedrich, 1871-1919, 53
Liibke, Helena, 208
"Likvidatsiia likholiet'ia," 248
Limitation of armament, 88
Lincoln, Robert T., 14
Lindov, G. D., 133
Literature and communism, 312
Literature--Censorship, 133
Literature, Russian, see Russian literature
Literaturnyi fond. Damskii komitet, 133
Litfond, 133
Lithuania--Agriculture, 43; History, 43, 45; History--German occupation, 1915-1918, 240; 1918-1945, 362; Nationalism, 642, 650; Revolutionists, 139; Views, 43
Lithuanian National Council in America, 650
Little, William Henry, 1937-   , 55
Litvinov, Maksim Maksimovich, 1876-1951, 139, 617
Liubimov, Dmitrii Nikolaevich, 1864-   , 56
Livermore, Edith, 57
Livingstead, Ivor M. V. Z., 58
Local administration, 494
Local government, 494
Lodygensky, Georges, 385

Loehr, Mrs., collector, 280
Longuevan, Joseph B., collector, 496
Lonjumeau, France. School of Higher Social Sciences (RSDRP), 2, 133
Lopukhov, V., see Muraveiskii, S.
Lorenz, Mrs. Otto, 41
Loucheur, Louis, 1872-1931, 201
Lovestone, Jay, 1898-   , 281
Luch Azii (periodical), Harbin, 543
Lucy, pseud., 139
Ludinkhausen-Wolff, Sergei Evgen'evich, Baron, 203
Lukomskii, Aleksandr Sergeevich, d. 1939, 386
Lunacharskii, Anatolii Vasil'evich, 1875-1933, 139
Lupolov, IA. M., 133
Lutheran Council, National, 617
Lutz, Ralph Haswell, 1886-1968, 554
L'vov. Biblioteka imeni Shevchenko, 133
L'vova, Mariia Vladimirovna, 108
Lwów, see L'vov
Lykes, Gibbes, 592
Lykes, William F. G., 592
Lyon, Bessie Eddy, 467, 593
Lyons, Marvin, collector, 34, 39, 121, 150, 195, 282, 383, 396

McCormick, Chauncey, 1884-1954, 594
McDonnell, Geoffrey, 497
McDuffee, Roy W., 283
McGinty, John, 600
MacKenzie, Natasha, 4
McLean, Katherine S., 595
Makarov, N., 284
Makhno, Nestor Ivanovich, 1889-1935, 387
Maklakov, Vasilii Alekseevich, 1870-1957, 139, 273, 285, 303, 652
Makowiecki, Zygmunt, 202
Maksimalist (Vladivostok), 133
Malamuth, Charles, 14
Malinovskii, Roman Vikentievich, 139, 140
Malyi teatr, 133
Manchuria--Description, 461; History, 484, 536, 598, 643, 653; Railroads, 527. See also Chinese Eastern Railway.
Manchuria--Social life and customs, 461
"Manchuria and Manchukuo," 484
Mandel'berg, V. E., 133
Mao Tse-tung, 1893-1976, 262
March Revolution, see Russia--History--March (February O.S.) Revolution, 1917
Margulies, M. S., "God interventsii," ms., 133
Mariia Feodorovna, Empress Consort of Alexander III, Emperor of Russia, 1847-1928, 52, 54, 59
Marine shipping, 414, 617
Maritime Province, Siberia--History, 456, 458, 476, 494; Japanese intervention in, see Russia--History--Allied intervention, 1918-1920--Japanese intervention
Maritime Province, Siberia. Komissiia po obsledovaniiu obstoiatel'stv sobytii 4-6 aprelia vo Vladivostoke, 498;

                    Vremennoe priamurskoe pravitel´stvo. Sibirskaia flotiliia,
          458, 494
Maritime Regional People´s Assembly, 12
Maritime shipping, 414, 617
Markov, Anatolii, 388
Markov, Sergei Leonidovich, 1878-1918, 366
Markov, Sergei Vladimirovich, 195
Markovskaia artilleriiskaia brigada, see under Istoricheskaia
     komissiia Markovskogo artilleriiskogo diviziona
Markovskii artilleriiskii divizion. Istoricheskaia komissiia, see
     Istoricheskaia komissiia Markovskogo artilleriiskogo diviziona
Martens, Ludwig Christian Alexander Karl, 1874-1948, 263, 286
Martov, IUlii Osipovich, 1873-1923, 133, 139, 389
Martynov, A. P., d. 1951, 60
Martynov, General, 651
Martynov, Zakhar Nikiforovich, 390
Marx, Karl, 133
Marxism, see Communism; Socialism
Masaryk, Tomás Garrigue, Pres., Czechoslovakia, 1850-1937, 499
Maslovskii, Evgenii Vasil´evich, 203
Mason, Frank Earl, 1893-1979, 287
Mason, Jack, 502
Masonic orders, 133
Masons (secret order), 133
Masquerade ball, St. Petersburg, 1903, 111, 119
"The Massacre of the Romanoffs," 34
Masury, George, 496
Materialism, Dialectical, 277. See also Socialism
Mathews, Sarah E., 1880-   , 561, 596
Matveev, General, 204
Matveev, Laura, 47
Maximova-Kulaev, Antonina Alexandrovna, 288
May, F. Curtis, 666
Mazour, Anatole Gregory, 1900-   , 273, 314
Mears, Eliot Grinnell, 445
Medals collection, ca. 1914-1974, 8
Medals, Military and naval, 8, 68
Medical care, 617
Medical care of veterans, 154
Medical profession, 288, 385, 425, 673
Medicine, 673
Meiendorf, Maria F., Baronessa, 1869-1972, 61
Meigs, Nadia, 4
Mel´gunov, Sergei Petrovich, 1897-1956, 110, 289
"Memoirs of a Russian Historian," 63
"Memorandum on Russian Affairs," 609
"A Memorandum on the Political Changes in Russia Since the
     Revolution," 271
"Memories of Russia, 1916-1919," 404
"Memuary ob otrechenii ot prestola rossiiskago Gosudaria Imperatora
     Nikolaia II," 103
Mendeleev Congress on Theoretical and Applied Chemistry,
     St. Petersburg, 1911, 12
Mendeleevskii s"ezd po obshchei i prikladnoi khimii, St. Petersburg,

175

1911, 12
Mennonite Central Committee, American, 617
Mennonites, 112
Men´shchikov, L. P., 133
Menshevik Party, see Rossiiskaia sotsial-demokraticheskaia rabochaia partiia
Meshcheriakov family, 108
Meyer, Henry Cord, 1913-   , 391
Michael, Grand Duke of Russia, 1878-1918, 69, 88
Michael, Louis Guy, 62
Middle East--World War, 1914-1918, see World War, 1914-1918--Campaigns--Turkey and the Near East
Mikhail Aleksandrovich, Grand Duke of Russia, 1878-1918, 69, 88
Miksys, Zibuntas, 1923-   , 45, 362
Milasius, Oskaras Vladislovas, 1877-1939, 45
Military aeronautics--China, 674
Military air pilots--Poland, 430
Military art and science, 295
Military attachés. See also Diplomatic and consular service; Diplomats
Military attachés, Russian--Denmark, 213; France, 153, 392; Japan, 164, Switzerland, 358; United States, 167; Yugoslavia, 332
Military aviation--China, 674
Military crimes, 160, 419
Military decorations, 8, 68
Military intelligence, 365
Military medals, 8, 68
Military offences, 160, 419
Military officers, see Russia. Armiia--Officers
Military Police, International, 12
Military power, 88, 295
Military relations, see Russia [or other country name]--Relations (military)
Military science, 295
Miliukov, Pavel Nikolaevich, 1859-1943, 12, 63, 133, 139, 227, 652
Miller, Evgenii Karlovich, 1867-1937, 133, 375, 392, 661, 665
Miller, Miriam, 583
Mineral lands, 478
Mines and mineral resources, 37, 478; Poland, 478; Siberia, 478. See also Coal; Gold mines and mining
Mining, 478
Ministers (diplomatic agents), see Diplomatic and consular service
Mir i trud (Berlin), 133
Mirbach-Harff, Wilhelm, Graf von, 1871-1918, 436
Miroliubov, Nikander Ivanovich, 1870-1927, 64
Miroshnikov, Lev Ivanovich, 65
Mirovicz, General, 205
Mirsky, N. Sviatopolk-, see Sviatopolk-Mirsky, N., collector
Mitchell, Anna V. S., 597
Mitkiewicz, Leon, 1896-1972, 393
Mohrenschildt, Dimitri Sergius von, see Von Mohrenschildt, Dimitri Sergius, 1902-
"Moi posliednie miesiatsy v dieistvuiushchei armii," 368
Moldavia--Politics and government, 70

Molotov, Viacheslav M., 12
Monarchs, 672. See also Russia--Court and courtiers
Monarkhicheskoe ob"edinenie Rossii, 669
Le Monde slave, 485
"Monetary Circulation and Currencies of the Russian Far East During the Revolution and Civil War," 511
Monetary question, 4, 5
Money, 4, 5
Money, Paper, 4, 5
Mongolia--Communism, 540, 546; Gold mines and mining, 14; History, 540-551
Moran, Hugh Anderson, 1881-   , 598
Moravskii, Valerian Ivanovich, 1884-1940, 500
Morocco, Russians in, 654
Morrow, C. H., 14
Moscow--Description, 461, 615; History, 294; Kreml´--Pictorial works, 117; Pictorial works, 2; Rumiantsovskii muzei, 323; Students´ societies, 45
Moscow Household Troops Regiment, 380
Moskovskii polk, 380
Moskovskii i Rumiantsovskii muzei, 323
Motion pictures, see Moving-pictures
Moving-pictures, 2, 12, 105, 137, 354
Mueller and Graeff photographic poster collection, ca. 1914-1945, 9
Mugan´, Azerbaijan, 345
Mukhanov, Mikhail Georgievich, 66
Muraveiskii, S., 132
Murav´eva, Ekaterina Ivanovna, 652
Murphy, Merle Farmer, 599
Murray, A. C., 501
Museum of Russian Culture, San Francisco, 60
Museums, 323
Mutiny--France, 256

NKVD, 365
"Na puti k krisizmu sotsial´nago rationalizma," 284
"Na sluzhbie v kitaiskoi armii," 676
"Nach der Feier," 202
Naczelny Komitet Narodowy, 206
"Nakaz bol´shogo i malago voiskovogo kruga Voiska terskago" (Order of the Large and Small Military Union of the Tersk Unit), 394
Nansen, Fritjof, 617
Narodnaia volia (partiia), 14, 133, 139
Narodno-trudovoi soiuz, 656
Narodnyi komissariat vnutrennikh del, 365
Narodovoltsy, 14, 133, 139
Nasha strana (Buenos Aires), 668
Natanson, M. A., 133
National consciousness, see Nationalism
National debts, 248
National Educational Television, 137
National Lutheran Council, 617
National planning, see Russia--Economic policy

National Polish Committee of America, 207
National Publishing Agency, Poland, see Krajowa Agencja Wydawnicza
Nationalism, 628, 634, 657; Finland, 35; Lithuania, 642, 650; Poland, 230, 238; Ukraine, 172
Natural science, 673
Naumov, Aleksandr Nikolaevich, 1868-1950, 67
Naval attachés, see Military attachés
Naval Conference, Washington, D.C., 1921-1922, 659
Naval history, 156. See also Russia. Morskoi flot; Russia. Voennyi flot
Naval operations during the Civil War, see Russia--History--Revolution, 1917-1921--Naval operations
Near East and Turkey--World War, 1914-1918, see World War, 1914-1918--Campaigns--Turkey and the Near East
Near East Relief, 617
Nechaev, S. G., 133
Nekrasov, Nikolai Vissarionovich, 290
Nekrasov, Vl. A., 133
Netherlands, see under Dutch travelers; The Hague
Nettlau, Max, 133
Neue Volks-Zeitung (New York), 133
New York. Amtorg Trading Corporation, 478; Finnish Information Bureau, 263, 272
New York Group of Assistance to the Russian Social-Democrat Workers' Party, 133
Newspaper Enterprise Association, 502
Newspapers, Russian, 14, 240
Nicholas I, Emperor of Russia, 1796-1855, 68
Nicholas II, Emperor of Russia, 1868-1918, 2, 12, 24, 27, 52, 57, 64, 69, 78, 95, 98, 102, 103, 105, 118, 121, 537, 596
Nicolaevsky, Boris I., 1887-1966, 133
Nicolai, Nathalie, 456
Nieroth, Theodore M., see Nirod, Feodor Maksimilianovich, Graf, 1871-
Nikolaev, Aleksandr Mikhailovich, see Nikolaieff, Alexander Mikhailovitch, 1876-
Nikolaevskii, Boris Ivanovich, see Nicolaevsky, Boris I., 1887-1966
Nikolai Nikolaevich, Grand Duke of Russia, 1856-1929, 66
Nikolaieff, Alexander Mikhailovitch, 1876-   , 653
Nikol'skii, Evgenii Aleksandrovich, 161
Nilus, Eugene Christian, see Nilus, Evgenii Khristianovich, 1880-
Nilus, Evgenii Khristianovich, 1880-   , 503
Nirod, Feodor Maksimilianovich, Graf, 1871-   , 395
N'iu-Iorkskaia gruppa sodeistviia R.S.-D.R.P., 133
Nobility, see Russia--Nobility
North America--Colonies, 14, 575
Northern Russia--History, 338
Northwest Russia, 364, 367, 407, 440
Northwestern government, see Russia (1917-1922. Civil War governments). Severo-zapadnoe pravitel'stvo
Nosovich, Anatolii, 396
Novaia russkaia kniga (Berlin), 133
Novaia zhizn' (New life) (1917-1918) Leningrad, 291
November Revolution, see Russia--History--November (October O.S.) Revolution, 1917

Nowak, Jan, 397
Nuorteva, Santeri, 263, 286
Nursing, 234

OGPU, 289
Ob"edinenie russkikh v Marokko, 654
Ob"edinennoe gosudarstvennoe politicheskoe upravlenie, 289
Oberstes polnisches National-Komitee, see Naczelny Komitet Narodowy
Oberuchev, K. M., 133
Oblastnoi komitet armii, flota i rabochikh Finliandii, 292
Obolenskii family, 106
"Oborona Mugani, 1918-1919: zapiski kavkazskago pogranichnika," 345
"Oborona revoliutsii i sotsial-demokratiia," 389
O'Brien, Charles A., 600
Obshchestva formirovaniia boevykh otriadov, 398
Obshchestva ob"edineniia i vzaimopomoshchi russkikh ofitserov
    i dobrovol´tsev, 399
Obshchestvo pomoshchi politicheskim zakliuchennym v sovetskoi Rossii,
    133
Obshchestvo russkikh veteranov Velikoi voiny. Vestnik, 512
Obukhova, V. S. (Zhitlovskaia, V. S.), 133
Ocean transporation, 414, 617
"Ocherk revoliutsionnykh sobytii v russkoi srednei Azii," 373
Ocherki po istorii revoliutsionnogo dvizheniia v srednei Azii, 132
Ochrana, see Russia. Departament politsii; Russia. Okhrannye
    otdeleniia
Ochrana collection, see Russia. Departament politsii. Zagranichnaia
    agentura, Paris
October Revolution, see Russia--History--November (October O.S.)
    Revolution, 1917
Odessa, 606; History--Posters, 11; Strelnikovskii trial, 142
Odintsov, Gleb Nikolaevich, 400
"Odyssey from Russia," 667
Offenses, Military, 160, 419
Officers, Military, see Russia. Armiia--Officers
Officials and employees, 104, 113, 120
Ogólny Zydowski Zwiazek Robotniczy "Bund" na Litwie, w Polsce i w
    Rosji, 133, 139
Oiderman, M., 401
Oil, see Petroleum
Oil-painting, 313, 325
Okhrana, see Russia. Departament politsii; Russia. Okhrannye
    otdeleniia
Okhrana collection, see Russia. Departament politsii. Zagranichnaia
    agentura, Paris
Olga Aleksandrovna, Grand Duchess of Russia, 1882-1960, 107, 400
"Olonetskaia Kareliia," 293
Omsk government, see Russia (1917-1922. Civil War governments).
    Vremennoe sibirskoe pravitel´stvo
Omsk government (Kolchak), see Russia (1917-1922. Civil War
    governments). Vremennoe rossiiskoe pravitel´stvo (Kolchak)
One Hundred Years of Revolutionary Internationals,
    Conference, Hoover Institution on War, Revolution

and Peace, Stanford University, 1964, 134
"Only My Memories," 660
"Opisanie boia 15 iulia 1916 goda pri der. Trysten, kol. Kurgan i der. Voronchin," 196
Orbison, Thomas James, 1866-1938, 601
Orekhov, V. V., 628, 634, 657
Orenburg--History, 579
Orenburg cossacks, see Cossacks; Russia (1917-1922. Civil War governments). Armiia. 2. Orenburgskii kazachii polk
"Organization of American Relief in Europe, 1918-1919," 554
Organizations--Bookplates and stamps, 133
Orientalism, 65
"The Origins of Bolshevism in Russian Central Asia," 136
Orlov, N. A., 133
Ornatskii, see Chicherin, Georgii Vasil´evich, 1872-1936
Orthodox Eastern Church, Russian, 19, 31, 88, 116, 119, 133, 421; United States, 671. See also Russkaia pravoslavnaia tserkov´ zagranitsei
Orton, Mrs. W. R., 475
"Ostatnia kampania konna," 379
Ostroukhov, P., collector, 504
Otorchi, Ulan, 546
Ouperoff, V. V., see Uperov, Vasilii Vasil´evich, 1877-1932
Out of My Past, 47
Ovcharenko, I. N., 133
Ovchinnikov, Anton Zakharovich, 505
Ozels, Oskars, 1889-1975, 402
"Ozero Tolbo: vospominaniia o nachalnom periode mongol´skoi revoliutsii," 546
Ozonation, 86
Ozonization, 86

Pacifism, 88, 411
Paderewski, Ignacy Jan, 1860-1941, 208
Painting, 313, 325
Paleologue, Sergei Nikolaevich, 1887-   , 403
Paley, Olga Valerianovna, 1865-   , 404
Palitsyn, Fedor Fedorovich, 1851-1923, 405
Panteleev, Dimitri, 515
Pantiukhov, Oleg Ivanovich, 1882-1974, 406
Pantuhoff, Oleg, Jr., 406
Paper money, 4, 5
Pares, Sir Bernard, 1867-1949, 506
Paris. Congress, 1856, 70; Peace Conference, 1919, 102, 178, 192, 197, 199, 208, 303; Peace Conference, 1919. Commission on Baltic Affairs, 209; Peace Conference, 1919. U.S. Division of Territorial, Economic and Political Intelligence, 210; School of Higher Social Sciences (RSDRP), 2, 133; Social Democrat Library, 133
Parizhskaia sotsial-demokraticheskaia biblioteka, 133
Parizhskii vestnik, 380
Parties, Political, 133, 139
Partiia eserov-maksimalistov. Zagranichnaia delegatsiia, see Partiia sotsialistov-revoliutsionerov

Partiia levykh sotsialistov-revoliutsionerov (Internationalistov), 436. See also Partiia sotsialistov-revoliutsionerov
Partiia narodnoi voli, 14, 133, 139
Partiia sotsialistov-revolutsionerov, 14, 123, 133, 135, 139, 141, 142, 340. See also Partiia levykh sotsialistov-revoliutsionerov (Internatsionalistov)
Partridge, Stanley N., 507
Parvus, see Helphand, Alexander, 1867-1924
Pash, Boris T., 407
Patouillet, Madame, 294
Patrick, "Lucy," 139
Paulin, Anatolii Nikolaevich Rozenshil´d-, see Rozenshil´d-Paulin, Anatolii Nikolaevich
Pavlonskii, GPU agent, 133
Pavlovskoe voennoe uchilishche, 334
Peace and Labor (Berlin), 133
Peace Conference, The Hague, 1899, 41
Peace Conference, 2d, The Hague, 1907, 41
Peace Conference, Paris, 1919, see Paris. Peace Conference, 1919
Peace movements, 88, 411
Peasantry, 145
Peasants, 145
Pechal´nye stranitsy russkoi revoliutsii, 387
Pedagogy, 565, 636
Penal institutions, 127, 289
Peresylnaia tiurma, 127
Periodicals, Russian, 634
Pershin, Dimitrii Petrovich, 547
Persia, see Iran
Personal health services, 617
Pertsov, Konstantin A., see Pertzoff, Constantin A.
Pertsov, V. A., 508
Pertzoff, Constantin A., 1899-   , 509
Pertzoff, V. A., see Pertsov, V. A.
1-aia zabaikal´skaia kazach´ia diviziia v velikoi evropeiskoi voine 1914-1918 g., 228
Peter I, the Great, Emperor of Russia, 1672-1725, 90
Peter and Paul Fortress, 12
Peterburgskaia gruppa russkikh sotsial-demokratov (Blagoevtsy), 133
Petrograd, see Saint Petersburg
Petrograd Children´s Colony, 559, 561
Petrograd Lancers, 224. See also Russia. Armiia. Kavaleriia
"Petrograd Lancers in Service to their Country," 224
Petrogradskaia detskaia koloniia, 559, 561
Petroleum, 448
Petroleum industry and trade--Baku, 412
Petropavlovskaia krepost´, 12
Petrov, Arkadii Nikolaevich, 510
Petrushevich, Ivan, 1875-1950, 408
Philipp, Werner, 10
Philosophy, 673
Physicians--Correspondence, reminiscences, etc., 288, 385, 425
Piatigorsk concentration camp, 353
Pickett, Carrie, 602

Picture postcards, see Postal cards
Pierce, Richard A., 136
"Pieredzejumi Riga Bermonta Dienas," 402
Pilots, Military (Aeronautics)--Poland, 430
Pirnie, Malcolm, 603
"Pisateliu Solzhenitsynu ot immigranta staroi revoliutsii," 664
Planning, Economic, see Russia--Economic policy
Planting, see Agriculture
Platonov, Valerian Platonovich, 1809?-   , 71
Plehve, Viacheslav Konstantinovich, 12, 47
Plekhanov, Georgii Valentinovich, 1856-1918, 12, 133, 139
Pleve, Viacheslav Konstantinovich, 12, 47
Plevitskaia, N., 133
Podtiagin, M. P. collection, see Russia. Voennyi agent (Japan)
Podvoiskii, Nikolai, 12
Pogodin, Mikhail Petrovich, 1800-1875, 32
Pogrebetskii, Aleksandr I., 511
Poland--Air pilots, Military, 430
Poland. Ambasada (U.S.), 409
Poland--Boundaries, 102, 409, 434; Economic conditions, 71, 594, 604; Foreign relations--1918-1945, 409; Foreign relations--Russia, 434
Poland, Georgians in, 426
Poland--History--Posters, 11; History--Revolution, 1830-1832, 46; History--Revolution, 1863-1864, 71; History--20th century, 212, 393, 397; History--German occupation, 1914-1918, 238; History--1918-1945, 208, 576; History--Wars of 1918-1921, 215, 341, 379, 409, 430, 574; History--Wars of 1918-1921--Armistices, 415; Independence movements--Posters, 11
Poland. Krajowa Agencja Wydawnicza, see Krajowa Agencja Wydawnicza
Poland--Mines and mineral resources, 478. See also Coal--Galicia
Poland. National Publishing Agency, see Krajowa Agencja Wydawnicza
Poland--Nationalism, 230, 238; Politics and government--1796-1918, 71, 72; Politics and government--1918-1945, 409, 594
Poland. Polskie Siły Powietrzne. 7. Kościuszko Squadron, 430
Poland--Posters, 275; Religion, 71; Revolutionists, 139; Social conditions, 604; Treaties, etc. Russia, Oct. 11, 1920, 415; Ukrainians in, 645; Views, 43
Poland. Wojsko Polskie--Cavalry, 379
Poland--World War, 1914-1918, 206, 207, 215, 238, 594, 604, 626; World War, 1914-1918--Territorial questions, 225
"Poland's Treason," 215
Poles in foreign countries, 397; in Lithuania, 43
Poletika, W. P. von, 211
Police, 85. See also Secret service
Police, International Military, 12
Police administration--China--Tientsin, 675
Police management--China--Tientsin, 675
Police spies, see Agents provocateurs
Polish Grey Samaritans, 604
Polish posters, 11, 275
Polish question, 177, 200, 202, 206, 208, 212, 225, 230
Polish-Russian War, 1919-1920, see Poland--History--Wars of 1918-1921

Polish subject collection, 1908-1981, 212
Political crimes and offenses, 133, 139, 289
Political history, 88, 295
Political offenses, 133, 139, 289
Political parties, 133, 139
Political prisoners, 133
Political Red Cross, 133
Political refugees, see Emigration and immigration; Refugees
Political satire, 133
Political science--Anecdotes, facetiae, satire, etc., 133
Political trials, 289. See also Political crimes and offences
Political violence, 139, 295. See also Revolutionists
Politicheskii krasnyi krest, 133
Politicheskii ob"edinennyi komitet, 655
Politics and government, see Russia [or other country name]--Politics
    and government
Das politische Leben in Russisch-Polen (Political life
    in Russian Poland), 72
"Die polnische Frage," 225
"Poltavskiia eparkhial'nyia diela," 410
"Polyphony of The First Circle: A Study in Solzenicyn's Affinity
    With Dostoevskij," 51
Popovskii, Mark Aleksandrovich, collector, 411
Population, Foreign, 92, 112, 667
"The Port Arthur Diary," 162
Port Arthur--Siege, 1904-1905, 162. See also Russo-Japanese War,
    1904-1905
Portugeisia, S. O., 133
"Posledniaia Rossiia," 455
Poslednie novosti, 227
"Posliednie piat' dnei tsarskago Petrograda, 23-28 fevralia
    1917 g.: dnevnik posliedniago Petrogradskago gradonachal'nika,"
    22
Posolskaia incident collection, 1920, 14
Possony, Stefan Thomas, 1913-   , 266, 283, 295
Post, Wilbur E., 412
Postage-stamps, 4, 6, 16
Postal cards, 12, 14, 207, 300, 536
Postcards, see Postal cards
Poster collection, 11
Posters, 9, 11, 14, 292, 565, 594, 598, 625; Polish, 275
Postnikova, E., 296
Pototskii, Sergei Nikolaevich, 1877-   , 213
Potresov, Aleksandr Nikolaevich, 133
Pravda (truth), 297
"Pravitel'stvo spaseniia revoliutsii," 292
Press--Archangel, Russia--translations of newspaper article extracts,
    1918-1919, 14
Pretrial detention, 289
Prianishnikov, Boris V., 656
Price, Arnold H., 214
Price, Hereward Thimbleby, 1880-1964, 214
Primorskaia oblast', see Maritime Province, Siberia
Prinas kum istoriiata na sotsializma v Bulgariia, 122

Prisoners, Political, 133
Prisoners of war, 198, 213, 235, 332, 382, 427, 575, 598, 617, 622; Austria, 182; Germany, 198, 214, 235, 427; Siberia, 182, 214
Prisons, 127, 289
"The Problem of Eastern Galicia," 100
"Problems of Central and Eastern Europe," 177
Production economics, Agricultural, 44, 50, 94
"Professional'nye soiuzy Rossii v pervye gody revoliutsii," 126
"Proiskhozhdenie kazakov: doklad," 336
"Prokliatyi korabl'," 455
Prokopovich, S. N., 133
Propaganda, Anti-communist, 656
Propaganda, Communist, 261
Propaganda, Russian, 14, 240, 312
Protection of children, 559, 561, 617
Protocols of the Elders of Zion, see
    Protocols of the Wise Men of Zion
Protocols of the Wise Men of Zion, 73, 133
Protokoly sionskikh mudretsov, see
    Protocols of the Wise Men of Zion
Proudhon, Pierre Joseph, 1809-1865, 32
"Providence or Chance? Reminiscences," 490
Provisional Government, see Russia (1917. Provisional Government)
Provisional Government of Autonomous Siberia, see Russia (1917-1922. Civil War governments). Vremennoe sibirskoe pravitel'stvo
Provisional Government Project, Hoover Institution, see Hoover Institution on War, Revolution and Peace. Russian Provisional Government Project
Provocateurs, see Agents provocateurs
Prussia--Foreign relations, 1815-1870, 46. See also Germany
Prussia, East (Province)--World War, 1914-1918--Pictorial works, 224
Public debts, 248
Public finance, see Finance, Public
Public policy, see Russia--Economic policy
Publishers and publishing--Bookplates and stamps, 133
Puchkov, F. A., 512
Purington, Chester Wells, 513

Quakers, 618
Quakers. American Friends Service Committee, 553, 617

"R.S.F.S.R., 1919-1920 g.g.," 296
"R.S.F.S.R., 21-yi god," 296
Raack, Richard C., 354
"Rabochaia kooperatsiia v pervye gody russkoi revoliutsii, 1917-1921," 126
"Rabochee vosstanie protiv sovetskoi vlasti," 446
"Rabochii vopros pri Arkhangel'skom pravitel'stve," 246
Radek, Karl, 1885-1939, 298
Railroad Congress, Petrograd, 1918, 291
Railroad Union. All-Russian Executive Committee, 133, 291
Railroads, 14, 216, 291, 343, 471, 481, 486, 536, 537; Manchuria, 527; Siberia, 14, 471, 481, 486, 501, 527. See also Chinese Eastern Railway; U.S. Advisory Commission of Railway Experts

to Siberia
Rakovskii, Khristian Georgievich, 1873-1941, 299
Ral´k, supplier of church furniture for the Russian court, 19
Ralli-Arbore, Z. K., 133
Ramplee-Smith, Winifred V., collector, 300
Rappoport, A. IU., 133
Raskin, A. G., 133
Raskol´nikov, F., "Otkrytoe pis´mo Stalinu," 133
Rasputin, Grigorii Efimovich, 1871-1916, 12, 26, 74, 133
Rathvon, N. Peter, 330
Ravich, A., pseud., see Varska, A. S.
Ravich, M. M., 133
Rayski, Ludomił, 1892-1976, 215
Razumnik, R. Ivanov-, "Po tiur´mam na rodine," ms., 133
Reames, Grace Belle, see Bungey, Grace Belle Reames
Rebellions, see Revolutions
"Rechnaia boevaia flotiliia na reke Kame v 1919 godu," 539
Reconstruction (1914-1939), 617; Economic aspects, 248, 278; Europe, 558; Pictorial works, 237. See also World War, 1914-1918
"Record of a Russian Year, 1921-1922: Daily Life in Soviet Russia," 599
Red Army, see Russia (1917-   R.S.F.S.R.). Armiia
Red Cross, Political, 133
Red Cross. Russia. Rossiiskoe obshchestvo krasnogo kresta, 151, 213, 304, 382
Red Cross. U.S. American National Red Cross, 3, 560, 561, 567, 569, 581, 590, 596, 600, 603, 605, 617; Commission to Russia, 591; Commission to Siberia, 250, 507, 559, 566, 593, 602
Red International of Labor Unions, 252
Red Myth, 137
Refugees, 161, 237, 303, 332, 356, 374, 375, 382, 403, 418, 419, 428, 450, 451, 452, 520, 552, 597, 611, 617, 631, 639, 641, 646, 647, 648, 656, 660, 665; Congresses, 437; Pictorial works, 407. See also Emigration and immigration; Russia--History--Revolution, 1917-1921--Refugees; Russians in [name of country]
Regional Committee of the Army, Navy, and Workers of Finland, see Oblastnoi komitet armii, flota i rabochikh Finliandii
Reilly, Sidney, 133
Reise, Lloyd, collector, 163
Relief, International, see Russia--History--Revolution, 1917-1921--Civilian relief; World War, 1914-1918--Civilian relief
Religion, 673; in Russia, see Russia--Religion
Religion and communism, 277, 565. See also Church and state, 1917-
"Reminiscences of Four Years with N.K.V.D.," 365
Repatriation, 617. See also Emigration and immigration
Reporters, American--Correspondence, reminiscences, etc., 287
Rerberg, Fedor Petrovich, 1868-   , 413
Research Program on the History of the Communist Party of the Soviet Union, Columbia University, 136
"A Résumé of Events in the Caucasus Since the Russian Revolution," 412
"The Retreat of the Hundred Thousand: An Article-Novelette," 463
Revel--Harbor, 414
"Revel´skaia gavan´ i bol´sheviki" (Revel harbor and the

Bolsheviks), 414
Revoliutsiia i korennoe naselenie Turkestana, 309
"Revoliutsiia na Dal'nem vostoke," 483
Revolution of 1905, see Russia--History--Revolution of 1905
Revolution, 1917-1921, see Russia--History--Revolution, 1917-1921
Revolution, March-November 1917, see Russia--History--Revolution, March-November 1917
Revolution, March (February O.S.) 1917, see Russia--History--March (February O.S.) Revolution, 1917
Revolution, November (October O.S.) 1917, see Russia--History--November (October O.S.) Revolution, 1917
"Revolution and Civil War in Siberia and the Far East," 532
Revolutionaries, see Revolutionists
"Revolutionary Movement in Petrograd," 319
"Revolutionary Odyssey of the White Rabbit," 342
Revolutionists, 14, 123, 124, 126, 127, 130, 133, 135, 139, 141, 142, 143, 144, 145, 190, 229, 262, 652; Armenia, 133, 139; Finland, 139; Latvia, 139; Lithuania, 139; Poland, 139; Ukraine, 133, 139
Revolutions, 295
Reynolds, Elliott H., 514
Riabukhin, N. M., 548
Richardson, Gardner, 606
Riga, Gulf of, 236
Riga, Treaty of, 1920, 415
Riga front--World War, 1914-1918, 205
Ringland, Arthur C., 607
Rizhskii zaliv, 236
Rodgers, Marvin, 608
Rodichev, Fedor Izmailovich, 1854-1933, 133, 301
Rodzianko, Mikhail Vladimirovich, 1859-1924, 12, 75
Roehrberg, Th., see Rerberg, Fedor Petrovich, 1868-
Rogers, Leighton W., 302
Rohrbach, Paul, 1869-1956, 391
Rokitiansky, Nicholas John, 1912-   , collector, 76
Romania--Foreign relations--Russia, 14, 70, 197; Politics and government, 70; World War, 1914-1918, 191
Romanov, House of, 12, 24, 33, 34, 52, 54, 58, 64, 69, 93, 95, 97, 105, 106, 115, 442, 596, 628, 634, 657, 669; Miscellania, 17; Portraits, caricatures, etc., 2, 12
Romanov, Vasili, Prince, 108, 116, 156, 166, 345, 448, 454
Romanovskii, Ivan Pavlovich, 1877-1920, 381
Romine, John W., 370
Ronzhin, Sergei Aleksandrovich, 216
Rosenbluth, Robert, 609
Rosenschild-Paulin, A. N., see Rozenshil'd-Paulin, Anatolii Nikolaevich
Ross, Fort (California)--Views, 76
"Rossiia dlia russkikh," 663
Rossiiskaia sotsial-demokraticheskaia rabochaia partiia, 2, 11, 126, 128, 131, 133, 138, 139, 140, 145, 184, 348, 389; Biblioteka, Paris, 133; German funds for, 133, 190, 227; New York group of assistance to, 133; St. Petersburg group (Blagoevtsy), 133; TSentral'nyi komitet, 389; Turkestanskaia organizatsiia, 136;

Zurich faction, 133. See also Communism
Rossiiskoe tsentral´noe ob"edinenie, 437
Rostovtseff, Fedor, 658
Roumiantzow Museum, 323
Royal visits, 2, 57
Rozenfel´d, O. I., 133
Rozenshil´d-Paulin, Anatolii Nikolaevich, 217
Rubber stamps, 133
Rubin, Jacob, 139
Rubinov, D. M., 133
Rudneff, Bertha, 218
Rudneff, Ilya Alexeevich, 1892-1969, 218
Rukhlov, Sergei Vasil´evich--Photograph, 12
Rulers, 672. See also Russia--Court and courtiers
Rumiantsovskii muzei, 323
Rural life, 145
Russia. Armiia, 146, 179, 185, 195, 329, 359, 368, 384, 386, 628
Russia. Armiia. Cossacks. See also Cossacks
Russia. Armiia. Cossacks. Kubansko-terskii plastunskii korpus, 189
Russia. Armiia. 10. armiia, 179; 10. korpus, 219, 413; Don Cadet Corps, 442; 20. korpus, 217; Glavnoe upravlenie General´nogo shtaba, 147, 161; Glavnyi shtab, 161; Kavaleriia, 350, 396, 443, 651. See also Russia. Armiia. 1. Ulanskii polk
Russia. Armiia. Kavkazskaia armiia, 220; Konvoi Ego Imperatorskogo Velichestva Gosudaria Imperatora Nikolaia II-go, 390; Kubansko-terskii plastunskii korpus, 189; Kubanskoe kazach´e voisko, 347. See also Cossacks
Russia. Armiia. Leib-gvardii egerskii polk, 637; Leib-gvardii finliandskii polk, 639; Leib-gvardii kirasirskii Ego Velichestva polk, 14; Leib-gvardii kirasirskii Eia Velichestva polk, 166, 400; Leib-gvardii moskovskii polk, 380; Leib-gvardii 1. strelkovyi Ego Velichestva polk, 406; Leib-gvardii ulanskii Ego Velichestva polk, 396. See also Russia. Armiia. Kavaleriia
Russia. Armiia--Medals, badges, decorations, etc., 8, 68; Officers, 12, 175, 231, 282, 372; Officers--Correspondence, reminiscences, etc., 14, 31, 104, 157, 166, 170, 173, 203, 333, 334, 347, 357, 367, 395, 406, 427, 431, 490; Officers--Portraits, 12, 151; Officers--Registers, 111; Organization, 147
Russia. Armiia. Pekhota, 179. See also Russia. Armiia. 5. pekhotnaia diviziia
Russia. Armiia. 1. zabaikal´skaia kazach´ia diviziia, 228. See also Cossacks
Russia. Armiia. 1. gvardeiskii korpus, 329; 1. ulanskii polk, 224. See also Russia. Armiia. Kavaleriia
Russia. Armiia. Petrograd Lancers, 224. See also Russia. Armiia. Kavaleriia
Russia. Armiia. 5. pekhotnaia diviziia, 233. See also Russia. Armiia. Pekhota
Russia. Armiia--Portraits, 400; Procurement, 164; Registers, 231; Regulations, 148
Russia. Armiiia. Shtab verkhovnogo glavnokomanduiushchego, see Russia. Shtab verkhovnogo glavnokomanduiushchego
Russia. Armiia. 34. samokatnaia rota, 384

Russia--Biography, 388; Biography--Portraits, 101; Civilization, 7,
     32; Colonies--North America, 14, 575; Commerce--Estonia, 414;
     Commerce--Germany, 79, 80; Commercial policy, 53, 145;
     Constitutional history, 188
Russia. Council of Ministers, see Russia. Sovet ministrov
Russia--Court and courtiers, 24, 26, 59, 120. See also Russia--Kings
     and rulers
Russia--Defenses, 223
Russia. Departament politsii, 133. See also Russia. Okhrannye
     otdeleniia
Russia. Departament politsii. Zagranichnaia agentura, Paris, 139,
     285
Russia--Description and travel, 115, 660; 1917-1945, 278, 287
Russia. Dom predvaretel'noe zakliuchenie, St. Petersburg, 133
Russia--Economic conditions, 44, 437, 571, 617; Economic conditions--
     1918-1945, 255, 313, 316, 318, 599, 609, 618; Economic policy,
     249, 258, 278; Foreign economic relations, 258
Russia--Foreign relations. See also International relations
Russia--Foreign relations, 13, 28, 245, 270, 287, 295, 304, 659;
     1894-1917, 63, 89; 1917-1945, 63; Austria, 20; China, 330;
     Czechoslovakia, 244; Denmark, 213; Estonia, 401; France, 114,
     285, 303; Germany, 57, 79, 80, 81, 82, 83; Great Britain, 346;
     Hesse, 81; Japan, 12, 165; Poland, 434; Romania, 14, 70, 197;
     Saxe-Weimar-Eisenach, 82; Treaties, 265; United States, 14,
     105, 106, 165, 266, 272, 283, 286, 304, 630; Wuerttemberg, 83
Russia. Gendarme Office, 133; Gosudarstvennaia duma, 12, 77, 133
Russia. Gosudarstvennaia duma--Collection (in Russian
     and English), 1906-1916, 77
Russia--Historiography, 15; History, 13, 14, 66, 117, 145, 355, 658;
     19th century, 144, 355, 633, 634; 19th century--Pictorial
     works, 11; Peter I, 1689-1725, 90; 20th century, 14, 43, 144,
     355, 437; 20th century--Pictorial works, 2, 11; Nicholas II,
     1894-1917, 40, 55, 56, 58, 61, 64, 69, 89, 104, 106, 107, 114,
     118, 121, 144, 150, 186, 195, 282, 385, 396, 400, 575, 596,
     633; Nicholas II, 1894-1917--Drama, 38, 52; Nicholas II,
     1894-1917--Pictorial works, 2, 12; Revolution of 1905, 12, 30,
     56, 133, 161; 1917-   , 24, 213, 359, 370, 375, 556, 570, 571,
     664, 669
Russia--History--Revolution, 1917-1921, 12, 14, 34, 129, 132, 133,
     243, 246, 247, 249, 253, 257, 259, 262, 266, 270, 271, 279,
     282, 284, 285, 287, 289, 293, 294, 295, 296, 299, 303, 304,
     305, 309, 311, 314, 316, 321, 322, 324, 325, 360, 532, 671.
     See also Ukraine--History--Revolution, 1917-1921
Russia--History--March (February O.S.) Revolution, 1917, 98, 118,
     121, 242, 269, 300, 302, 317, 333, 384
Russia--History--Revolution, March-November 1917, 22, 186, 227, 245,
     264, 273, 274, 280, 283, 290, 291, 292, 297, 301, 312, 315,
     319, 320, 410; Pictorial works, 2, 12
Russia--History--November (October O.S.) Revolution, 1917, 62
Russia--History--Revolution, 1917-1921--Anti-Bolshevik accounts and
     counterrevolutionary movements, 14, 27, 31, 33, 39, 47, 52, 61,
     67, 75, 88, 93, 106, 107, 113, 114, 115, 123, 124, 133, 135,
     142, 143, 164, 170, 173, 175, 186, 191, 274, 289, 303, 328-454,
     455, 457, 477, 522, 531, 535, 547, 567, 569, 575, 628, 633,

637, 648, 656, 660, 661, 664. See also Mongolia--History;
 Siberia--History--Revolution, 1917-1921
Russia--History--Revolution, 1917-1921--Atrocities, 12, 14, 250, 289
Russia--History--Revolution, 1917-1921--Campaigns, 213, 366, 448,
 641; Caucasus, 375; Crimea, 375, 413, 452; Kuban region, 254;
 Northwest, 364, 367; South, 337, 375, 452; Southwest, 377;
 Ukraine, 241. See also Siberia--History--Revolution, 1917-1921
Russia--History--Revolution, 1917-1921--Chronology, 344
Russia--History--Revolution, 1917-1921--Civilian relief, 260, 307,
 552-622, 624-626; Pictorial works, 610. See also Food relief;
 World War, 1914-1918--Civilian relief
Russia--History--Revolution, 1917-1921--Finance, 53, 511; Foreign
 participation, 463, 466, 499, 568; Foreign participation--
 Pictorial works, 591; Foreign public opinion, 242, 266, 283;
 Hospitals, 288, 385, 425; Kronshtadt Rebellion, 1921, 133;
 Miscellanea, 4; Naval operations, 407, 428, 447, 454, 458,
 491, 494, 539; Pictorial works, 2, 12, 311, 325, 481, 536;
 Posters, 9, 11, 292, 565, 625; Reconstruction, 248, 255,
 258, 308; Refugees, 87, 213, 218, 285, 375, 418, 419, 451, 452,
 523, 552, 559, 611, 631, 644, 652. See also Refugees
Russia--History--Revolution, 1917-1921, Collection, 14
Russia--History--Allied intervention, 1918-1920. See also Siberia--
 History--Revolution, 1917-1921
Russia--History--Allied intervention, 1918-1920, 2, 12, 29, 243, 247,
 303, 306, 339, 348, 356, 358, 367, 378, 412, 413, 422, 432,
 438, 448, 454, 455, 461, 462, 466, 475, 477, 481, 485, 488,
 492, 497, 502, 509, 515, 525, 527, 532, 564, 568, 575, 598,
 600; American intervention, 261, 354, 435, 445, 459, 465, 467,
 474, 475, 476, 479, 480, 495, 514, 516, 524, 528, 530, 564;
 British intervention, 261, 338, 364, 441; Canadian
 intervention, 497; Czech intervention, see Ceská druzina;
 French intervention, 485; Japanese intervention, 472, 476, 477,
 480, 498, 502, 513, 522, 523; Latvian intervention, 517
Russia--History, Naval, 156
Russia--History--Posters, 11; Study and teaching--France, 658
Russia--Industries, 201, 249, 327, 437; Pictorial works, 37
Russia. Kabinet Ego Imperatorskago Velichestva.
 Ispolnitel´naia kommissiia po ustroistvu zemel´
 Glukhoozerskoi fermy, 78
Russia--Kings and rulers, 672. See also Russia--Court and courtiers
Russia. Konsul´stvo, Breslau, 79; Konsul´stvo, Leipzig, 80;
 Legatsiia (Hesse) 81; Legatsiia (Saxe-Weimar-Eisenach), 82;
 Legatsiia (Wuerttemberg), 83; Ministerstvo imperatorskogo
 dvora, 84; Ministerstvo inostrannykh del, 304; Ministerstvo
 iustitsii, 120; Ministerstvo vnutrennykh del, 133
Russia--Miscellanea, 14
Russia. Morskoi flot, 236, 448. See also Russia. Voennyi flot
Russia--Naval history, 156; Nobility, 31, 54, 106, 107, 108, 111,
 119, 120, 186, 633
Russia, Northern--History, 338
Russia, Northwest, 364, 367, 407, 440
Russia--Officials and employees, 104, 113, 120
Russia. Okhrannye otdeleniia, 14, 55, 60, 85, 133, 139, 285, 300.
 See also Russia. Departament politsii

Russia--Politics and government, 10, 13, 133; 1881-1894, 48; 1894-1917, 24, 26, 40, 47, 67, 77, 113, 118, 126, 449; 1917-   , 249, 316

Russia. Posol´stvo (France), 303; Posol´stvo (U.S.), 304

Russia--Relations (general) with China, 268; Relations (military) with France, 153; with Germany, 152; with Iran, 203; with Japan, 164

Russia--Religion, 116, 565; 1917-   , 421, 439, 636

Russia. Shtab verkhovnogo glavnokomanduiushchego, 221

Russia--Social conditions, 23, 49, 53, 66, 99, 342, 437, 565, 644; 1917-   , 563, 599, 618, 641, 657; 1917-   --Pictorial works, 571, 575, 636

Russia, Southeastern, 133

Russia, Southern, 337, 383, 417, 451, 452

Russia, Southwestern, 377

Russia. Sovet ministrov, 222; Verkhovnaia rasporiaditel´naia komissiia, 133

Russia--Views, 2, 12, 32, 37

Russia. Voenno-morskoi agent (Germany), 152; Voenoe ministerstvo, 223; Voennyi agent (France), 153; Voennyi agent (Japan), 164

Russia. Voennyi flot, 428; Officers, 156; Procurement, 152. See also Russia. Morskoi flot

Russia. Zhandarskie upravlenii, 133

Russia (1917. Provisional Government), 188, 264, 286; Ministerstvo revoliutsionnaia oborona, 133; Photographs, 12; Vserossiiskoe uchreditel´noe sobranie, 133, 305

Russia (1917-   R.S.F.S.R.). Amurskaia flotiliia, 494; Chrezvychainaia komissiia po bor´be s kontr-revoliutsiei i sabotazhem, 12, 133, 282, 289; Armiia, 251; Sovet narodnykh komissarov, 306; Treaties, etc. Poland, Oct. 11, 1920, 415; Tsentral´naia komissiia pomoshchi golodaiushchim, 307; Voenno-morskoi flot. Amurskaia voennaia flotiliia, 494

Russia (1917-1922. Civil War governments). Armiia, 359, 364, 392, 661; Armiia. Istoricheskaia komissiia Markovskogo artilleriiskogo diviziona, 366; Armiia. Markovskaia artilleriiskaia brigada, 366; Armiia. Terskoe kazach´e voisko, 349, 361, 394. See also Cossacks

Russia (1917-1922. Civil War governments). Armiia. Ufimskaia kavaleriiskaia diviziia, 384; Armiia. 2. Orenburgskii kazachii polk, 535. See also Cossacks

Russia (1917-1922. Civil War governments). Dobrovol´cheskaia armiia, 133, 304, 375, 378, 382, 386, 522; Dobrovol´cheskaia armiia. Glavnyi kaznachei, 416; Dobrovol´cheskaia armiia. Kornilovskii polk, 170, 347, 438, 452; Donskaia armiia, 337, 417; Flot, 428; Ispolnitel´naia komissiia soveshchaniia chlenov Uchreditel´nogo sobraniia, 133; Kaspiiskaia flotiliia, 447; Morskoi flot, 428; Russkaia narodnaia armiia, see Russkaia narodnaia armiia (Russian people´s army)

Russia (1917-1922. Civil War governments). Severo-zapadnoe pravitel´stvo. Armiia, 364, 367; Severo-zapadnoe pravitel´stvo. Eiserne Division, 402; Voennyi flot, 428; Vooruzhennye sily iuga Rossii, 75, 304, 375, 382, 437, 451, 452, 641; Vooruzhennye sily iuga Rossii. Nachal´nik snabzheniia, 418; Vooruzhennye sily iuga Rossii. Sudnoe

otdielenie, 419; Vremennoe rossiiskoe pravitel´stvo (Kolchak), 89, 470, 520, 531, 534. See also Russia (1917-1922. Civil War governments). Vremennoe sibirskoe pravitel´stvo
Russia (1917-1922. Civil War governments). Vremennoe sibirskoe pravitel´stvo, 500, 510, 515, 534. See also Russia (1917-1922. Civil War governments). Vremennoe rossiiskoe pravitel´stvo (Kolchak)
Russia (1923- U.S.S.R.). Komitet gosudarstvennoi bezopastnosti, 51; Ob"edinennoe gosudarstvennoe politicheskoe upravlenie, 289; Narodnyi komissariat vnutrennikh del, 365; Vysshii sovet narodnogo khoziaistva, 278; Voenno-morskoi flot. Amurskaia voennaia flotiliia, 494
Russian All-Military Union, see Russkii obshchevoinskii soiuz
Russian Archive (Berlin), 133
Russian Central Asia, see Soviet Central Asia
Russian Civil War in Georgia--newspaper clippings, 14
"Russian Experience, 1910-1917," 62
Russian Historical Archive and Repository, 31, 54, 66, 68, 111, 151, 334, 637
Russian literature, 13, 110, 312
Russian Military Cemetery (France), 239
Russian National Committee, 659
Russian National Progressive Party, 672
Russian newspapers, 14, 240
Russian officer--photograph, 1839, 12
Russian Orthodox Church, see Orthodox Eastern Church, Russian
Russian Orthodox Church Outside of Russia, see Russkaia pravoslavnaia tserkov´ zagranitsei
Russian People´s army, see Russkaia narodnaia armiia
Russian periodicals, 634
Russian pictorial collection, 1887-1977, 12
Russian Provisional Government, see Russia (1917. Provisional Government)
Russian Provisional Government Project, Hoover Institution, see Hoover Institution on War, Revolution and Peace. Russian Provisional Government Project
The Russian Provisional Government, 1917, 264
"The Russian Public Debt," 308
Russian Railway Service Corps, see U.S. Russian Railway Service Corps
Russian Red Cross, see Red Cross. Russia. Rossiiskoe obshchestvo krasnogo kresta
Russian Republican League (Paris), 133
Russian Review, 13, 671
Russian revolutionary movements, 19th century--Posters, 11
Russian Revolutionary Social-Democrat League Abroad, 133. See also Rossiiskaia sotsial-demokraticheskaia rabochaia partiia
Russian School of Higher Social Sciences (RSDRP), 2, 133
Russian Social Democrat Union, 133. See also Rossiiskaia sotsial-demokraticheskaia rabochaia partiia
Russian Social Democratic Archive (Berlin), 133
Russian Social Democratic Workers Party, see Rossiiskaia sotsial-demokraticheskaia rabochaia partiia
Russian subject collection, 1700-1975, 14

Russian Volunteer Army, see Russia (1917-1922. Civil War
    governments). Dobrovol´cheskaia armiia
Russians in China, 520, 638, 644, 646, 647, 674, 675, 676; in Europe,
    375, 452; in Finland, 641; in foreign countries, 14, 23, 61,
    88, 99, 105, 107, 133, 139, 143, 304, 342, 350, 356, 376, 382,
    451, 628, 629, 634, 641, 655, 657, 659, 662, 668, 669; in
    France, 229, 380, 652; in Germany, 631; in Great Britain, 672;
    in Hungary, 87; in Mongolia, 542, 549; in Morocco, 654; in
    San Francisco, 649; in the East (Far East), 64, 500, 520, 523,
    547, 663; in the United States, 92, 334, 630, 632, 633, 635,
    636, 638, 649, 660, 670; in Turkey, 452, 597, 611; in
    Yugoslavia, 332, 403. See also Refugees
"Russie," 423
"Russie: Bulletin des anneés 1917-1922" (Russia: Report on
    the years 1917-1922), 15
Russiian, Viktor Nikolaevich, 85
Russing, John, 224
Russkaia narodnaia armiia (Russian people´s army), 420
Russkaia pravoslavnaia tserkov´ zagranitsei, 654. See also Orthodox
    Eastern Church, Russian
Russkaia respublikanskaia liga (Paris), 133
Russkaia vysshaia shkola obshchestvennykh nauk v Parizhe, 2, 133
Russkii akademicheskii soiuz (Berlin), 133
Russkii arkhiv (Berlin), 133
Russkii obshchevoinskii soiuz, 628, 661, 665
Russkii sotsial-demokraticheskii arkhiv (Berlin), 133
Russkiia vedomosti (Russian news) (Moscow), 421
Russkoe aktsionernoe obshchestvo dlia primeneniia ozona, 86
Russkoe obozrenie (Chicago), 533
Russkoe slovo (Russian word), 140
"Russland und die Weltpolitik, 1917-1920: Studien zur Geschichte der
    Interventionen in Russland," 348
Russo-Japanese War, 1904-1905, 14, 97, 157, 161, 165, 170, 395;
    Pictorial works, 158, 159, 163, 168. See also Port
    Arthur--Siege, 1904-1905
Russo-Polish War, 1919-1920, see Poland--History--Wars of 1918-1921
Russo-Romanian relations--Report, 14
Russo-Turkish War, 1877-1878, 149; Reparations, 155
Ryskulov, T., 309

SRs, see Partiia sotsialistov-revoliutsionerov
Sabine, Edward G., collector, 610
Sabler, V. K., 133
Sachs, Johannes, 225
Safonov, Ludmila, 1897-   , 660
Saint Petersburg. Agence télégraphique, 169; Aleksandro-Nevskaia
    lavra, 421; Costume ball, 1903, 111, 119; Dom predvaritel´noe
    zakliuchenie, 133; History, 294; History--1917-1921, 22, 118,
    269, 280, 317, 319, 320; History--1917-1921--Pictorial works,
    2, 12, 311, 325; Kazanskii sobor, 119; Malyi teatr, 133; Maps,
    99; Mendeleevskii s"ezd po obshchei i prikladnoi khimii, 1911,
    12; Peresylnaia tiurma, 127; Petrograd Children´s Colony, 559,
    561; Petropavlovskaia krepost´, 12; U.S. Consulate, see U.S.

   Consulate, Leningrad; Zimnii dvorets, 12, 111, 119
Saint Petersburg group of social democrats (Blagoevtsy), 133
Saint Petersburg Union of Struggle for the Liberation of the Working
   Class, 133
Saint Serafim of Sarov, 116
Sakharov, Konstantin Viacheslavovich, 1881- , 516
Salnais, Lilija, 517
Salnais, Voldemars, 1886-1948, 517
Samara--History, 579, 610, 624
Samarin, IUrii Fedorovich, 1819-1876, 32
Sambain, 139
Samsonow, Michael S., 1900-1973, 8, 87
San Francisco. American Russian Institute, 12
San Francisco, Russians in, 649
San Francisco. Yuba Manufacturing Co., see Yuba Manufacturing
   Company of San Francisco
Sankt-Peterburg, see Saint Petersburg
Sapon´ko, Angel Osipovich, 1876-1944, 88
Sarov, Saint Serafim of, 116
Satire, Political, 133
Save the Children Fund, London, 617
Savich, N. V., 226
Savidge, Evan, pseud., see Petrushevich, Ivan, 1875-1950
Savin, Petr Panteleimonovich, 661
Savinkov, Boris Viktorovich, 1879-1925, 139, 422
Savintsev, Lieutenant, 518
Saxe-Weimar-Eisenach--Foreign relations--Russia, 82
Sazonov, Sergei Dmitrievich, 1861-1917, 12, 89
Schakovskoy, Princess, 423
Schakovskoy, Wladimir, Prince, 1904-1972, 423
Schauman, Georg Carl August, 1870-1930, 424
Schlüsselburg Archive, 133
Schneider, Alan, 425
Schneider, Leo Victor, 1890-1963, 425
School of Higher Social Sciences (RSDRP), 2, 133
Schuyler, Eugene, 90
Schwartz, S. M., 133
Schwarz, Alexis von, see Shvarts, Aleksei Vladimirovich fon,
   1874-1953
Science, 673
Scipio, Lynn A., 1876- , collector, 611
Scoville, Ogden, 638
Sea transportation, 414, 617
Seals (Numismatics), 133
Secret service, 14, 55, 60, 85, 139, 289. See also Espionage
"Selostus Torminnastaan Elintarpeiden Hankkimiseksi Amerikasta
   Suomeen Vuosina 1918-1919," 619
"Semeinaia khronika ot Krotkovykh do Meshcheriakovykh," 108
Semenov, Evgenii Petrovich, 1861- , 133, 227
Semenov, Grigorii Mikhailovich, 1890-1945, 14, 519, 522, 523
Semenov, IU. F., 133
Semionoff, Evgenii Petrovich, see Semenov, Evgenii Petrovich, 1861-
Semkovskii, S. IU., 133
Serafim, Saint, of Sarov, 116

193

Seraphim, Sister, 50
Serbia--World War, 1914-1918, 253
Serebrennikov, Ivan Innokentievich, 1882-   , 520
Serfdom, 321
Servitude, 321
Sevastopol´--History, 413
Sevastopoulo, Marc, 91
Sevastopoulo family, 91
Severo-zapadnoe pravitel´stvo, see Russia (1917-1922. Civil War governments). Severo-zapadnoe pravitel´stvo
"Severo-zapadnyi front grazhdanskoi voiny v Rossii 1919 goda" 440
Shakovskoi, Vladimir, Prince, see Schakovskoy, Wladimir, Prince, 1904-1972
Shalikashvili, Maria, 426
Shalikashvili, Dimitri, 426
Shapiro, B. (Secretary of N.Y. faction of the SR Party), 133
Shapiro-Lavrova, Nadezhda L., 521
Shaplen, Joseph, 133
Shatskii (Zinoviev, Grigorii Evseevich, 1883-1936), 133, 139
Shchavinskii, podpolk, ed., 366
Shchepikhin, Sergei Afanasevich, 522
Shcherbachev, Dmitrii Grigor´evich, 1855-1932, 427
Shevchenko, Taras, 1814-1861, 133
Shevchenko Library, Lvov, 133
Shevelev, Klavdii Valentinovich, 1881-   , 428
Shil´nikov, Ivan Fedorovich, 228
Shingarev, Andrei Ivanovich--Photograph, 12
Shinkarenko, Nikolai Vsevolodovich, 1890-1968, 429
Shipping, 617; Baltic Sea, 414
Shkuro, Andrei Grigor´evich, 1887-1947, 662
Shlissel´burgskii arkhiv, 133
Shneyeroff, M. M., 1880-   , 141
Shreider, G. I., 133
Shrewsbury, Kenneth O., 430
Shtakel´berg, Baron, 133
Shteinraikh, N. I., 133
Shternberg, Roman Fedorovich Ungern-, Baron, see Ungern-Shternberg, Roman Fedorovich, Baron, 1887-1921
Shulman, Shirley, 538
Shupak, N. O., 133
Shupak, S. D., 133
Shutko, IAkov, collector, 229
Shvarts, Aleksei Vladimirovich fon, 1874-1953, 431
Shvarts, S. M., 133
Shvetzoff, Dimitrii Andreevich, 1902-   , 395, 432
Siberia, American intervention in, see Russia--History--Allied intervention, 1918-1920--American intervention
"Siberia and Eastern Russia," 476
Siberia, British intervention in, see Russia--History--Allied intervention, 1918-1920--British intervention; Czech intervention in, see Ceská druzina
Siberia--Description and travel, 133, 278, 461; Economic conditions, 534
Siberia. Far eastern region, see Far eastern region, Siberia

Siberia. Far Eastern Republic, see Far Eastern Republic
Siberia, French intervention in, see Russia--History--Allied
	intervention, 1918-1920--French intervention
Siberia--History--Revolution, 1917-1921, 14, 64, 89, 133, 164, 214,
	303, 304, 356, 453, 455-477, 479-539, 542, 551, 559, 560, 561,
	564, 566, 568, 575, 587, 590, 593, 595, 596, 598, 600, 602,
	605, 617, 625; Pictorial works, 2, 354, 469, 476, 480, 497,
	507, 538. See also Russia--History--Allied intervention, 1918-
	1920
Siberia. International Military Police, 12
Siberia, Japanese intervention in, see Russia--History--Allied
	intervention, 1918-1920--Japanese intervention; Latvian
	intervention in, see Russia--History--Allied intervention,
	1918-1920--Latvian intervention
Siberia. Maritime Province, see Maritime Province, Siberia
Siberia--Mines and mineral resources, 478. See also Gold mines
	and mining
Siberia--Prisoners of war, 182, 214; Views, 469; Railroads, see
	Railroads--Siberia
Siberia. Vremennoe sibirskoe pravitel'stvo, see Russia (1917-1922.
	Civil War Governments). Vremennoe sibirskoe pravitel'stvo
Siberia--World War, 1914-1918, 593
"A Siberian Experience," 596
Siberian Flotilla, 458, 494
Siberian provisional government, see Russia (1917-1922. Civil War
	governments). Vremennoe sibirskoe pravitel'stvo
Sibirskaia flotiliia, 458, 494
"Sievero-zapadnyi front grazhdanskoi voiny v Rossii 1919 goda," 440
Sionskie protokoly, see
	Protocols of the Wise Men of Zion
"La situation agricole en Arménie occidental," 94
Skalskii, Vladimir Evgenievich, 433
Skoblin, Nikolai, 133, 665
Skoptsy, 133
"Slaviane v Amerikie" (Slavs in America), 92
Slavophilism, 32
Slavs in Canada, 92; in Latin America, 92; in the United States, 92,
	627, 666
Slusser, Robert M., 265
"Sluzhba General'nago shtaba v divizii i korpusie," 147
"Sluzhba v Glavnom shtabie i Glavnom upravlenii General'nago shtaba,"
	161
Smirnoff, V. N., 133
Smirnov, Mikhail, 539
Smirnov, V. N., 133
Smith, Henry Bancroft, 1884-   , 612
Smith, Jack A., 523
Smith, Jessica, 613
Smolin, I. S., 93
Snigirevskii, Konstantin Vasil'evich, d. 1937, 154
"Sobstvennyi Ego Velichestva konvoi v dni revoliutsii," 121
"Sobytiia v Mongolii-Khalkhie, 1920-1921 godakh," 545
Social conditions, see Russia [or other country name]--Social
	conditions

Social democracy, see Socialism
Socialism, 124, 128, 130, 133, 140, 145, 279; international, 129, 133, 134, 262. See also Communism; Dialectical materialism
Socialism and American Art in the Light of European Utopianism, Marxism and Anarchism, 125
Socialism and art, 125
Socialism in the Balkan Peninsula, 299; in Bulgaria, 122; in France, 256
Socialist Revolutionary Party, see Partiia sotsialistov-revoliutsionerov
Société agricole arménienne, 94
Societies--Bookplates and stamps, 133
Societies, Students'--Moscow, 45
Society of Friends, 618; American Friends Service Committee, 55, 617
Society to Aid Political Prisoners in the Soviet Union, 133
Sociology, 88
Soiuz bor´by za osvobozhdenie rabochego klassa, 133. See also Rossiiskaia sotsial-demokraticheskaia rabochaia partiia
Soiuz russkikh sotsial-demokratov, 133. See also Rossiiskaia sotsial-demokraticheskaia rabochaia partiia
Soiuz vol´nogo kazachestva, 133. See also Cossacks
Sokolnicki, Michał, 1880-1967, 230
Sokolnikov, Grigorii IAkovlevich, 1888-1939, 310
Sokolnitskii, V., 549
Sokolov, Boris Fedorovich, 1893-   , 311
Sokolov, Nikolai Alekseevich, 1882-1924, 95
"Soldier Under Three Flags: The Personal Memoirs of Lev Pavlovich Sukacev," 438
Solicitors, 143
Solovei, Dmytro, 96
Solovetskii Islands, 289
Solov´ev, Sergei Mikhailovich, 1820-1879, 32
Solski, Wacław, 1896-   , 312
Solzhenitsyn, Aleksandr Isaevich, 1918-   , 51, 664
"Soobrazheniia ob ustroistvie obuchenii i upotroblenii budushchei russkoi kavalerii," 651
Sosnowski, Jerzy Jan, 200
Soudakoff, Peter, 74, 97
Southeastern Russia, 133
Southern Russia, 337, 375, 383, 417, 451, 452, 567
Southwestern Russia, 377
Sovet ministrov, see Russia. Sovet ministrov
Sovet narodnykh komissarov, see Russia (1917-   R.S.F.S.R.). Sovet narodnykh komissarov
Sovet oppozitsii Man´chzhurii i Dal´niago vostoka, 663
Sovereigns, 672. See also Russia--Court and courtiers
Soviet Central Asia, 132, 136, 373; Bibliography, 279
Soviet Far East, see Far eastern region, Siberia
Soviet Policy in Public Finance, 1917-1928, 310
"Soviet-Polish Dispute," 434
Soviet Treaty Series Project, Hoover Institution, see Hoover Institution on War, Revolution and Peace. Soviet Treaty Series Project
Soviet Union. Posol´stvo (U.S.), 260

Spalding, Clara, 313
Spalding, Merrill Ten Broeck, 313
Speaks, John, 610
Specie, 4, 5
Spies, see under Espionage; Secret service
Spies, Police, see Agents provocateurs
"Spravki o glavnokomanduiushchikh frontami, komandirakh armiiami, komandirakh korpusov i proch" (List of commanding officers of the Russian Imperial Army, arranged by units, at the time of the First World War), 231
Sprigg, Rodney Searle, 1894-   , 524
Spying, see under Espionage; Secret service
Srednaia aziia, see Soviet Central Asia
Stackelberg, Rudolf von, Baron, 98
Stafford, Clayton I., 435
Stalin, Iosif, 1879-1953, 14, 139, 279
Stamps, n.d., 16
Stamps, Hand, 133
Stamps, Postage, 4, 6, 16
Stamps, Rubber, 133
Stanfield, Boris, 1888-   , 314
Stanford University. Library, 72
Stankevich, Vlad. Bened., 133
Starynkevich, Konstantin Sokratovich, 133
State and agriculture, 44, 145, 211; Germany, 211
State and church, 1917-   , 276, 421, 439. See also Communism and religion
State and industry, 145
State Department, see U.S. Department of State
State planning, see Russia--Economic policy
State visits, 2, 57
Statesmen, 67, 71, 111
"Stat´i i rechi o srednei Azii i Uzbekistane," 279
Steffens, Joseph Lincoln, 1866-1936, 272
Steinberg, Isaac Nachman, 1888-1957, 436
Steinfeldt, Eric, collector, 525
Stenbock-Fermor, Elizabeth, 91
Stenbock-Fermor, Ivan, Graf, 1897-   , collector, 99
Stepanov, Aleksandr Stepanovich, 526
Stepanova, Vanda Kazimirovna, 232
Stephens, Frederick Dorsey, 1891-   , 614
Stepniak, Sergius, see Kravchinskii, Sergei Mikhailovich, 1852-1895
Stepno-Badzheiskaia volost´ collection, 14
Stevens, John Frank, 1853-1943, 527
Stewart, Ella W., 623
Stines, Norman Caswell, Jr., 1914-1980, 315
Stockholm. International Socialist Conference, 1917, 133, 297
Stolypin, Petr Arkad´evich, 1867-1911, 12, 69, 118, 133
Ston, N. I., 133
Stone, Naum Il´ich, 133
Storage warehouses, 617
Story, Gertrude A., 615
Story, Russell McCulloch, 1883-1942, 615

"The Story of Baron Ungern-Sternberg," 548
Strait of Irbe, 236
Strategy, Communist, 341
Strelnikovskii trial, Odessa, 142
Strobridge, William S., 528
Stroev, V., "Neveroiatnye skazki," ms., 1930, 133
Strong, Anna Louise, 287
"The Struggle for a Democracy in Siberia: Reminiscences of a
    Contemporary," 468
Struve, Gleb P., 437
Struve, Nikita, 641
Struve, Petr Berngardovich, 1870-1944, 133, 437
Student Friendship Fund, 565
Student movements, 279
Students, 139, 565, 670
Students' societies--Moscow, 45
Submarine warfare, 176
Subversive activities, 669
Sukacev, Lev Pavlovich, 1895-1974, 438
Sukacev, Natalie, 438
Sukennikov, M., 133
Sukhomlinov, Vladimir Aleksandrovich--Photograph, 12
Sullivant, Robert Scott, 1925-   , 100
"Summer of 1919, from Kurgan to Spassk," 508
Sunzhenskii line, 349
Supreme Economic Council, 278
Supreme Economic Council (Allied and Associated Powers), 585
Supreme Economic Council and American Relief Administration Documents
    Project, see Hoover Institution on War, Revolution and Peace.
    Supreme Economic Council and American Relief Administration
    Documents Project
Supreme War Council. American Section, 257
"Sur les routes de mon passé," 114
Sutleff, Helen B., 514
Sutton, Antony, 138
Suvorin Theater, 133
Sviatikov, S. G., 133
Sviatopolk-Mirsky, N., collector, 101
"Svodki o politicheskom i ekonomicheskom polozhenii v Sovetskoi
    Rossii za 1922 god" (Summaries of the political and economic
    situation in Soviet Russia for 1922), 316
"Svoim i chuzhim: o tragedii 22 sentiabria," 665
Swinnerton, C. T., 317
Switzerland, Russian military attachés in, 358
Sworakowski, Witold S., 1903-1979, 102, 190, 434
Swords, 18
Sychev, E., 529
Syny Israilia (play), 133
Szamuely, Tibor--Photograph, 12

Tabernacle (Church furniture), 19
Tal´, Georgii Aleksandrovich von, 103
Talbot, Earl, 567
Tallinn--Harbor, 414

Taneev, Sergei Aleksandrovich, 1887-1975, 104
Taneyew, Tinatine, 104
Tapping, Amy Pryor, 604
Tarsaidze, Alexandre Georgievich, 1901-1978, 105
Tatishchev family, 106
Tatistcheff, Alexis Borisovich, 1903-   , 106
Tchernigovetz, Nikolai, 664
Tchitcherin, George V., see Chicherin, Georgii Vasil´evich, 1872-1936
Teatr Suvorina, 133
Ten Broeck Spalding, Merrill, see Spalding, Merrill Ten Broeck
Tenure of land, 50, 145
Terrorism, 139
Tersk region, 361
Terskoe kazach´e voisko, see Russia (1917-1922. Civil War
    governments). Armiia. Terskoe kazach´e voisko
Thetford (Vermont) Historical Society, 490
Third International, see Communist International
Thompson, Donald C., 105
Tientsin, China--Police administration, 675
Tikhon, Patriarch of Moscow and All Russia, 1865-1925, 439
Timofievich, Anatolii Pavlovich, d. 1976, 107
Tkachev, P., 133
Tolstaia, M. P., see Tolstoy, M. P.
Tolstaia, Mariia Alekseevna, 108
Tolstaia, Sofiia Andreevna, 1844-1919, 109
Tolstoi, Lev Nikolaevich, 1828-1910, 109, 110, 411
Tolstoy, Leo, graf, see Tolstoi, Lev Nikolaevich, 1828-1910
Tolstoy, Beatrice, 640
Tolstoy, Ilia, 640
Tolstoy, M. P., 111
Tolstoy Foundation, 109
Tomiloff, P. A., see Tomilov, P. A.
Tomilov, P. A., 440
"Totals of the Struggle Against Famine in 1921-22: Collection of
    Articles and Reports," 307
Trade--Estonia, 414; Germany, 79, 80
Trade-unions, 126, 281; United States, 281
Trade-unions and communism, 281
Transcaucasia, 14, 346, 578; History--Revolution, 1917-1921, 412
Transportation, 259, 571, 617
"Transportnyia sredstva i transportirovanie," 259
Trans-Siberian Railroad, 486, 501. See also Railroads
Travelers, 133; Dutch, 115
Treat, Payson J., 1879-1972, 165, 268
Treaties, 265
Treaty of Brest-Litovsk, Feb. 9, 1918 (Ukraine), 180
Treaty of Riga, 1920, 415
Treloar, George D., 441
Trest, 133
Trials (Political crimes and offenses), 289. See also Political
    crimes and offenses
Tribunal Arbitral, The Hague, 1912, 155
"Trinadtsat´ let Oktiabria" (Thirteen years of October), 318
Triska, Jan F., 265

Troianovskii, Aleksandr Antonovich, 139
Troitskosavsk, 551
Trotskii, Lev, 1879-1940, 2, 12, 14, 97, 133, 139, 314
Trotzky, Ilja, 183
Troyanovskii, Aleksandr Antonovich, 139
Trubetskoi, Vladimir S., Kniaz´, 166
Trufanov, Sergei Mikhailovich, 2, 133
Truman, Harry S., Pres. U.S., 1884-1972, 635
The Trust, 133
Trysten (village), 196
"The Tsarist Secret Police," 55
"TSarskii listok," 133
Tschebotarioff, Gregory Porphyriewitch, 1899-   , 442
Tschebotarioff, Ludmila, see Safonov, Ludmila, 1897-
TSentral´naia komissiia pomoshchi golodaiushchim, see Russia
    (1917-   R.S.F.S.R.). TSentral´naia komissiia pomoshchi
    golodaiushchim
TSereteli, Iraklii Georgievich, 1882-1959, 133
Tsiliga, A., "V strane velikoi Izhi," 133
Tsion, S. A., 133
Tsurikov, N., 665
Tsushima, Battle of, 1905, 158. See also Russo-Japanese War,
    1904-1905
Tuban, Mark R., collector, 17
Turkestan--History, 136; Revolution, 1917-1921, 309, 357
Turkey--Boundaries--Armenia, 444
Turkey, Georgians in, 426
Turkey--History--Revolution, 1918-1923, 247
Turkey and the Near East--World War, 1914-1918, see World War,
    1914-1918--Campaigns--Turkey and the Near East
Turkey, Russians in, 452, 597, 611
Turkish-Russian War, 1877-1878, see Russo-Turkish War, 1877-1878
Turrou, Leon G., 616
Turskii, Kaspar, 133

Uchreditel´noe sobranie, see Russia (1917. Provisional Government).
    Vserossiiskoe uchreditel´noe sobranie
Ufa-Urals district, 589
Ufimskaia kavaleriiskaia diviziia, 384
Uget, Sergei Antonovich, 1884-   , 304, 308
Ughet, Serge, 304, 308
Uhlan, see Ulan
Ukraine--Boundaries, 408; Cooperative societies, 96, 408;
    History--1917-   , 133, 299, 409; History--Revolution,
    1917-1921, 2, 11, 133, 241, 247, 249, 303, 339, 360, 387, 391,
    408, 477, 555, 573, 575, 588, 592, 605; History--Revolution,
    1917-1921--Posters, 11; Nationalism, 172; Religion, 410;
    Revolutionists, 133, 139; Social conditions, 645; World
    War,1914-1918, 172
Ukrainian Communist Party, 241
Ukrainians in Canada, 408; in foreign countries, 133, 139; in Poland,
    645; in the United States, 92, 408
Ulanskii polk, 224. See also Russia. Armiia. Kavaleriia
"Ulany Ego Velichestva, 1876-1926" (His Majesty´s Lancers,

1876-1926), 443
"Ulany Ego Velichestva, 1876-1926: Imperator Aleksandr II; Imperator Nikolai II," 396
Ul'ianov, Aleksandr Il'ich, 139
Ul'ianov, Vladimir Il'ich, see Lenin, Vladimir Il'ich, 1870-1924
Underground, Anti-communist, see Anti-communist movements
Ungern-Shternberg, Roman Fedorovich, Baron, 1887-1921, 541, 543, 545, 547, 548, 551
Ungern-Shternberg (Roman Fedorovich, Baron) collection, 1921, 550
Union of Cossack Volunteers, 133. See also Cossacks
Union of Russian Social Democrats, 133. See also Rossiiskaia sotsial-demokraticheskaia rabochaia partiia
Union of Struggle for the Liberation of the Working Class, 133
Unions, Trade, see Trade-unions
United States. See also headings beginning with "American"
U.S. Advisory Commission of Railway Experts to Russia, 14, 29, 343, 471, 481, 486, 527, 537. See also Railroads
U.S. American Expeditionary Forces, see U.S. Army. A.E.F., 1917-1920
U.S. American National Red Cross, see Red Cross. U.S. American National Red Cross
U.S. American Relief Administration, 554, 555, 558, 562, 570, 572, 574, 578, 580, 581, 583, 584, 585, 601, 606, 608; American Relief Administration. Coal Commission, 576; American Relief Administration. European Children's Fund, 562, 572, 601; American Relief Administration. Russian Operations, 1921-1923, 553, 556, 557, 563, 571, 573, 575, 579, 582, 586, 589, 592, 599, 603, 607, 609, 610, 614, 616, 617, 620, 624; American Relief Administration. Russian Operations, 1921-1923. Historical Division, 307
U.S.--Anti-communist movements, 390; Communism, 252, 281
U.S. Army. A.E.F., 1917-1920, 239, 459, 465, 467, 473, 474, 476, 487, 495, 496, 507, 514, 524, 528, 530, 562, 564, 600; Army. A.E.F., 1917-1920--Pictorial works, 354, 480, 537, 538; Army. Camp Fremont, California, 528, 595; Army. Camp Kearny, California, 595; Army. 8th Division, 528; Army. Mission to Armenia, see U.S. Military Mission to Armenia
U.S. Army--Officers--Correspondence, reminiscences, etc., 459, 465
U.S. Army. 31st Infantry, 474, 487, 495, 496; 348th Field Artillery, 562; 27th Infantry, 14, 476
U.S.--Art, 125
U.S. Committee Upon the Arbitration of the Boundary Between Turkey and Armenia, 444
U.S.--Communism, 252, 281
U.S. Congress, 266; Consulate, Leningrad, 319; Department of State, 283, 319; Department of State. The Inquiry, see Paris. Peace Conference, 1919. U.S. Division of Territorial, Economic and Political Intelligence
U.S.--Diplomatic and consular service, 29, 479; Diplomatic and consular service--Russia, 29
U.S. Division of Territorial, Economic and Political Intelligence, see Paris. Peace Conference, 1919. U.S. Division of Territorial, Economic and Political Intelligence
U.S. Federal Security Agency, 666; Food Administration, 554, 594,

626

U.S.--Foreign relations--1913-1921, 199; Foreign relations--Finland, 263; Foreign relations--Russia, 14, 105, 106, 165, 266, 272, 283, 286, 304, 630
U.S. Grain Corporation, 612, 617
U.S.--Labor and laboring classes, 281
U.S. Library of Congress, 199
U.S., Russian military attachés in, 167
U.S. Military Mission to Armenia, 445; Navy, 482, 617
U.S., Russian Orthodox Church in, 671
U.S. Russian Railway Service Corps, 471, 481, 537. See also U.S. Advisory Commission of Railway Experts to Russia; Railroads
U.S., Russians in the, see Russians in the U.S.
U.S., Slavs in the, 92, 627, 666
U.S.--Trade-unions, 281
U.S., Ukrainians in the, 92, 408
U.S. War Trade Board. Bureau of Research, 271
U.S.--World War, 1914-1918, 530; World War, 1939-1945, 627
University of California, 670
Unruh, B. H., 112
"An Unwritten Chapter," 616
Uperov, Vasilii Vasil´evich, 1877-1932, 233
Upovalov, Ivan, 446
Ural cossacks, see Cossacks
Ural Mountains region, 589
"Urginskiia sobytiia 1921 goda," 544
Uriev, V., 93
Urquhart, Leslie, 320
"Usluzhlivyi liberal," 279
"Ustav unutrennei sluzhby," 148
Ustrialov, Nikolai Vasil´evich, 1890-   , 531
Uzbekistan--Bibliography, 279
"Uzhasy goloda i liudoedstva v Rossii v 1921-22 gg.," 324

"V chem byla sila Rasputina," 26
V dvukh vekakh, 355
"V Zabaikal´ie i na primorskom fronte v 1920-22 g.g.," 535
Vagner, Ekaterina Nikolaevna, 142
Vail, Edwin H., 618
Vainshtein, S. L., 133
Vakar, N. P., 133
Vaksmut, A. P., 447
Valakh, Meir, see Litvinov, Maksim Maksimovich, 1876-1951
Valentinov, N., see Vol´skii, Nikolai Vladislavivich, 1879-1964
Valkeapaeae, P. J., 619
Varneck, Elena, 162, 310, 446, 484, 511, 512, 521, 532, 547, 548, 549, 550, 551, 676
Varnek, Tat´iana Aleksandrovna, 234
Varska, A. S., 533
Vasil´ev, Dimitrii Stepanovich, d. 1915, 167
Vasil´ev, E., 235
Vatatsi, Mariia Petrovna, 1860-   , 113
Verkhovnaia rasporiaditel´naia komissiia, 133

Vernadsky, George, 1887-1973, 321
Vernadsky, Nina, 322
Verstraete, Maurice, 1866-   , 114
Veselovzorov, Major General, 148
Vesselago, George M., 1892-   , 448
<u>Vestnik Obshchestva russkikh veteranov Velikoi voiny</u>, 512
Veterans--Medical care, 154
Viazemskii, Sergei, Prince, <u>see</u> Wiasemsky, Serge, Prince
Viazemskii, Sergei Sergeevich, d. 1915, 236
Victor, George, 667
Vignaux, Paul, 133
Vikzhel´, 133, 291
Viliatser, I. A., 133
Vinaver, Maxim Moiseevich, 449
Vinaver, Rose Georgievna, 449
Vinogradoff, Igor, <u>collector</u>, 115
Vinogradov,   kap., ed., 366
Vinogradov, A. K., 323
Violin, IA. A., 324
Vishniak, Mark Veniaminovich, 1883-1976, 133, 143
Visits of state, 2, 57
Visual arts, 25, 117
Vitkovskii, Vladimir K., 450
Vitte, Sergei Iul´evich, Graf--Photograph, 12
Vladimir Kirillovich, Grand Duke of Russia, 1917-   , 668, 669
"Vladimir Oskarovich Kappel´: vospominaniia uchastnika beloi
     bor´by," 453
Vladimirov, Ivan Alekseevich, 1870-1947, 325
Vladivostok--History, 455, 458, 465, 491, 498, 517, 566; Views, 476,
     480, 525
Vnutrenniaia liniia, 133
"Voevyia dieistviia 1. Zabaikal´skogoi kazach´ei divizii v velikoi
     voine 1914-1918 goda," 228
Vogel, Faith Bugbee, 465
Voisko terskago, <u>see</u> Russia (1917-1922. Civil War governments).
     Armiia. Terskoe kazach´e voisko
Voitinskii, V. S., 133
Voitsekhovskii, Sergei L´vovich, 1900-   , 669
Volga Kama Bank, 456
Volkhovskii, Feliks Vadimovich, 1846-1914, 144
Volkonskii, Vladimir Mikhailovich, 1868-1953, 116
Volkov, Boris, 551
Volmar, George von, 133
Volodin, M. M., 133
Vologodskii, Petr Vasil´evich, 534
Vol´skii, Nikolai Vladislavovich, 1879-1964, 133, 145, 285
Vol´skii, Vera, 145
Volunteer Army, <u>see</u> Russia (1917-1922. Civil War governments).
     Dobrovol´cheskaia armiia
Von Arnold, Antonina R., 670
Von Etter, Maria, <u>see</u> Etter, Maria von
Von Gerngros, Aleksandr Alekseevich--Photograph, 12
Von Lampe, Aleksei Aleksandrovich, <u>see</u> Lampe, Aleksei Aleksandrovich
     von, 1885-1960

203

Von Leuchtenberg, Nikolai Nikolaevich, Herzog, see Leikhtenberg, Nikolai Nikolaevich, Gertsog fon
Von Mirbach-Harff, Wilhelm, Graf, 1871-1918, 436
Von Mohrenschildt, Dimitri Sergius, 1902-   , 671
Von Poletika, W. P., see Poletika, W. P. von
Von Schwarz, Alexis, see Shvarts, Aleksei Vladimirovich fon, 1874-1953
Von Tal´, Georgii Aleksandrovich, see Tal´, Georgii Aleksandrovich von
Von Volmar, George, 133
Vooruzhennye sily iuga Rossii, see Russia (1917-1922. Civil War governments). Vooruzhennye sily iuga Rossii
Voronchin (village), 196
Vorontsov-Dashkov, Ilarion, see Woronzow-Daschkow, Hilarion, Graf, collector
Vorotovov, Colonel, 535
Voskevich, P., collector, 12
"Vos´maia kamskaia strelkovaia diviziia v sibirskom ledianom pokhode," 512
"Vospominaniia F. I. Rodicheva o 1917 godu," 301
"Vospominaniia ob Ungernskom periode vo vneshnei Mongolii," 541
"Vospominaniia sotsialdemokrata," 126
"Vospominaniia starago plastuna o velikoi voinie, 1914-1917," 189
Votkinsk--History, 446
Voyce, Arthur, d. 1977, 117
"Vozdushyia voiska," 193
"Vozstanie v Irkutsk," 529
Vpered, 133
Vrangel´, Mariia D., 451
Vrangel´, Petr Nikolaevich, Baron, 1878-1928, 356, 375, 422, 450, 451, 452
Vrangel´ army camp (Gallipoli)--Photograph, ca. 1921, 12
"Vremennoe polozhenie ob upravlenii Terskim voiskom," 361
Vremennoe rossiiskoe pravitel´stvo (Kolchak), see Russia (1917-1922. Civil War governments). Vremennoe rossiiskoe pravetel´stvo (Kolchak)
Vremennoe sibirskoe pravitel´stvo, see Russia (1917-1922. Civil War governments). Vremennoe sibirskoe pravitel´stvo
Vserossiiskaia chrezvychainaia komissiia po bor´be s kontr-revoliutsiei i sabotazhem, see Russia (1917- R.S.F.S.R.). Chrezvychainaia komissiia po bor´be s kontr-revoliutsiei i sabotazhem
Vserossiiskaia fashistskaia partiia, 629
Vserossiiskii ispolnitel´nyi komitet Zheleznodorozhnogo soiuza (Vikzhel´), 133, 291
Vserossiiskii tserkovnyi s"ezd, Moscow, Jan.-Feb. 1918, 421. See also Orthodox Eastern Church, Russian
Vserossiiskoe uchreditel´noe sobranie, see Russia (1917. Provisional Government). Vserossiiskoe uchreditel´noe sobranie
Vsesoiuznyi mendeleevskii s"ezd po teoreticheskoi i prikladnoi khimii, St. Petersburg, 1911, 12
"Vstriechnyi boi divizii i korpusa," 185
"2-i Orenburgskii kazachii polk v 1918-1920 g.g.," 535
Vulikh, T. I., 133

Vyrypaev, V. I., 453
"Vyslushai, delai," 74
Vysshii sovet narodnogo khoziaistva, 278

Wachhold, Allen, 620
Wagner, Ekaterina N., see Vagner, Ekaterina Nikolaevna
Walach, Meir, see Litvinov, Maksim Maksimovich, 1876-1951
Wallach, Meyer, see Litvinov, Maksim Maksimovich, 1876-1951
Wallachia--Politics and government, 70
Wallen, E. Carl, 1889-1961, 621
Walsh, Phyllis J., 169
Walsh, Warren B., translator, 22, 118
War, Prisoners of, see Prisoners of war
War guilt (World War I), 181, 222
War of 1914, see World War, 1914-1918
War propaganda (World War I), see World War, 1914-1918--Russian propaganda
War Trade Board. Bureau of Research, 271
Wardwell, Allen, 250
Warehouses, 617
Warfare, Submarine, 176
Washington, Harold George, 1892-1961?, collector, 536
Washington, D.C., Conference on the Limitation of Naval Armaments, 1921-1922, 659
Water quality management, 86
Water transportation, 414, 617
Wayne, Roy E., 237
Weidmann, Ingeborg K., 129
Weimar-Eisenach-Saxe--Foreign relations--Russia, 82
Weinstein, S. L. (Vainshtein, S. L.), 133
Wells, Helen, 591
Wertheim, Maurice, 412
Westermann, William Linn, 1873- , 444
Western Reserve Historical Society, 502
Whitcomb, John M., collector, 326
White Russian (anti-Bolshevik) governments, see Russia (1917-1922. Civil War governments)
"White Russian Emigrants and the Japanese Army in the Far East," 523
Whitehead, James H., collector, 537
Why is Communism Intrinsically Evil? 276
Wiasemsky, Serge, Prince, 672
Willis, Edward Frederick, 1904- , 622
Wilson, Samuel Graham, 623
Winship, North, 319
Winter Palace, 12, 111, 119
Wiren, Nicholas, 18
Wiskowski, Wlodzimierz, collector, 238
Witte, Sergei IUl´evich, Graf--Photograph, 12
Wolfe, Henry Cutler, 1893-1976, 624
Wolff, Sergei Evgen´evich Ludinkhausen-, Baron, 203
Wolkoff, A. de, 156
Woltner, Margarete, 112
Woolf, Paul N., collector, 168
"The Work of Okhrana Departments in Russia," 85

Workingmen's associations, see Trade-unions
Workers, see Labor and laboring classes
World Alliance of Young Men's Christian Associations, 625
"A World Destroyed: Memoirs," 645
World politics, 88, 295
World War, 1914-1918, 75, 98, 105, 115, 161, 164, 169-240, 294, 304, 329, 333, 357, 363, 377, 380, 385, 386, 390, 395, 405, 406, 413, 429, 431, 437, 438, 464, 628, 634. See also Reconstruction (1914-1939)
World War, 1914-1918--Aerial operations, 193, 218; Baltic provinces, 171, 209; California, 595; Campaigns--Carpathian Mountains, 205; Campaigns--Eastern, 189, 196, 204, 217, 219, 221, 236, 329, 333, 380, 384, 405, 413, 431, 464; Campaigns--Riga front, 205; Campaigns--Romania, 191; Campaigns--Serbia, 253; Campaigns--Turkey and the Near East, 173, 203, 253, 431; Campaigns--Turkey and the Near East--Caucasus, 173, 220, 621; Campaigns--Turkey and the Near East--Dardanelles, 24; Campaigns--Turkey and the Near East--Gallipoli, 24; Campaigns--Western, 253; Causes, 181, 222; Civilian relief, 213, 554, 574, 577, 578, 581, 584, 605, 608, 612, 621, 622, 625. See also Food relief; Russia--History--Revolution, 1917-1921--Civilian relief; World War, 1914-1918--Hospitals, charities, etc.; Civilian relief--Armenia, 623; Civilian relief--Baltic states, 580; Civilian relief--Estonia, 351; Civilian relief--Finland, 619; Civilian relief--Latvia, 601; Civilian relief--Poland, 594, 604, 626; Destruction and pillage, 253; Diplomatic history, 199, 200; Finance, 174, 201; Finland, 205; France, 229; Germany, 240; Hospitals, charities, etc., 151, 234. See also World War, 1914-1918--Civilian relief
World War, 1914-1918--Internment camps, see Prisoners of war
World War, 1914-1918--Military supplies, 133; Naval operations, 236; Naval operations, American, 482; Naval operations--Submarine, 176; Peace, 177, 183, 192, 200, 209, 210, 253; Peace conference, Paris, 1919, see Paris. Peace Conference, 1919
World War, 1914-1918--Peace treaties--Brest-Litovsk, Feb. 9, 1918 (Ukraine), 180; Pictorial works, 2, 12, 180, 239, 253, 591; Poland, 206, 207, 215, 238; Posters, 9, 11; Prisoners and prisons, see Prisoners of war
World War, 1914-1918--Prussia, East (Province)--Pictorial works, 224; Railroads, see World War, 1914-1918--Transportation
World War, 1914-1918--Reconstruction, see Reconstruction (1914-1939)
World War, 1914-1918--Refugees, 161, 213, 237. See also Revolution, 1917-1921--Refugees
World War, 1914-1918--Regimental histories, 228; Regimental histories--20. korpus, 217; Regimental histories--10. armiia, 179; Regimental histories--Kubansko-Terskii plastunskii korpus, 189; Regimental histories--1. Ulanskii polk, 224; Regimental histories--Austria--Legiony Polskie, 206; Romania, 191; Russian propaganda, 14, 240, 312; Secret service, 365; Siberia, 593; Supplies, 133; Tactical history, see World War, 1914-1918--Campaigns
World War, 1914-1918--Territorial questions, 192, 210; Territorial questions--Bessarabia, 197; Territorial questions--Poland,

225; Transportation, 14, 216, 471, 486; Treaties, see World War, 1914-1918--Peace
World War, 1914-1918--Ukraine, 172; United States, 530; War work--Red Cross, 581, 603, 605. See also Red Cross. U.S. American National Red Cross; War work--Y.M.C.A., 587, 598, 625. See also Young Men's Christian Associations; War work--Y.W.C.A., 595, 617; War guilt, 181, 222; War materials, 133
World War I pictorial collection, 1914-1919, 239
World War I subject collection, 1914-1920, 240
World War, 1939-1945--France, 133; Indochina, French, 347; United States, 627
Woronzow-Daschkow, Hilarion, Graf, collector, 111, 119
Woyciechowski, Serge, see Voitsekhovskii, Sergei L´vovich, 1900-
Wrangel, see Vrangel´
Wuerttemberg--Foreign relations--Russia, 83
Wullus collection, see Germany. Oberste Heeresleitung
Wynkoop, Nancy, 186

Xenia, Grand Duchess, see Kseniia Aleksandrovna, Grand Duchess of Russia

Y.M.C.A., see Young Men's Christian Associations
Y.W.C.A., 595, 617
Yakunin, Nicholas T., 639
Yakutsk--History, 494
Yaremenko, A. N., see IAremenko, A. N.
Yelsky, Isadore, 1896-1958, 538
Young Men's Christian Associations, 564, 565, 568, 587, 611, 615, 617, 625. See also World War, 1914-1918--War work--Y.M.C.A.
Young Women's Christian Associations, 595, 617
Yourieff, W., 93
Yuba Manufacturing Company of San Francisco, 478
Yudenitch, N. N., see IUdenich, Nikolai Nikolaevich, 1862-1933
Yugoslavia, Russian military attachés in, 332
Yugoslavia, Russians in, 332, 403
Yurchenko, Ivan, 673

Zagranichnaia delegatsiia Partii eserov-maksimalistov, see Partiia sotsialistov-revoliutsionerov
Zagranichnaia liga Russkoi revoliutsionnoi sotsial-demokratii, 133. See also Rossiiskaia sotsial-demokraticheskaia rabochaia partiia
Zaitzevsky, Olga P., 329
Zakhartchenko, Constantine L., 1900-   , 167, 674
Zakhartchenko, Mrs. Constantine L., 243
"Zapiski kirasira," 166
"Zapiski o plienie," 235
"Zapiski velikoi voiny 1914-1918 g.," 232
Zaporogians, see Cossacks
Zaria (Berlin), 446
Zasulich, Vera, 139
Zavadskii, Sergei Vladislavovich, 120
Zavadskii, Vladislav Romual´dovich, 1840-1910, 120
Zavarin, Konstantin Nikolaevich, 539

Zavarin, Natalie N., 539
Zawodny, Jay K., 327
Zborovskii, M. S., 133
Zebrak, Nicholas A., 675
Zemstvo, 494
Zershchikov, K., 121
Zheleznodorozhnyi soiuz. Vserossiiskii ispolnitel´nyi komitet, 133, 291
"Zheliczn´yia dorogoi v voennoe vremia," 216
Zhenevskii komitet pomoshchi politicheskim zakliuchennym, 133
Zhitlovskaia, V. S. (Obukhova, V. S.), 133
Zhitomirskii, Moishe, 139
Zholnerovich, Vanda Kazimirovna, see Stepanova, Vanda Kazimirovna
Zholondkovskii,   , polk, ed., 366
Zhordaniia, Noi Nikolaevich, 133
"Zhurnal voennykh dieistvii shtaba X-go armeiskago korpusa," 219
Zimnyi dvorets, 12, 111, 119
Zinkin, Harold, collector, 19
Zinoviev, Grigorii Evseevich, 1883-1936 (Shatskii), 133, 139
Zionism, 139. See also Jews
Znamia truda, Moscow, 291
Znamiecki, Alexander, 626
Zubets, Vladimir Aleksandrovich, 676
Zundelevich, A., 133
Zundelevich, L., 133
Zurich faction, RSDWP, 133
Zvegintsov, Nikolai, 454
Zvezdin, S. L., 133